D0409834

Thomas Pyles

Thomas Pyles

Selected Essays on English Usage

Edited by

John Algeo

A University of Florida Book

University Presses of Florida

Gainesville / 1979

Library of Congress Cataloging in Publication Data

Pyles, Thomas, 1905 –
    Selected essays on English usage.

    ''A University of Florida book.''
    ''The writings of Thomas Pyles'': p.

    1. English language in the United States—Collected
works. I. Algeo, John. II. Title.
PE2802.P9   410   78–18833
ISBN 0–8130–0546–6

The University Presses of Florida is the scholarly
publishing agency for the State University
System of Florida.

TYPOGRAPHY BY TYPO-GRAPHICS
ORLANDO, FLORIDA

PRINTED IN FLORIDA

Acknowledgments

PERMISSION to reprint the essays by Thomas Pyles in this collection has been kindly given by the following:

Columbia University Press for "The Pronunciation of Latin in English: A Lexicographical Dilemma," *American Speech*, 22 (1947), 3–17; "Onomastic Individualism in Oklahoma," *American Speech*, 22 (1947), 257–64; "Bollicky Naked," *American Speech*, 24 (1949), 255; "British Titles of Nobility and Honor in American English," *American Speech*, 28 (1953), 69–79; " 'Task Force' Makes 'Breakthrough,' " *American Speech*, 35 (1960), 155–56; "Sweet Are the Usages of Diversity," *American Speech*, 45 (1970), 252–60.

The Johns Hopkins Press for "Tempest in Teapot: Reform in Latin Pronunciation," *ELH*, 6 (1939), 138–64; "Dan Chaucer," *MLN*, 57 (1942), 437–39; "Innocuous Linguistic Indecorum: A Semantic Byway," *MLN*, 64 (1949), 1–8; "Ophelia's 'Nothing,' " *MLN*, 64 (1949), 322–23; "That Fine Italian *A* in American English," in *Philologica: The Malone Anniversary Studies*, edited by Thomas A. Kirby and Henry B. Woolf (Baltimore, 1949), pp. 290–95.

The National Council of Teachers of English for "Linguistics and Pedagogy: The Need for Conciliation," *College English*, 10 (1949), 389–95; "The English of VIPs," *College English*, 16 (1955), 356–61; "The Role of Historical Linguistics," *College English*, 26 (1965), 292–98; "English Usage: The Views of the Literati," *College English*, 28 (1967), 443–54.

The University of Alabama Press for "The Auditory Mass Media and U," in *Studies in Linguistics in Honor of Raven I. McDavid, Jr.*, edited by L. M. Davis (University, 1972), pp. 425–34.

The American Name Society for "Bible Belt Onomastics; or, Some Curiosities of Antipedobaptist Nomenclature," *Names*, 7 (1959), 84–100.

Basic Books for Chapter 12, "Dictionaries and Usage" by Thomas Pyles, in *Linguistics Today*, edited by Archibald A. Hill, ©1969 by Basic Books Inc., Publishers, New York.

The University of Florida Press for "Inkhornisms, Fustian, and Current Vogue Words," in *All These to Teach: Essays in Honor of C. A. Robertson*, edited by R. A. Bryan, A. C. Morris, A. A. Murphree, and A. L. Williams (Gainesville, 1965), pp. 1–14.

The Modern Language Association of America for "The Pronunciation of Latin Learned Loanwords and Foreign Words in Old English," *PMLA*, 58 (1943), 891–910.

The *New York Times* for "Subliminal Words Are Never Finalized," *New York Times Magazine*, 15 June 1958, pp. 16, 55, 57, 58, ©1958 by The New York Times Company. Reprinted by permission.

The essays are printed here with only minor changes suggested or approved by the author. Added matter has been enclosed in square brackets.

The following persons helped in the preparation of the manuscript: Adele S. Algeo, O. C. Dean, Louise Hanes, April Maddox, and Thomas Pyles, Jr.

Contents

Contents

Onomastica

Pseudodoxia Epidemica Linguistica

Foreword

IF one sign of a living entity is that it changes the substance of which it is made while preserving a continuity of form, no one can doubt that languages are in that respect living entities. The twenty-one essays collected here bear witness to the vitality of English and to its integrity in the midst of great variety in use. Originally published during a thirty-four-year period, the essays are grouped under five major topics: the pronunciation of Latin in England and America, currently voguish forms of expression, unwitting indecorum in the use of taboo words, curiosities in the bestowal of names and titles, and the murky realm of lay linguistics. Although diverse in their subject matter, these essays present a consistent view of English usage and of the attitudes that English speakers have taken toward it. They range from a technical study of Latin orthoepy in Old English times to a popular treatment of vogue words in our own day. Yet through all of them there runs a single thread: a view of change and continuity in the English language, set forth with the precision, craft, and style that Thomas Pyles's students and colleagues look forward to in all his work. The essays are gathered together here for the benefit of students of English and in honor of their author, a scholar who, by his example, has set and continues to set a standard in matter and manner to which all linguists would do well to aspire.

Orthoepia Classica

The first usage problem of which we have any record among English speakers is the correct pronunciation of Latin words, which has presented difficulties

ix

for the inhabitants of the British Isles, and for their linguistic descendents throughout the world, from the time of the Conversion to the present day. Even in Old English times the influx of learned Latin borrowings, some of which were freely adapted to an English context but many of which were treated as foreignisms, presented an orthoepical challenge. On the one hand, there was pressure to give Latin words the pronunciation they had in the literary Latin of the educated classes on the Continent. On the other hand, there was a tendency to treat spellings of Latin words as representing the sounds they stood for in English and to follow the native pattern in placing stress. On the whole, anglicizing tendencies won out (selection 1: "The Pronunciation of Latin Learned Loanwords and Foreign Words in Old English"). After the Great Vowel Shift had changed the phonetic value of the tense vowels for English speakers, the discrepancy between the English pronunciations of Latin and the various continental pronunciations was sharply increased. The question of the correct pronunciation of Latin was consequently much debated. The traditional English method of sounding Latin competed first with the Italian and then with the "reformed" pronunciation, which sought to re-create a Latin pronunciation approximating that of the classical period (selection 2: "Tempest in Teapot: Reform in Latin Pronunciation"). By the mid-twentieth century, while dictionaries continued to record the traditional phonetic value for Latin used in an English context, the "reformed" or "classical" pronunciation had so completely won out in the teaching of Latin in the schools that the practice of English speakers wavered between the two methods and, as often as not, settled on a hybrid pronunciation, incorporating inconsistent and unpredictable elements of each system (selection 3: "The Pronunciation of Latin in English: A Lexicographical Dilemma"). More recent dictionaries have recorded this mixed pronunciation, which has clearly become the new standard—neither traditional nor reformed, but a tertium quid.

De Temporibus et Moribus

Uncertainty in the pronunciation of Latin has extended to loanwords from other languages, even long-established ones, with the result that what are thought of as more "authentic" pronunciations are replacing the anglicizations that English speakers have favored at least since the reign of Alfred the Great. Thus, in the pronunciation of foreign words, recent years have witnessed "the triumph of a little learning over the traditions of centuries of cultivated usage" (selection 4: "That Fine Italian A in American English").

The content of the lexicon as well as the pronunciation of individual items reflects a striving for fashionableness—according to the standards of fashion that are favored in "this Great Republic," as H. L. Mencken was wont to call it. Fondness for the fancy word has, however, a long, if not an honorable, tradition among English speakers. The influx of technical or pseudo-technical jargon into the general vocabulary of present-day English, whereby the hip speaker demonstrates his know-how and with-it-ity (selections 5: "Subliminal Words Are Never Finalized" and 6: " 'Task Force' Makes 'Breakthrough' "), can be seen as a metempsychosis of a practice that was all the rage among fashionable savants of the English Renaissance (selection 7: "Inkhornisms, Fustian, and Current Vogue Words"). The study of the usage of modern men of mode—or at least of men and women of reputation and influence—which should be taken into account by anyone who presumes to deal authoritatively with linguistic standards in our time, has been made more convenient by the advent of the modern mass media. The auditory media also promise to be a force in spreading the usage of those same Very Important Persons. Their language, as it is displayed on important occasions with pomp and circumstance, contrasts strikingly with that which books dealing with English usage have prescribed and proscribed (selection 8: "The English of VIPs"). These new standards for English— and standards they clearly are—will, with the benefit of the media, surely be increasingly admired and emulated. We may confidently expect that they will supplant that older variety of cultivated English that, in accord with the innovation of A. S. C. Ross, can be called by the undemocratic but serviceable term "U" (for *upper class*), a variety of English distinguished by such currently unfashionable virtues as tradition and elegance (selection 9: "The Auditory Mass Media and U").

Semantica et Etymologia

Currently fashionable speakers who would pride themselves on their linguistic delicacy may unwittingly use expressions whose earlier history was indecorous in the extreme. An expression's meaning at any given time is, of course, the meaning in which it is used at that time. The earlier history of a word, often involving a variety of obsolete or archaic senses, has no direct bearing on its current use. That fact, however, is not always appreciated by the linguistically naive, who are much given to the etymological fallacy—an assumption that words have "real" meanings (often those of some earlier stage of their history or of their component parts) that are as unalterable as the law of the Medes and the Persians. The study of etymology itself began with some such assumption, and lay linguistics has never put it aside. A particularly fitting joke on literal etymologizers is that a goodly number of expressions that were once indelicate in their senses or associations have passed into common use. Many an etymologically indecent phrase has entered genteel colloquial use with no consciousness on the part of its users of the "true meaning" of the idiom, and many an obscure phrase in English literature from Shakespeare through Browning, not to mention Chaucer on the one hand or present-day authors on the other, requires more honest glossing than is generally given it (selections 10: "Innocuous Linguistic Indecorum: A Semantic Byway," 11: "Bollicky Naked," and 12: "Ophelia's 'Nothing' ").

Onomastica

Personal names and titles are aspects of language that allow man's creative impulse to express itself and that reveal much about the name- and title-bearers and the society in which they live. Titles define one man's obligations and prerogatives with respect to another, but their appropriate use requires an intimate acquaintance with the social structure of the group to which they are native. It is hardly surprising, therefore, that titles should often be misused by those not privy to their intricacies, who are by no means limited to the uneducated. A famous misuse of one title by Spenser established a new tradition for its use in literary contexts (selection 13: "Dan Chaucer"). If the English have had trouble with their own titles, it is more than can be reasonably expected that others should be able to keep them straight. The American may dearly love a lord, but he has a hard time remembering what to call him (selection 14: "British Titles of Nobility and Honor in American English"). What the American lacks, however, in command of the terminological intricacies of the British peerage, he more than compensates for by the imaginativeness with which he has bestowed names upon his offspring. Perhaps in no other aspect of American life has the citizen been less oppressed by the weight of tradition than in the giving of names: here his individualism has had full scope for expression (selection 15: "Onomastic Individualism in Oklahoma"). The untrammeled freedom with which Americans have created new personal names and the folksy humor with which they have combined old ones is due, in part, to the fact that in large areas of the country there have been relatively few restraints, such as those provided by the traditional forms of public christening, to inhibit the fancies of parental name-givers (selection 16: "Bible Belt Onomastics; or, Some Curiosities of Antipedobaptist Nomenclature").

Pseudodoxia Epidemica Linguistica

The new standards of usage—whether in pronunciation, syntax, diction, naming, or whatnot—have not yet been accepted, or even recognized, by many self-appointed guardians of the language. But that fact is hardly surprising inasmuch as those same pundits often have only very imperfect knowledge about the more old-fashioned standard or, for that matter, about linguistic matters in general. The American's attitude toward his own language has been molded by what the schools teach about it; and in turn widely, albeit uncritically, held attitudes toward correctness determine what the schools teach. Lay linguistics reinforces and is reinforced by school-marm grammar, the two combining to create a view of language at sharp variance with the facts, present and past, as they can be ascertained by anyone with the patience to investigate impartially and thoroughly the actual use of language. What is taught in the schools about English usage should take account of those facts (selection 17: "Linguistics and Pedagogy: The Need for Conciliation"). The present state of English and its future both rest upon a long prior development; one of the clearest differences between the professional linguist and the lay linguist is that the latter has no sense of historical perspective. For him, what is, is what has always been, and consequently any change is perceived as degeneration. One of the great contributions of nineteenth-century linguistics—a contribution still not fully appreciated—is that it made possible an historical and thus liberating view of language and of language change (selection 18: "The Role of Historical Linguistics"). Unfortunately, some otherwise quite literate and liberated persons are not familiar with the results of linguistic research or have not understood their implications. The practitioners of lay linguistics are by no means limited to the humble and uneducated, but include in their numbers some very distinguished men of letters, whose views are issued to the world with a self-confidence that is matched only by their ill-informedness (selection 19: "English Usage: The Views of the Literati"). Lay linguists, famous and humble alike, are wont to look to the Dictionary for support of their views. The opinion that the business of dictionaries is to support some particular notion of what is good, beautiful, and true in language is one of the cardinal tenets of lay linguistics, and the discovery that dictionaries instead report present and past linguistic facts, as well as their makers have been able to ascertain them, may be a disillusioning experience (selection 20: "Dictionaries and Usage"). There is a well-established, scholarly tradition for the study of language that seeks to discover the facts of usage rather than to legislate about them. To discover facts is not, however, to celebrate them or to make them moral imperatives. The linguistic scholar talks as he pleases and is pleased to allow others the same right—whether he personally finds their speechways agreeable or not (selection 21: "Sweet Are the Usages of Diversity").

   Today English usage is clearly in flux. Whether we look to the pronunciation of learned Latinisms, fashionable additions to the vocabulary from various technical subjects, the sometimes unconscious extension of vulgarisms to general use, or the fruitier examples of name giving, we see the language in change. There has, however, never been a time when English was not in flux. There is thus no justification for stoutly opposing new forms merely on the grounds of their newness. Change is a sign not of decay but of vitality in language, and although some changes will inevitably be distasteful to those who place value on tradition and elegance, the English of Alfred, of Chaucer, and of Shakespeare maintains continuity with the English of today and of tomorrow.

Omnia mutantur, nihil interit.

J.A.

Orthoepia Classica

1

The Pronunciation of Latin Learned Loanwords and Foreign Words in Old English

THE obvious and very necessary distinction between learned and popular loanwords was first made by A. Pogatscher in his *Zur Lautlehre der griechischen, lateinischen und romanischen Lehnworte im Altenglischen*.[1] E. Sievers[2] made a further division, realizing that a distinction, recognized by Pogatscher (for example, on p. 31), but not stressed by him sufficiently for Sievers's purposes, should be made between two classes of learned borrowings. With an approach somewhat different from that of Pogatscher, he at first distinguishes two groups, loanwords (*Lehnwörter*) and foreign words (*Fremdwörter*), designating by the former term such words as are a part of the vocabulary of living communication and bear a more or less native stamp; by the latter, such words as exist for the most part only in learned literature and are distinctly felt as foreign, such as proper names like *Caesar* and *Suetonius*. The loanwords of his first division Sievers further subdivided into popular loanwords, the earliest of all borrowings, and learned loanwords, taken over later than the popular words and owing their adoption to more or less cultural influences such as, in the case of the Old English learned borrowings, the church. These last are to be distinguished, he points out, from foreign words in that they are part of a living vocabulary, even though their use is limited to a certain class of speakers. What Sievers has done simply amounts to extracting from Pogatscher's learned words those bookish words which are distinctly felt as foreign and making of them a third class, which he calls foreign words.[3]

1. *Quellen und Forschungen*, 64 (Strassburg, 1888), 23–24.
2. *Zum angelsächsischen Vocalismus* (Leipzig, 1900), pp. 3–5.
3. These foreign words, mostly eye-words in that their use was confined largely to writing,

3

Even in its earliest known forms English is not entirely lacking in borrowed elements. The earliest OE loanwords are, however, popular in origin and therefore rest upon a purely oral tradition. Most were brought with them by the English when they left the Continent, and have to do with the ordinary business of daily life, for instance, *wīn*, *strǣt*, *piper*. With these and somewhat later popular borrowings this study will concern itself only incidentally, for their phonological development is that of the English language itself, but will instead deal with that particular group of Latin borrowings[4] comprising learned loanwords and foreign words.

The conversion of the English to Christianity introduced a group of words, all of them learned in origin, for instance (*a*)*postol*, *circul*, *martyr*, *templ*. While there are a few instances of oral transmission, these words were as a rule taken over first in their written forms, the vowels of their stressed syllables being directly transliterated (though their quantity, as will be seen, depends on various circumstances), in contrast to the orally transmitted popular words; and, as we should expect, these learned words, their use in the nature of things confined to a more or less restricted circle of educated men, were spoken according to the customary learned pronunciation of the time—the oral Latin of church, cloister, and school.

Of the learned words and foreign words whose pronunciation is the subject of the present paper, it may be pointed out that some preserve their foreign flavor even to the point of retaining their Latin inflexional endings; these may be classed without difficulty as foreign words. Others are assimilated to the borrowing language to the extent that they take on the OE inflexional endings, without, however, undergoing the phonetic changes characteristic of the popular loans (though such a word may ultimately become popular, and its subsequent development be that of the borrowing language); these may usually be classed as learned loanwords. A third group is in a sense intermediate, with foreign endings in subject case and native endings in oblique cases; this group may be classed with the first as comprising foreign words. Naturally, we shall encounter borderline cases where it will be impossible to determine with any exactness to which of these three groups a given word belongs, since lines of demarcation are not always clearly

------

would seem to have had no such fixed traditional pronunciation as the learned loanwords, though I am strongly of the opinion that, when they were used orally, their pronunciation was likely to conform to the pattern of the learned loanwords much more closely than Sievers's metrical tests would indicate for their pronunciation in verse.

4. Words of Greek and Hebrew origin are also considered, inasmuch as most of these came into English via Latin.

drawn, and since our evidence is sometimes incomplete. Likewise, it must be borne in mind that oral and literary transmission may take place side by side, as with *clēric* and *cānonic*, words closely associated with the church, with no native synonyms readily accessible.

It is necessary also to take into consideration the situation on the Continent, whence came those teachers, like Abbo of Fleury, who were to impart the rudiments of Latin to the English; likewise, we must take care to differentiate between the colloquial Latin of the folk, that is, Vulgar Latin, a language already advanced in its development in early OE times, and the literary Latin of the educated classes. We cannot, of course, always be certain of the relation of the literary to the colloquial Latin in the various periods, as Meyer-Lübke points out; we may, however, conclude with him that "im allgemeinen liegt die Sache so, dass die gesprochene Sprache sich langsam veränderte, während die Schriftsprache festblieb."[5] By the sixth century the disparity between Vulgar Latin and the literary Latin of the educated seems to have become especially significant, for Gregory of Tours, though he himself wrote in the vernacular Latin of his time, complains in the Praefatio of his *Historia Francorum* that his acquaintances understood only popular Latin.[6]

The sections which follow will give the details, as nearly as they may be deduced, of the pronunciation of literary Latin in OE times.[7] I have not been here concerned so much with piling up examples by including every Latin word which appears in OE literature as with formulating those general principles which governed the pronunciation of Latin learned loanwords and foreign words in OE.[8]

---

5. *Einführung in das Studium der romanischen Sprachwissenschaft,* dritte neuarbeitete Auflage (Heidelberg, 1920), p. 120.

6. Cf. H. Berger, *Die Lehnwörter in der französischen Sprache ältester Zeit* (Leipzig, 1899), p. 7.

7. Since, for reasons to be discussed at various points in the course of this paper, I do not agree with Sievers as to the extent of the phonological importance of the useful distinction between learned loanwords and foreign words, I shall not distinguish between the two classes except where such a distinction seems to me important.

8. Some of the illustrative words have been documented, particularly those which show or seem to show deviations from the principles deduced or synthesized. Practically all these words may be traced to their sources, however, through the indexes in Pogatscher, pp. 210–20; Otto Funke, *Die gelehrten lateinischen Lehn- und Fremdwörter in der altenglischen Literatur* (Halle, 1914), pp. 195–99, 205–9; and Mary S. Serjeantson, *A History of Foreign Words in English* (New York, 1936), pp. 307–54. Serjeantson includes an appendix, pp. 271–88, listing pre-Conquest loans from Latin, and devotes her second chapter to a discussion of such words. She is, however, concerned with cultural history rather than with phonology, which is dealt with in a brief note, pp. 289–92.

I. STRESS AND QUANTITY

A. STRESS

When a loanword is naturalized to the extent that it takes on the inflexional system of the borrowing language, that language exerts a strong influence so to regulate the stressing of the borrowed word that there shall be no contradiction to its own stress system: this is a basic law. And, since the Germanic word has initial stress, Latin loanwords not originally stressed on the first syllable customarily shift their stress in accordance with the Germanic principle. The same is true, if perhaps to a somewhat lesser extent, of foreign words, as will be shown later; even these cannot escape the strong tendency to initial stress which is characteristic of the Germanic languages. Opinions vary as to the uniformity of this shift, particularly with regard to the foreign words; but, when all the evidence, along with all the probabilities, has been considered, it would appear that we are justified in assuming that the same phonetic generalizations hold true alike for learned loanwords and foreign words in OE, and I have therefore not hesitated to group the two classes of words in the present study, interesting though the distinction between them made by Sievers may be. I find no convincing evidence that any of the foreign words in use in OE were customarily treated differently from the learned loanwords; on the contrary, there is metrical evidence based on alliteration[9]—the only sort which seems to me in any way conclusive—that foreign words whose original stress was not initial were made to conform to the Germanic principle.[10] Since this metrical treatment agrees with what we may be sure of on linguistic grounds in the case of learned loanwords, I cannot agree with Funke's contention that each foreign word requires an individual treatment.[11]

---

9. Funke (p. 61) concludes that we dare not unqualifiedly depend on the metrical handling of the rare word for its pronunciation in prose. This is true enough as a general principle, but when the metrical treatment of the foreign words under discussion agrees, as we shall see, with the metrically and linguistically demonstrable treatment of learned loanwords, it seems a fairly safe assumption that, allowing of course for individual differences, they fitted into the same general scheme.

10. Alliteration in the line "Comêta be naman cræftgleawe men" (*Chronicle*, 975, MS A, in *Two of the Saxon Chronicles*, ed. Earle and Plummer, Oxford, 1892, 1:120) indicates that the obviously foreign *comēta* was not stressed on the penultimate syllable, as it was in Latin. Even the word *reliquias*, in which the *re-* might have been regarded as a prefix, like the *a-* in (*a*)*postol*, (*a*)*pistol*, had initial stress, as shown by the alliteration in the *Menologium* preceding the *Chronicle* in MS C (*Two of the Saxon Chronicles*, Appendix A, 1:275).

11. P. 59. He holds that we must presume the retention of the Latin stress position, in speech if not in poetry. However, as Funke himself points out, many of these words appear

Certainly individual variations must have been heard then as now, but, in the absence of better evidence, the preponderating number of foreign words demonstrably stressed initially, along with the influence of the whole body of learned loanwords, unquestionably indicates that foreign words were treated in much the same manner as the learned loanwords, that is, according to the school pronunciation of the time, which in turn followed the native stress pattern.

All Latin disyllables and all trisyllables with antepenultimate stress would naturally have unchanged stress position in OE: *Ádam*, *cálic*, *círcul*, *cléric*, *Dídimus*, *Élene*, *Énos*, *fénix*, *Jácob*, *Lúcifer*, *mártyr*, *órgan*, *palm*, *prólogus*, *sanct*, *Sódoma*, *tábule*, *témpl*. Latin words of three or more syllables in which the principal accent was not originally on the initial syllable were arbitrarily stressed heavily on that syllable in OE. In this group of words the syllable receiving the principal accent in Latin usually received a secondary stress in OE:[12] *áltàre*, *Cálèndas*, *cástèlles*, *cómèta*, *crístàllus*, *gígàntas*, *mágìster*, *sácèrdas*;[13] a great many trisyllabic proper names such as *Álbàno*, *Ándrèas*, *Cáldèas*, *Dámàsco*, *Égỳpta*, *Jóhànnes*, *Mária*, *Mártìnus*, *Phílìppus*, *Rómàne*, and the month names *Áprèlis*, *Agùstus*, *Séptèmbris*, *Óctòber*, *Nóvèmbris*, *Décèmbris;* four-syllabled words with penultimate Latin stress, *Áffricànus*, *Apollìnus*, *Bábilòne*, *básilìsca*, *Cónstantìnus*, *Fílistìna*, *Hólofèrnus*, *Júliàna;* four-syllabled words with antepenultimate Latin stress,[14] *Ássỳria*, *Béthùlia*, *Bítthìnia*, *Bóètius*, *cómmèdia*, *Éusèbius*, *Grégòrius*, *Itàlia*, *Láurèntius;*[15] a few names of five

---

in OE in double form, that is, both as foreign words with Latin inflexion and as loanwords with native inflexion. He therefore assumes, according to the degree in which a word has laid aside the intrinsic character of the *Fremdwort*, i.e., its foreign inflexion, that variations in stress and also in quantity occurred. See also J. W. Bright, "Proper Names in Old English Verse," *PMLA*, 14 (1899), 347–68, who contends that the stressing of proper names in verse had no such pretension to uniformity as Sievers and Pogatscher believe. Nevertheless, it seems reasonable to infer that, on the comparatively rare occasions when such proper names were used orally in OE times, they were stressed according to the contemporary school pronunciation.

12. Because a learned loanword or a foreign word was not likely to be completely isolated from its original, it is reasonable to infer that a Latin word of three or more syllables with the accent not on the initial syllable bore in OE a secondary stress (sometimes approaching full stress) on the syllable originally stressed in the Latin word. The inference has some support in the fact that in a few isolated cases the syllable stressed in the original bears the alliteration in verse, a most unlikely occurrence if the Latin stress had not in some degree been retained. Cf. M. Rieger, "Die alt- und angelsächsische Verskunst," *Zeitschrift für deutsche Philologie*, 7 (1876), 11, note.

13. When such Latin trisyllables appeared in OE in disyllabic form, the secondary accent was lost: *cálend*, *gígant*, *sácerd*.

14. Following Sievers's metrical system, Pogatscher, p. 25, believes that these words had a second principal stress and classifies them under Sievers's Type A.

15. When the *i* in words in *-ia*, *-ius* was pronounced [j], the syllable count would obviously

8 Orthoepia Classica

and six syllables, *Bártholomèus*, *Éthiòpia*, *Mácedònia*, *Mármedònia*, *Nábochodonòssor*.

B. Quantity in Stressed Syllables

1. Closed Syllables

In closed syllables the vowel was short, as in Vulgar Latin,[16] the length of the syllable being due to the consonant group: *balsam*, *cantic*, *circul*, *martyr*, *organ*, *sanct*, *templ;* (in syllables receiving the OE secondary stress) *calèndas*, *castèlles*, *magìster*, *sacèrdas*. Spellings with doubling of consonants following either the OE or the Latin principal stress indicate a wavering in vocalic length: *Affrica*, *Annanias*, *Benniamin*, *Channaneum*, *Effessia*, *zefferus*. It is noteworthy that in these last, all of them foreign words, the spelling has changed because of a variation in pronunciation; we should expect, in words such as these above all others, literal transcription. The doubling seems to indicate that what was principally expected of the stressed syllable was length, and that either the long vowel or the long consonant satisfied this demand. In Latin words of four syllables ending in *-ia*, *-ius* with antepenultimate stress (becoming secondary stress in OE), the vowel stressed originally is short when the *i* in the ending was pronounced [j] in OE (with concomitant reduction of syllable count): *Calvàrje*.

2. Open Syllables

In the Romanic dialects from the sixth century on, short stressed vowels in open syllables underwent lengthening, although it is not altogether clear whether this lengthening occurred in all vowels uniformly and simultaneously; furthermore, possible dialectal differences in development must be taken into consideration. That the Latin colloquial language favored *schōla*, *stōla*, *sōnus*, *cōcus* (< *cŏquus*), all with short vowels in Classical Latin, is certain, but there can also be no doubt that the school influence was conservative and frequently opposed the newer pronunciation. Abbo of Fleury, for instance, on whose *Quaestiones Grammaticales* Funke's study is based, makes a point of enjoining on the English the classical

be reduced, but the same syllables would receive the stress: (as three syllables) *Assỳria* [-ja], (as four syllables) *Mármedònia* [-ja]. [Here and elsewhere, for typographical convenience, the following substitutions have been made: *th* for Old English thorn and eth, and *g* for Old English yogh.]

16. Meyer-Lübke, *Einführung*, p. 141: "Vokale in geschlossener Silbe werden nämlich durchweg gekürzt, in offener durchweg gedehnt." Though "der Zeitpunkt dieser Veränderung lässt sich nicht genau bestimmen" (p. 142), it is certain that it took place well before the beginning of the period of borrowing with which we are here concerned.

shortness in *datus, status*, etc.,[17] and Funke assumes the same in England for the school of Bede and the circle of Aldhelm, since Classical Latin was the inspiration and model for these learned men, with their high regard for the rules of classical metrics. The question is, however, Did they observe classical metrical principles in the pronunciation of prose? Here we have some evidence, for Ælfric in the introduction to his Grammar tells us that prose and verse were distinguished in pronunciation: "Miror ualde, quare multi corripiunt sillabas in prosa, quae in metro breues sunt, cum prosa absoluta sit a lege metri; sicut pronuntiant *pater* brittonice et *malus* et similia, quae in metro habentur breues."[18] But even without such a clear statement it would seem reasonable to suppose that such a distinction was generally made.[19] It is, in fact, demonstrable that a strongly popular influence exerted itself in churchly circles at the very time that the more highly educated of the clergy were breaking lances for the classical quantities,[20] and we may safely conclude that in England, as elsewhere, originally short stressed vowels in Latin words were pronounced long when they appeared in open syllables.

It would seem, then, that we may go clear back to Pogatscher and accept his generalization that "in gelehrten Entlehnungen gelten die haupttonigen Silben als lang" (p. 31), despite the strictures of Sievers (*Zum angel-sächsischen Vocalismus*), who criticizes him for generalizing on too narrow grounds,[21] and who has, largely by making half-verses fit into his famous metrical patterns, attempted to demonstrate shortness in many foreign words, e.g., *Abeles*, *Elene*, *Gomorra*, which he concludes must exhibit resolved stress ($^\prime$xx). But, while such deviations from what was almost certainly the general rule may have existed as peculiarities of individual speakers, we cannot be sure that exceptions based solely on Sievers's verse-types are altogether to be trusted. The difficulty about such tests is that they will frequently work both ways. Pogatscher's conclusion quoted at the beginning of this paragraph is made partly on the basis of Sievers's own work. In 1885 Sievers wrote, "Als allgemeines Gesetz gilt, dass die betonter Silben der Fremdnamen als lang gelten."[22] Again, in his *Altgermanische*

17. Cited by Funke, p. 46.

18. *Ælfrics Grammatik und Glossar*, ed. J. Zupitza (Berlin, 1880), p. 2.

19. Ælfric's reference is, of course, to Latin poetry. We can infer nothing as to the treatment of loanwords in OE poetry from what he says.

20. For examples see Funke, p. 47.

21. Sievers believes that one can at most speak of an approximate fixity of length in two-syllabled forms like *Adam*, *Jacob*, etc., and their oblique cases.

22. "Zur Rhythmik des germanischen Alliterationsverses," zweiter Abschnitt, *Beiträge zur Geschichte der deutschen Sprache und Literatur*, 10:492.

Metrik (Halle, 1893), he declares, "Gelehrte Fremdnamen und Fremdwörter überhaupt dehnen in der Regel die Vocale aller Tonsilben" (p. 124), pointing out in a note that "viersilbige Paroxytona schwanken in der Quantität der ersten Silbe" and "auch bei dreisilbigen Wörtern kommt gelegentlich Kürze der erste Silbe vor" (p. 125). Somewhat before 1900, however, he had come to the conclusion, largely through the application of the metric tests, that his rule for length was not to be too rigidly adhered to, even for disyllables:

> Sie [d.h. diese Regel] wird bei genauerem Zusehen . . . tatsächlich durch so viele Ausnahmen durchbrochen, dass man höchstens bei zweisilbigen Formen . . . von einer annähernden Festigkeit der Länge reden kann. Bei den drei- und mehrsilbigen Formen aber finden sich zahlreiche Belege für Kürze, und zwar zum Teil auch bei Namen, die andererseits nur mit Länge gelesen werden können.[23]

A single example will suffice to illustrate how the application of the Sievers Types may turn out in the hands of different investigators. Sievers assumes a short *e* in *fenix* (< Lat. *phoenix*), at least in the pronunciation of the author of the poem of that name, putting such half-lines as "se is fenix haten" (86b), "and fenix byrneð" (218b), and "swa fenix beacnað" (646b) into Type C (x ´x| ´x);[24] using the same method of investigation, Pogatscher, pp. 35–36, puts the half-lines in question into Type A (´x| ´x) with anacrusis, so that *fenix* constitutes no exception to his rule for the length of stressed syllables in learned loanwords and foreign words. Obviously, then, little help in determining quantity lies in this method, at the same time too arbitrary and too flexible. I should be inclined to infer length in *fenix*, according to the principle of the English school pronunciation which prescribed length in stressed open syllables, for, while not denying the possibility that the *Phoenix* poet, as well as many of his contemporaries, may have pronounced the *e* short, I can see no reason for thinking so beyond the fact that there must have been variations in the pronunciation of vowel quantities then as now.[25] Certainly we cannot assume shortness on the basis of Sievers's metrical treatment of the word. In the absence of better evidence than this, it is reasonable to infer length in the open stressed syllables of *all* learned loanwords and foreign words in OE, regardless of their classical quantities: *Ábimèlech*, *Áprèlis*, *clēric* (< *clēricus*), *cōc*

---

23. *Zum angelsächsischen Vocalismus*, p. 6.
24. "Zur Rhythmik des germanischen Alliterationsverses," p. 499.
25. It should be borne in mind that the words in question are foreign words, i.e., bookish words and proper names, rarely spoken.

(< cŏcus, cŏquus), cómèta, córòna, crēda, fīfele (< fĭbula), grād (<grădus), láctŭca, nōn (<nōna), Óctòber, sōn (<sŏnus), tītul.

K. Luick's belief that Latin trisyllables with antepenultimate accent were pronounced with short first syllables in OE, e.g., clĕricus, fīfele, etc., must be mentioned here.[26] Luick explains in a note that

> die abweichende Quantitierung der Proparoxytona erklärt sich als Übertragung einer englischen Sprechgewohnheit. Nach der Zeit der älteren Synkope von Mittelvokalen . . . gab es im heimischen Wörtmaterial keine Wörter der Form $^?$xx (ohne Nebenton), sondern nur $^?$x und $^?$xx: Dreisilbler mit nur *einem* Akzent hatten immer Kürze in erster Silbe. Danach sprach man auch im Lateinischen clĕricus statt clēricus u. dgl.[27]

But'oblique cases of OE disyllables with length in the vowel of the first syllable correspond to the pattern of clēricus, for example, līnenes. Furthermore, the fact that the words in question were learned would tend to isolate them from the English *Sprechgewohnheit*.

Those vowel lengthenings which took place in open syllables are, as we have seen, a result a Romance sound-law, and would therefore be expected to appear in words in which the Latin principal accent was on the first syllable, that is, in Latin disyllables and in Latin trisyllables with antepenultimate accent. This does not, however, account for the vowel length which undoubtedly occurs in syllables not stressed in Latin, e.g., OE Mēsopotamie (< Lat. Mĕsopotamia), māgister (< Lat. măgister). Pogatscher, pp. 49–50, points out that some of the lengthening which occurs in syllables not originally stressed, particularly in polysyllabic words, rests on the carrying over to OE poetry of accentual and quantitative characteristics current in late Latin accentual poetry. More important for our purposes, because their treatment rests on a purely English basis, are those words in which length occurs in a syllable immediately before a Latin accent preserved in OE, e.g., mágìster (< Lat. măgíster). This lengthening may be explained as an analogical phenomenon in agreement with native word types. Inasmuch as secondary stress had disappeared after short initial syllables, as in cyninga, words of the type $^{'\,\smile}$x were not present in OE at the time of the learned borrowings. Therefore, all loanwords

---

26. *Historische Grammatik der englischen Sprache* (Leipzig, 1921), 1.1:200. Luick came to this conclusion earlier in "Zu den lateinischen Lehnwörtern im Altenglischen," *Archiv*, 126 (1911), 35–39, in which he presents evidence to show that shortening in trisyllables occurred much earlier than it is generally thought.

27. *Historische Grammatik*, p. 201, note 1.

originally stressed ˘ˊx combine preservation of the Latin accent with
lengthening of the syllable stressed in OE, in agreement with the familiar
OE type ˊˉx. In native words of two syllables secondary stress was apparently
lost very early,[28] and Latin disyllables in OE therefore had none; however,
in loanwords of two syllables derived from trisyllabic Latin paroxytones,
the influence of the trisyllabic original, usually coexistent in OE with the
disyllable, might have caused the length to be retained in the first syllable
even when the secondary accent was lost, e.g., *cálend–cálèndas*, *gígant–*
gígàntas, *sácerd–sácèrdas*.

C. QUANTITY IN UNSTRESSED SYLLABLES

Vowels in unstressed syllables of loanwords and foreign words seem to
have been treated precisely like those in unstressed syllables of native words,
as we should expect. They therefore require no special treatment here.

II. QUALITY

A. VOWELS

1. In Stressed Syllables

Inasmuch as most learned loanwords and foreign words are, except for
the endings of the former, transcribed literally, it follows that there must
be divergence from the original pronunciation; this is inevitable when a
word goes over from the phonetic system of one language into that of
another. The most momentous changes in regard to vowels, those having
to do with quantity, have been discussed in the preceding section. All that
need be said of the quality of stressed vowels in learned loanwords and
foreign words is that the letters representing them were given the pronunciation those symbols had in the borrowing language.[29] It should be pointed
out in passing that the diphthongs *ae*, *oe* had been smoothed in Latin to

28. Cf. Pogatscher, pp. 22–23; Funke, pp. 54–56.

29. This statement holds equally for ME as for OE, and for ModE as well, up to the
introduction of the "reformed" or "classical" pronunciation in the nineteenth century, a
procedure which has caused considerable confusion in the pronunciation of Latin learned
loanwords and foreign words in Present English. As the late G. C. Moore Smith has put
the matter in a letter to me (11 June 1939), "When I was a boy, we had only one pronunciation
of Latin, and Latin phrases or short quotations were in familiar use among educated people,
but when all the vowels were changed, no one dared to quote a word of Latin lest he should
not be understood, and Latin became for the first time a dead language." For a review of
the situation in ModE, see my "Tempest in Teapot: Reform in Latin Pronunciation," *ELH*,
6 (1939), 138–64 [selection 2 of this collection].

open and close *e* respectively long before the period of OE learned borrowing. In late Latin the sounds were confused, as *ae* for *oe*, *e* and *oe* for *ae*, *e* in spellings indicate.[30] In OE open stressed syllables, original *ae* and *oe* appear as *ē*, for example, *fēnix* (< *phoenix*).

Popular loanwords, whose transmission was oral, present quite a different story; their history is much more complicated than that of the learned loanwords, inasmuch as they underwent all the changes in form that took place in native words. With them, however, we are not here concerned.

2. In Unstressed Syllables

In general the vowels of unstressed syllables were preserved literally and treated like the unstressed vowels in OE. The most important changes are those affecting the Latin endings, such as the loss of the final unstressed vowel in *nōn*, *scōl*, *sōn*, etc., and of entire final unstressed syllables in *clēric*, *cōc*, *grād*, etc., though all these words also appeared as foreign words with the Latin endings. English inflexional endings appear, as in *scōlu* (< Lat. *schŏla*). These changes have more to do with inflexion and gender than with pronunciation, however, and are adequately dealt with by Funke, pp. 112–34, and Pogatscher, pp. 155–65. Svarabhakti vowels frequently appear, e.g., *cēder* (< *cĕdrus*), *fēfer*, *-or* (< *fĕbris*), *plaster* (< *(em)plastrum*), *temp(e)l* (< *templum*).

B. CONSONANTS

1. Labials

Latin *p*

Unchanged in OE in learned loanwords and foreign words: *Āpollīnus*, *baptista*, *cāpitul*, *part*, *plaster*, *prīm*. It was not pronounced in initial *ps-*, as indicated by the fact that in the *Psalms* the word *psalterium* always alliterates with words beginning with *s*; but this is hardly to be regarded as an exclusively OE loss, since it had occurred long before in the Romance dialects, where it even drops out of the spelling of popular words, e.g., It., Span., Port. *salmo* (cf. ON *sálmr*).

The Greek aspirated explosive φ [ph] developed first to the affricate [pf], and then to the fricative [f], the sound used in post-Augustan Latin and taken over into OE, e.g., *fēnix* (< *phoenix*).[31]

---

30. Cf. C. H. Grandgent, *An Introduction to Vulgar Latin* (Boston, 1907), pp. 88, 90.

31. In Old Latin the voiceless stop *p* was used for the representation of the Greek [ph], as reflected in older loans, e.g., *ampulla*.

Latin *b*

Always retained initially in learned loanwords and foreign words: *Bābilōne*, *baptista*, *bāsilisca*, *Bitthīnia*. The fact that intervocalically it was interchangeable with *v* as early as the second century in Vulgar Latin is indicative of the bilabial sound of the Greek *β* which the Latin sound developed. This sound is represented in OE usually by *f*, sometimes by *b* (=[v]), rarely by *v* (*u*): *sāfīne*, *-a* (*Leechdoms*, *Wortcunning*, *and Starcraft*, ed. Cockayne, London, 1864, 1.34; 2.100, 120, 250), *sābīna* (1.34, 190), *sāuīna*, *-e* (1.190; 3.16, 22, 58), *Galua* (*Orosius*, Lauderdale MS, ed. Sweet, *EETS* 79, p. 208), *fīfele* (Wright-Wülcker, *Anglo-Saxon and Old English Vocabularies*, London, 1884, 1.403), *fēfer*, *-or* (John 4.52, Lindisfarne, Rushworth, and Corpus MSS, ed. Skeat), *fēber* (Cambridge MS), *Trēfia* (*Orosius*, p. 186).

Abbo of Fleury implies that final *b* was pronounced like *p* in his pronunciation and that of his school,[32] but that this pronunciation was ever common in England is doubtful.

Latin *f*

Unchanged as a rule: *fals*, *Februārius*, *Fīlistīne*, *firmamentum*, *font*, but occasionally geminated medially, e.g., *Affrica* (*Orosius*, p. 8), *zefferus* (*Riddles*, 41.68, in Grein-Wülcker, *Bibliothek der angelsächsischen Poesie*, 3.1.210). The gemination may have been to show English readers that the *f* is not [v] (cf. below, under *v*), as well as to indicate consonantal length with concomitant shortness of vowel in the stressed syllable (see above, "Stress and Quantity," I, B, 1).

Latin *v*

Unchanged: *vīgīlia*, *vēnab(u)lum*, *vers*, and as *f*: *fers* (*Ælfrics Gram*., ed. Zupitza, p. 218), *Firgilies* (Metrical version of verses in Boethius, 30.3, in Grein-Wülcker, *Bibliothek der angelsächsischen Poesie*, 3.2.56). Medieval Latin sometimes has *f* for *v* also: *fespa*, *difortium* (Wright-Wülcker, *AS and OE Vocabularies*, 1.21 and 17). Presumably the spelling with *f* indicates unvoicing, under Irish influence perhaps, though it may be only a matter of spelling. Sievers says, "Ältere lehnwörter ersetzen . . . das lat. *u* ziemlich regelmässig durch *f*,"[33] though his examples indicate that he has in mind OE intervocalic *f*. Intervocalic *f* seems likewise to have been voiced at the end of the Vulgar Latin period.[34] Inasmuch as *f* was frequently voiced both in OE and Vulgar Latin, we might conclude that such a spelling

32. Cited by Funke, p. 27.
33. *Angelsächsische Grammatik*, 3d ed. (Halle, 1898), sec. 205.
34. Grandgent, p. 135.

as *fers* does not necessarily indicate any divergence from the pronunciation to be expected. But the whole matter is doubtful.

2. Dentals

Latin *t*

Unchanged as a rule: *templ, tītul, trāmet, quātern*. (Cf. popular *lǣden*: learned *lātīnus*.)

Except when it was preceded by *s* (as in *quaestio*), *t* before *e* or *i* in hiatus had been assibilated to [ts] in Vulgar Latin by the fourth century.[35] This is the sound it probably had in the OE school pronunciation,[36] e.g., *pālendse* (< *palantia*) (*Orosius*, p. 272), *drācentse* (< *dracontea*) (Cockayne, *Leechdoms*, 1.106). (Cf. popular *plǣtse*, Luke, 10.10, Rushworth MS, ed. Skeat.) Abbo says that *ci* was pronounced like *ti* in *laetitia, iustitia*[37]—he is, of course, referring only to the final *t(ia)* in these words— which according to him was spoken as *tz*. The *z*, as Funke, p. 32, points out, must mean to Abbo simple *s*, not the *sd*-sound of which Priscian speaks;[38] therefore, *te, ti* in hiatus = *ce, ci* in any position = [ts].[39]

The Latin pronunciation of *th* (< Gk. *θ*) was simply [t], since Latin had nothing to correspond to the Greek aspirate [th]. When Greek *θ* [th] shifted to [θ], that sound was too foreign to Latin, and [t] continued to be used, though *θ* is transliterated by *th* from the middle of the second century B.C. There was, however, no excuse for the English to mispronounce the newer sound of *θ*, which was perfectly familiar to them; and that it was pronounced [θ] in OE is indicated by many spellings with thorn. This pronunciation did not exist for long,[40] but was revived in modern times.

35. Grandgent, pp. 116–18.
36. Cf. *c* in the same position, below.
37. Quoted by Funke, p. 32.
38. H. Keil, *Grammatici Latini* (Leipzig, 1855–80), 2:36.
39. Cf. Pogatscher, pp. 184–94.
40. Countless spellings, e.g., *Agaton, Cartage, Tisbee, Trace*, indicate that the usual ME pronunciation was simply [t]. Since *t* and *th* had thus come to be equated in loanwords and foreign words, a quite natural confusion arose, and words with *t* were often incorrectly spelled with *th*, e.g., *Anthaeus, bithumen, Pathmos, Sathanas*.

There must, however, have been many speakers in England who pronounced Latin *th* as [θ] in ME times, though evidence on the matter is scant. The ending *-t* of the Latin verb, third person singular, sometimes became [θ], perhaps by analogy with the English ending *-th*, and the familiar English sound must have been carried over to other Latin *t-* and *d-* sounds: Chaucer, for example, rimes *savith-significavit* (*Prologue to Canterbury Tales*, 661– 62; but see B. ten Brink, *Chaucers Sprache und Verskunst*, 3d ed., rev. E. Eckhardt, Leipzig, 1920, sec. 326, who apparently believes either that *savith* was pronounced with [t] or that the rime is inaccurate). Palsgrave warns against this type of blunder as late as 1530, as does

Abbo of Fleury, according to the manuscript edited by Angelo Cardinal Mai on which Funke bases many of his conclusions, says, "Sed aspirationes bene vos, Angli, pervidere potestis: habent sonum vestrae litterae, et qui pro θ frequentius B scribitis, sicut pro digammate effertis L."[41] The *L* is Mai's reading, but Henry Bradley, who saw a rotograph of the pages, says that the letter resembles capital *P*.[42] The text at this point has undoubtedly been properly emended, in part by M. H. Jellinek,[43] and completely by Bradley, who saw that the copyist of Mai took the two halves of an insertion in the manuscript to be the first lines of columns, and that the French scribe of Abbo, taking an original thorn and wynn for Latin letters (he apparently took the first for a minuscule *b*, the second for a *P*), substituted *B* and *P* in what Abbo certainly wrote: "Sed aspirationes bene uos Angli peruidere potestis, qui pro θ frequentius [thorn] scribitis, qui pro digamma [wynn],"[44] a clear statement of what we should expect even in the absence of such testimony.

The usual non-English medieval pronunciation of θ was [ts],[45] but there

---

Salesbury in 1567 (A. J. Ellis, *On Early English Pronunciation*, part 3, *EETS*, extra ser. 14, pp. 759, 767), but we may fairly assume, quite apart from the Chaucer rime, that it is much earlier. This pronouncing of final *t* as [θ] seems, indeed, to have been a trick of the schools in late medieval times. The *Brevissima Institutio*, a portion of Lily's *Latin Grammar*, warns specifically against this "fault," an admonition reflected in John Hart's *Orthographie* (1569). H. M. Ayres, "A Note on the School Pronunciation of Latin in England," *Speculum*, 1 (1926), 440–43, reprints the pertinent section of the *Institutio*.

41. Cited with his own emendations, which lead him to some amazing conclusions, by Funke, p. 29. I have used Funke's punctuation in the passage, but have restored Mai's readings. *Digammate* for original *digamma* is Mai's emendation.

42. "On the Text of Abbo of Fleury's *Quaestiones Grammaticales*," *Proceedings of the British Academy*, 10 (1921–23), 174–75, note.

43. "Zur Aussprache des Lateinischen im Mittelalter," *Aufsätze zur Sprach- und Literaturgeschichte* ("Wilhelm Braune zum 20 Februar 1920 dargebracht von Freunden und Schülern," Dortmund, 1920), p. 26.

44. The passage is further interesting in showing a learned survival of the classical pronunciation of digamma.

45. Grandgent, p. 139; cf. Erasmus, in Jellinek. *C* before *e* and *i* had the same sound, a pronunciation reflected in the Chaucerian *Cithero*: the spelling probably indicates a fashionable continental school pronunciation; since *c* before *e*, *i* had ceased to be [ts] in France in Chaucer's day, *th* is used in order to ensure the [ts] pronunciation. (Pronunciation with [t] or [θ] is unthinkable here.) If *Cithero* and its variant *Scithero* are Chaucer's own spellings and not merely scribal, the equation of *th* with *c* indicates that Chaucer used, in this word at least, a continental pronunciation of *th*. (The fact that the word in question is a proper name, a *Fremdwort*, is here probably of some significance.) However, we may be sure that such a pronunciation was not frequent in England in OE times, though it may have been employed as something of an affectation in later times. *Anthaeus, Pathmos, Sathanas*, all Chaucerian, indicate that, if *Cithero* is really Chaucer's own, he was not consistent in his pronunciation of *th* in foreign words, for in these examples the *th* has its more usual ME value of [t].

is no reason to suppose that the English, with the sound properly described for them and being perfectly familiar with it, did not use [θ].

Latin *d*

Unchanged in all positions: *Dāvid*, *dēmon*, *discipul*, *grād*, *cēder*. Abbo of Fleury says that in his pronunciation and that of his school, final *d* (*b*, *g*) was spoken as *t* (*p*, *k*),[46] but there is no evidence that such unvoicing was widespread in England.

In *Orosius*, Greek δ and Latin *d* are often represented by eth and thorn [for which *th* is substituted here], e.g., *Archimethes* (Lauderdale MS, p. 194), *Methia* (p. 10), *Perthica* (pp. 144, 148; *Perdica* also appears, p. 146, lines 12, 13, 15), *Sarthinia* (p. 202). The appearance of the forms with eth and thorn is so frequent that they cannot be ascribed merely to scribal carelessness. Pogatscher, pp. 176–77, thinks these reflect Alfred's own pronunciation, and may indicate that he knew something of contemporary Greek in which δ was pronounced like OE eth. On the other hand, the pronunciation of *d* as eth may rest on a Galloromanic basis, since intervocalic *d* became [ð], probably at the end of the Vulgar Latin period, in Gaul and elsewhere.[47]

3. Sibilants

Latin *s*

S seems to have been pronounced exactly as in native words, i.e., voiceless initially and finally, voiced between voiced sounds: *Andrēas*, *Jōhannes*, *Jōseph*, *Mēsopotāmie*, *sācerd*, *sēraphīn*. The OE practice agreed with the voicing which seems to have taken place in a late school pronunciation of Latin. In a tenth-century tractate on pronunciation, *s* between vowels is described as "weak," which can point only to voicing.[48] There is also evidence that intervocalic *s* may have been voiced in certain regions at the very end of the Vulgar Latin period.[49] Abbo of Fleury allows himself to be influenced by the popular language to the extent of recommending

---

46. Quoted by Funke, p. 27. Cf. Jellinek, pp. 18–19. Grandgent, p. 119, points out that in Vulgar Latin "at the end of a word there was hesitation between *d* and *t*; *d* may have been devocalized before a voiceless initial consonant, and possibly at the end of a phrase," as such spellings as *aput*, *capud*, *quot*, *set* indicate.

47. Grandgent, p. 119.

48. Reference in Grandgent, p. 125, note.

49. Meyer-Lübke, *Historische Grammatik der französischen Sprache* (Heidelberg, 1913), pp. 126–27.

this voiced intervocalic *s*, if that indeed is what he means by his "levi sono ubique sola."[50]

Sc and *sch* will be treated below, under *c*.

Latin (< Greek) *z*

Except initially, *z* had the sound of [ts] in OE, as such alternate spellings as *dracentse-draconze* and, in native words, *betsta-bezt, milts-milze* indicate. Initially, as in *zefferus*, it was probably [s], though direct evidence is lacking.

Priscian declares that the letter *z* is found only "in Graecis dictionibus," includes it with *x* under "consonantes duplices," and describes its sound as *sd*.[51] In Vulgar Latin it was pronounced [dj]; *di* often occurs for *z* and vice versa.[52]

4. Velars

Latin *c*, *ch* (< Greek χ), *k*, *q*, *x*

Initially and medially before *a*, *o*, *u*, and before *l*, *r*, Latin *c* had the sound [k]: *cālend, clēric, cōc, cristallus, scōla*.

In all positions *c* before *e* and *i* was pronounced [ts] in Vulgar Latin.[53] This was also the medieval school pronunciation, and seems to have been widely used in England, though, because of its strangeness initially, there must have been many who used the native palatal *c* in this position, and probably in other positions before front vowels. Evidence on this point is, however, lacking. Pronunciation as [k] must also have been fairly frequent, inasmuch as this pronunciation, dating from classical times, was the one used in Ireland.[54] The spelling of the popular loanword *yntse* (also appearing as *yndse*), from Latin *uncia*, reproduces the Romance assibilation as it was heard in England.[55] We cannot be sure, but it seems probable that the *c* before *e, i* in the following words was by some speakers pronounced [ts], by others exactly as in native words: *cālic* (< *calicem*), *cēder, cīlic* (< *cilicem*), *circul, crūc* (< *crucem*), *pūmic* (< *pumicem*). The spelling

50. Quoted by Funke, p. 19.
51. Keil, 2:36.
52. Grandgent, pp. 140–41.
53. For the Latin development of this sound from original [k], see Grandgent, p. 111; Meyer-Lübke, *Einführung*, pp. 160–64.
54. See M. H. Jellinek, "Über Aussprache des Lateinischen und deutsche Buchstaben-namen," *Akademie der Wissenschaften in Wien*, 212 Band, 2 Abhandlung (Wien und Leipzig, 1930), 12–13.
55. Modern *inch* is from a different form: *ynce* with [č], in which the assibilation is English, not Romance. See Pogatscher, pp. 186–87.

mertze (< *mercem*) (Wright-Wülcker, *Vocabularies*, 1.32) leaves little doubt
as to the pronunciation of that word. Pogatscher, p. 190, points out that
the assumption of [ts] explains the ME *pomys* and *c(h)alice* in a simple
way, but that the ME forms could also rest upon later contamination with
the corresponding French forms.

Sc was likewise palatalized in Vulgar Latin before *e* and *i*. As for the
later school pronunciation, according to Abbo *c* in the combination *sc* was
spoken "ut fere videatur sonare G, maxime S praecedente, ut suscipio,
suscepi, suscepit."[56] He is apparently referring to the pronunciation of *g*
before *e*, *i*, which was [j̑],[57] and Funke, pp. 36–37, argues that it follows
that *sc* before *e*, *i* was pronounced [sč], but does not insist that this was
a general pronunciation. Jellinek, however, points out that if Abbo had
pronounced *sc* as [š], he would probably have expressed himself in the
same terms.[58] Since the combination *sc* had the sound [š] in OE, one is
inclined to assume this pronunciation, at least for initial position, simply
because of the probabilities—for satisfactory evidence is lacking. It must
be obvious that Abbo's phonological equipment is sadly deficient; furthermore, one may be sure that he was the type of man who leaned over
backwards to satisfy his own notions of "correct" pronunciation and is
therefore not always to be relied upon. It will be noticed, nevertheless,
that in discussing *sce*, *sci* he gives examples of medial position only, which
fact leads one to suspect that he had that position only in mind (though
his general plan seems to indicate that the consonants under discussion
had the same pronunciation initially and medially); that is, even assuming
that he is describing the sound [sč], as Funke interprets his words, he
may simply have neglected to describe the sound of the combination in
initial position—where he might well have pronounced it [š]. This is
argumentum ab silentio, but it is the best we may do under the circumstances. I find no OE learned loanwords with *sc* before *e*, *i*; and only one
foreign word, *Sciththia* (with its derivative *Sciththeas*) (Metrical versions
of verses in Boethius, 1.2, in Grein-Wülcker, *Bibliothek der angelsächsischen Poesie*, 3.2.2, where it alliterates with *sceldas*).

Abbo condemns, in a passage badly misunderstood by Funke, pp. 33–
34, but correctly interpreted by Jellinek,[59] the pronunciation of *ce*, *ci* as
que, *qui*. His condemnation is interesting in showing that the classical

56. Entire passage quoted by Jellinek, "Zur Aussprache des Lateinischen im Mittelalter,"
p. 20.
57. See under *g*, below.
58. "Zur Aussprache des Lateinischen im Mittelalter," p. 21.
59. "Zur Aussprache des Lateinischen im Mittelalter," pp. 21–22.

tradition still existed in the pronunciation of those people who spoke *c* alike before all vowels. The sound of *c* in this condemned, though classically orthodox, pronunciation was [k]; inasmuch as Abbo equates *ce*, *ci* with *que*, *qui* as an example of what *not* to do with *c* before a front vowel, we must infer that *que*, *qui* were in his pronunciation [ke], [ki]: no other value of *c* could possibly be equated with *q*. As for the pronunciation of *qu* before *a*, *o*, *u*, we must again argue from silence: since Abbo nowhere says that *qu* varied in pronunciation according to the following vowel, we may assume that it was always [k]. The silence of the *w*-sound in *qu*, and also in *gu* (see below, under *g*) was not universal in Abbo's day and even later; the Thurot tractate cited by Grandgent, p. 125, note, and other authorities cited by Jellinek, "Zur Aussprache des Lateinischen im Mittelalter," pp. 23–24, do not agree with Abbo in their descriptions of the sound. In Vulgar Latin *qu* was [kw], but it was reduced to [k] before *o* and *u* by the first or second century.[60] Since the sound of the Classical Latin *qu* was perfectly familiar to the English in such native words as *cwethan*, *cwic*, *cwōmon*, and since there are rare occurrences of *qu* for *cw* in the oldest texts,[61] it would seem probable that the pronunciation [kw] was used in England in all positions. The evidence is, however, unsatisfactory, and we cannot be too certain, for to an Englishman living in the period of the learned borrowings the tradition which equated *qu* with *cw* in the oldest texts may well have been lost.

Latin *ch* (< Greek χ) was pronounced [k] in OE, as it was also in Latin.[62] Abbo says this by inference when he complains of the custom of transliterating χ by *x* because of the similar appearance of the letters. Though the text printed by Cardinal Mai has *Kereas* as a transliteration of χηρηας, the manuscript, as Bradley, p. 179, has shown, has χηρηα and *s.kerea* (explained by Bradley, doubtless correctly, as a scribal misreading of *cherea*). We find both *c* and *ch* in OE, for example, *scōla*, *chōr*. According to Jellinek's interpretation of Abbo,[63] which seems to me undoubtedly correct, after *s* and before *e*, *i*, the *ch* was pronounced as if no *h* followed the *c*; that is, *sche*, *schi* were pronounced like *sce*, *sci*.

Priscian includes *x* with *z* under "consonantes duplices."[64] Its sound was [ks] in Classical Latin, and, though the [k] tended to be lost in Vulgar

---

60. Grandgent, p. 107.

61. Sievers, *Angelsächsische Grammatik*, sec. 208.

62. From the middle of the second century B.C. the spelling *ch* occurs in Latin as a transcription of χ, but the sound of the Greek letter was foreign to the Romans, who pronounced it [k].

63. "Zur Aussprache des Lateinischen im Mittelalter," pp. 24–25.

64. Keil, 2:10.

Latin under varying circumstances,[65] it certainly had the pronunciation [ks] in OE.[66]

Latin *g*

Taken over into OE as *g*, initially and medially: *gīgant*, *Gōmorra*, *grād*, *Grēgōrius*.

In Abbo's description, *g* (and *k*) before *a*, *o*, *u* "sonant in faucibus," that is, they are velar. As to the pronunciation of *g* before *e*, *i*, he says nothing more helpful than the equivocal "Constat igitur ex his quae dicta sunt C et G pene aequaliter pronunciari, sequente qualibet vocali." This can hardly point to complete identity, but only to similarity, as Funke, p. 31, points out. Speaking of the pronunciation of *sc*, Abbo also tells us that it "videatur sonare G," which, though not very accurate phonetically, points to the assibilation of *g* which we may be sure of on other grounds. Furthermore, says Abbo, *lego*, *legam*, *lege*, *legi*, like *vinco*, *vincam*, *vince*, *vinci*, "mutato cum vocalibus sono dicimus," in the same passage condemning the pronunciation of *ge* as *gue*: "stultum est dicere pingue pro pinge."[67] In addition to furnishing evidence that the classical pronunciation of *g* still lingered on in the speech of a few purists, the passage indicates the assibilation of *g* before front vowels. In another connection, when his students seem to have asked him whether the rule that *g* is hard before *o* (and *a*) applies when the *o* (or *a*) is followed by *e* in the same syllable, Abbo replies that it does not have its velar sound: "non inpinguatur."[68] The assibilation of *c* before front vowels has already been treated; in similar manner *g* was assibilated in late clerical Latin to [ĵ] before front vowels.[69] This sound, which prevailed in the continental school pronunciation, it probably had in OE.

It is impossible to speak with any certainty concerning the pronunciation of *gu*, though Abbo, by direct statement and by implication, makes himself fairly clear. Whether the *u* was generally pronounced or not it is difficult to say; Abbo makes it plain that in his pronunciation, at least, it was not, when in the passage cited in the preceding paragraph he warns against equating *ge* and *gue*; for the only way such an equation can well be understood, in spite of Funke's amazing interpretation, is by assuming the

65. Grandgent, p. 108.
66. Sievers, *Angelsächsische Grammatik*, sec. 209.
67. The passage is quoted by Funke, p. 33, who misunderstands it.
68. The passage is quoted by Bradley, p. 174, and given in the following paragraph. It will be remembered, of course, that the original diphthongs had been smoothed.
69. For its development in early popular and clerical Latin see Meyer-Lübke, *Einführung*, pp. 164–65, and Grandgent, pp. 109–10.

"mispronunciation" [ge] instead of [ǰe] for *ge*. The equation which Abbo condemns is quite parallel with that which he cites for *ce*, *ci* and *que*, *qui*. In the light of Abbo's general method, we may infer that what he says of *gue* is applicable also to *gui* and, by implication from his silence, to *gu* followed by back vowels. In another passage already mentioned, Abbo writes, "De littera G scitote quia si non sequatur V propter diptongum non inpinguatur, ut lagoena, tragoedia." Since the original diphthong *oe* (as well as *ae*) had been smoothed, we might assume from his "si non sequatur V" that Abbo's implication is that *gu* before *e* (and *i*) was pronounced [g], not [gw]; in other words, inasmuch as he tells us that *g* alone before [e] did not have its velar sound if not followed by *u*, we may infer that it did have that sound when followed by *u*.

It is difficult to come to any conclusion about the pronunciation of *gu* in OE. This much we may say, however, that, whether or not it was itself pronounced, the *u* prevented the assibilation of *g*. The situation in Vulgar Latin fails to throw much light on the subject as far as OE is concerned.

There is no evidence that final *g* was commonly unvoiced in England, despite Abbo's statement that in his pronunciation and that of his school final *g* (*d*, *b*) was spoken as *k* (*t*, *p*).[70]

Latin *h*

In words whose transmission was not exclusively literary, Latin *h* is lost: *iācin(c)tus* (< *hyacinthus*), *istoriam*. In purely literary words it is retained in the spelling and pronounced like English *h*; *hōlocaustum*, *Hōlofernus*, *hostiārius*.[71]

Priscian says that *h* is only "nota aspirationis."[72] It was weak at all times in Latin, probably disappearing first when medial.[73] There is no trace of it in the Romance languages.

Latin *ch*, *ph*, *th* in words of Greek origin have already been treated under *c*, *p*, *t*.

5. Liquids and Nasals

Latin *l*, *m*, *n*, *r*

Liquids and nasals always appear unchanged in learned words and foreign words and therefore require no special treatment here.

70. Cf. above, under *b* and *d*.
71. But cf. its loss in popular proper names, e.g., *Ercol* (*Hercules*), *Elene*.
72. Keil, 2:12 and 36.
73. Grandgent, p. 106.

6. Semivowels

Latin j

Pronounced [j] in OE, as in Latin: *iānuarius*, *Iōhannes*, *iūniperus*. Latin *i* (as well as *e*) in hiatus lost its syllabic value by the first century at least.[74] This loss was probably characteristic of the OE pronunciation of Latin also, occurring in such words as, for example, *Assyria*, *psalterium*.

Latin v (= w)

Though originally [w], *v* became, probably early in the Empire, the bilabial fricative [β].[75] The sound of [w] naturally occurs in early popular loans in OE, for example, *wīn* (< *vinum*). The treatment of the later sound has already been discussed under labials, above. A new [w], however, developed in Latin from *u* in hiatus, which was probably so pronounced in OE.

III. SUMMARY

Old English treated Latin learned loanwords and foreign words precisely according to the native pattern in regard to stress, that is, the principal stress was placed on the first syllable. Classical quantities were not observed except in syllables with OE secondary stress, because another system of pronunciation than the classical, namely, the so-called school pronunciation, was used. The principal characteristics of this system in regard to quantity have been described and discussed. The vowels of Latin were given the pronunciation that the letters representing them had in OE.[76] The consonants have required a somewhat more detailed discussion, but an unmistakable conclusion in regard to them is that, despite the efforts of continental teachers like Abbo and the fact that we are dealing with a special class of words whose use would in the nature of things be confined to educated men, a group most likely to pride themselves upon their linguistic abilities, there was here also a strong tendency towards anglicization.

---

74. Grandgent, pp. 93–94.
75. Grandgent, pp. 135–36.
76. These values would, of course, approximate those of Classical Latin (and of Vulgar Latin as well) much more closely than would be the case in the modern period. The Great Vowel Shift has made the English pronunciation of Latin, up to the time of the "reform," differ radically from the classical, as well as from any contemporary continental pronunciation.

Tempest in Teapot: Reform in
Latin Pronunciation

EVIDENCE abounds to show that from the earliest times the English, despite the efforts of foreign teachers, made little effort to conform to any model in the pronunciation of Latin save that of their own language. Indeed, the same conformity to the pattern furnished by the vernacular is to be observed in the pronunciation of Latin by the various continental nations. The Great Vowel Shift, which was well under way at the beginning of the Modern English period, has, however, made the English pronunciation of Latin differ more radically from the classical pronunciation than does that of any continental nation. This vowel shift caused different values to be assigned to the various letters, and these new values were of course carried over into the pronunciation of Latin words. Latin in the mouths of Frenchmen, Germans, Spaniards, and Italians has *approximately* the same vowels, though the Frenchman's are likely to show nasalization; but the Englishman's vowels are so different from these as to be incomprehensible to a foreign Latinist, because the pronunciation of Latin in England has followed closely the development of the English language. No other cause for the English pronunciation of Latin need be sought for. As Henry Bradley says:

> It is sometimes imagined that the modern English way of pro-
> nouncing Latin was a deliberate invention of the Protestant reformers.
> For this view there is no foundation in fact. It may be conceded
> that English ecclesiastics and scholars who had frequent occasion to
> converse in Latin with Italians would learn to pronounce it in the
> Italian way; and no doubt the Reformation must have operated to
> arrest the growing tendency to the Italianization of English Latin.
> But there is no evidence that before the Reformation the un-English

pronunciation was taught in the schools. The grammar-school pronunciation of the early nineteenth century was the lineal descendant
of the grammar-school pronunciation of the fourteenth century.[1]

Though for convenience' sake we speak of *a* continental pronunciation
of Latin, there can be no doubt that there are many continental pronunciations, that each nation has made its pronunciation of Latin conform to
its own sound-system. For instance, the name *Cicero* is [sisero] to a
Frenchman, [tsitsero] to a German, [čičero] to an Italian. There is, indeed,
considerable diversity in continental practice, even in liturgical use. Priests
are quite likely to pronounce Latin exactly like their own vernacular. F.
Brittain reports that

> a French priest reciting the *Gloria Patri* . . . will say: *Sicǜt erat in
> prēsipio*; a Spanish priest will announce the Gospel as *Inithium sancti
> ebanhelii*; a German priest will end the Lord's prayer with *in zaecula
> zaeculorum*; and a Portuguese cantor will sing *Adeshtǝ*, *fidele*sh,

and that a Roman Catholic of his acquaintance "laments that, whenever
he has heard a Frenchman giving a mere Latin quotation, he has never
understood a word of it, owing to the absence of stress-accent and the
disfigurement of the Latin by the French phrase-accent."[2] Erasmus, in his
De Recta Latini Graecique Sermonis Pronuntiatione (Basiliae, 1528) deplores the complete absence of any international pronunciation of Latin,
with consequent confusion: "One would have thought all Babel had come
together." A large part of this confusion he attributes to the practice of
various nations of pronouncing Latin in their own way, and proceeds to
give examples of contemporary pronunciations of Latin, many chosen, as
we should expect, from Dutch usage. It is not surprising that the national
pronunciations have without exception the same phonetic peculiarities as
the vernacular: the French, Erasmus informs us, pronounce Latin *u* in their
own way, and prefix *e* to words beginning with *st* and *sp*; the Germans
confuse *b* and *p*, saying *pipere* for *bibere* and *biper* for *piper*; some of
the Spaniards, like the French, prefix *e* to initial *sp* and *st*, and confuse
b and *v*, saying *bibit* for *vivit*.[3] He concludes that it would be best to
return to the pronunciation of classical times, his conclusions agreeing to
a surprising extent with those of modern scholarship.

1. Introduction to J. Sargeaunt's *Pronunciation of English Words Derived from the Latin*,
SPE Tract 4 (Oxford, 1920), p. 5.
2. *Latin in Church* (Cambridge, 1934), pp. 28–29.
3. Erasmus is of course referring to the Spanish fricative [β]. Spain has been called
"Felix natio, ubi vivere est bibere."

It is obvious from what Erasmus says that there was no standardized pronunciation for ecclesiastical or diplomatic purposes; but it must be equally obvious that most English speakers of Latin were perfectly aware of the fact that they were giving to their vowels qualities which they did not elsewhere have. There must also have been many who could change over to a vowel system resembling the continental (we may use the singular here for the sake of convenience, though bearing in mind that no two languages have vowel systems precisely alike) with little more difficulty than is experienced today by an Englishman in using the "reformed" pronunciation of Latin. This fact probably explains the famous story of the conversation in Latin between Queen Elizabeth and the Polish ambassador. I do not think that, in view of what Erasmus tells us of Latin pronunciation in the reign of Henry VIII, we are justified in assuming that Elizabeth habitually used any pronunciation of Latin other than the traditional English one, though she undoubtedly knew the non-English vowel qualities. Likewise, when the Duke of Stettin-Pomerania visited England in 1602, and his party lost their way, they were directed in Latin by an English gentleman, according to the diary of Frederic Gerschow, a scholar who accompanied the Duke and who recorded the incident. Later, on reaching their destination, they got what they wanted through the intermediary of a learned parson. Joan Parkes, who recounts the incident,[4] thinks that the fact that the Duke could understand the Latin of the gentleman and the parson indicates that the vowels had not yet changed so as to be radically different from continental vowels. But, as Zachrisson has shown, the vowels changed much earlier than has been thought, and G. C. Moore Smith is undoubtedly correct in his explanation that the learned parson may have accommodated his pronunciation a little to the needs of the foreigner.[5]

Only a short time after the publication of Erasmus's book, John Cheke (1514–57) and Thomas Smith (1513–77), two young Cambridge students who were later to become the great classical scholars of the time in England, attempted to reform the pronunciation of Greek,[6] which apparently was given the contemporary Greek pronunciation, i.e., with ι, η, υ, $\epsilon\iota$, $o\iota$, $\upsilon\iota$ all sounded as [i]. Smith and Cheke "well perceived how the vulgar sounding of the Greek was, and concluded it evidently false, that so many different letters and diphthongs should have but one and the same sound."[7] Their

---

4. "English Vowel-Sounds in Latin," *Notes and Queries*, 27 February 1932, p. 152.
5. *Notes and Queries*, 19 March 1932, p. 212.
6. Their views are set forth in Cheke's *De Pronuntiatione Graecae Potissimum Linguae* (Basiliae, 1555) and Smith's *De Recta et Emendata Linguae Graecae Pronuntiatione* (Paris, 1568).
7. John Strype, *Life of Sir Thomas Smith* (Oxford, 1820), p. 8.

scheme was to do away with giving "one and the same sound" to so many letters by substituting English vowels; but there can be little doubt that the usual English pronunciation of Greek before the reform of Cheke and Smith, though under the influence of the contemporary Greek pronunciation of Classical Greek, was distinctly national.

As to the pronunciation of Latin there can be no doubt. Lipsius tells us in 1586 that the English pronounce *regina*, *amicus*, *vita* as *regeina*, *ameicus*, *veita*, i.e., they substituted the contemporary English value of the letter *i* for the continental value [i] with which Lipsius was most familiar.[8]

Thomas Coryat, the traveler, furnishes us with another early record of the difference between English and continental Latin, when he tells us why he decided to use the Italian pronunciation:

> The Italian when he uttereth any Latin word wherein this letter i is to be pronounced long, doth always pronounce it as a double e, viz. as ee. As for example: he pronounceth feedes for fides: veeta for vita: ameecus for amicus, &c. but where the i is not to be pronounced long he uttereth it as we doe in England, as in the words, impius, aquila, patria, Ecclesia: not aqueela, patreea, Eccleseea. And this pronunciation is so general in all Italy, that every man which speaketh Latin soundeth a double e for an i. Neither is it proper to Italy only, but to all other nations whatsoever in Christendome saving to England. For whereas in my travels I discoursed in Latin with Frenchmen, Germans, Spaniards, Danes, Polonians, Suecians, and divers others, I observed that every one with whom I had any conference, pronounced the i after the same manner that the Italians use. Neither would some of them (amongst whom I was not a little inquisitive for the reason of this their pronunciation) sticke to affirm that Plautus, Terence, Cicero, Hortensius, Caesar, and those other selected flowers of eloquence amongst the auncient Romans, pronounced the i in that sort as they themselves doe. Whereupon having observed such a generall consent amongst them in the pronunciation of this letter, I have thought good to imitate these nations herein, and to abandon my old English pronunciation of *vita*, *fides*, and *amicus*, as being utterly dissonant from the sound of all other Nations; and have determined (God willing) to retayne the same till my dying day.[9]

Shakespeare's *Merry Wives of Windsor*, written around the turn of the century, gives us a good idea of the English pronunciation of Latin—as

8. *De Recta Pronuntiatione Latinae Linguae Dialogus* (Antwerp, 1628), p. 23.
9. *Coryat's Crudities*, reprint of original edition of 1611 (Glasgow, 1905), 2:59–60.

well as the Welsh mispronunciation. Sir Hugh Evans, the Welsh parson, is displaying young William Page's progress in Latin to Mistress Page:

> EVANS. What is "fair," William?
> WILL. *Pulcher.*
> MISTRESS QUICKLY. Polecats! There are fairer things than polecats, sure.
> EVANS. . . . What is he, William, that does lend articles?
> WILL. Articles are borrowed of the pronoun, and be thus declined, *Singulariter, nominativo, hic, haec, hoc.*
> EVANS. *Nominativo, hig, hag, hog* . . . Well, what is your accusative case?
> WILL. *Accusativo, hinc.*
> EVANS. I pray you, have your remembrance, child. *Accusativo, hing, hang, hog.*
> QUICK. "Hang-hog" is Latin for bacon, I warrant you.
> EVANS. Leave your prabbles, 'oman. What is the focative case, William?
> WILL. O, — vocativo, *O*.
> EVANS. Remember, William; focative is *caret*.
> QUICK. And that's a good root.
> EVANS. . . . What is your genitive case plural, William?
> WILL. . . . Genitive, *horum, harum, horum*.
> QUICK. Vengeance of Jenny's case! Fie on her! Never name her, child, if she be a whore.
> EVANS. For shame, 'oman.
> QUICK. You do ill to teach the child such words. He teaches him to hick and hack, which they'll do fast enough of themselves, and to call "horum,"—fie upon you![10]

Drummond of Hawthornden reports Ben Jonson as telling him that "Scaliger writtes ane epistle to Casaubone, wher he scorns his [Casaubon's? But he was a Frenchman who lived in London in 1610–1614. The editor suggests "us"] Englishe speaking of Latine, for he thought he had spoken English to him."[11]

Somewhat later, Samuel Sorbière, a French traveler to England, gives us additional testimony as to the strangeness of the English pronunciation

10. 4:1.

11. *Ben Jonson's Conversations with William Drummond of Hawthornden*, Shakespeare Society (London, 1842), p. 33. An editorial note says, "This seems to allude to a curious passage in a letter of Scaliger, addressed, not to Casaubon, but to Stephanus Ubertus, in 1608." F. Brittain, *Latin in Church*, p. 35, tells that Scaliger was visited by some unknown Englishman in Leyden in 1608, and after listening to a long discourse in Latin from his visitor, which he did not even recognize as Latin, expressed his regret that he did not understand English very well.

of Latin: "Les Anglais s'expliquent en latin d'un certain accent, et avec
une prononciation qui ne le rend pas moins difficile que leur langue."[12]

It is not surprising that Milton, with his predilection for Italy, should
have preferred the Italian pronunciation to the English. He expresses himself
very clearly on the subject in his *Tractate on Education*, in which he advises
teachers of Latin to encourage "a distinct and clear pronunciation, as near
as may be to the Italian, especially in the vowels," proceeding, "for we
Englishmen, being far northerly, do not open our mouths in the cold air
wide enough to grace a southern tongue: but are observed by all other
nations to speak exceeding close and inward; so that to smatter Latin with
an English mouth is as ill a hearing as Law French."[13] Thomas Ellwood,
the Quaker, was employed at one time to read to Milton. He tells us:

> At my first sitting to read to him, observing that I used the English
> pronunciation, he told me, if I would have the benefit of the Latin
> tongue, not only to read and understand Latin authors, but to converse
> with foreigners, either abroad or at home, I must learn the foreign
> pronunciation. To this I consenting, he instructed me how to sound
> the vowels; so different from the common pronunciation used by the
> English, who speak Anglice their Latin, that—with some other
> variations in sounding some consonants in particular cases, as *c* before
> *e* and *i* like *ch*, *sc* before *i* like *sh*, &c.—the Latin thus spoken seemed
> as different from that which was delivered, as the English generally
> speak it, as if it were another language.[14]

However, Milton had finally to give in, in this as well as in other more
important matters, for, writing in 1661, he says in his *Grammar* that "Few
will be persuaded to pronounce Latin otherwise than their own English."[15]

Samuel Pepys tells amusingly of the discomfiture of an "Oxford scholar
in a Doctor of Law's gowne" who, at a dinner at the Spanish Ambassador's,
"though a gentle sort of scholar, yet sat like a fool for want of French
or Spanish, but knew only Latin, which he spoke like an Englishman."[16]

Pepys's contemporary, John Evelyn, hearing the exercises at Westminster

12. *Voyage en Angleterre* (Paris, 1664). The passage is quoted in G. B. Hill's edition of
Samuel Johnson's *Lives of the Poets* (Oxford, 1905), 1:133. Cf. also H. Neville, *Plato Redivivus*
(London, 1681), p. 12, in which another continental European, this time an Italian, speaks of
the English pronunciation of Latin.

13. *Prose Works*, ed. C. Symmons (London, 1806), 1:277–78.

14. *The History of Thomas Ellwood Written by Himself*, Morley's Universal Library, no.
32 (London, 1885), pp. 134–35.

15. *Prose Works*, 3:441.

16. *Diary*, 5 May 1669.

School, condemned "their odd pronouncing of Latin, so that out of England none were able to understand it, or endure it."[17] One suspects that Evelyn here is making a show of his cosmopolitanism. That a continental pronunciation of Latin may have had some currency in England in the seventeenth century, though not in the schools, is faintly implied by this remark and perhaps by Pepys's. The only two rimes I have come upon in English poems which indicate any other pronunciation of Latin than the English come from this period: one is from Sir John Denham's "A Dialogue between Sir John Pooley and Mr. Thomas Killigrew" and is as follows:

> And I will rub my Mater pia
> To find a Rhyme to Gonorrheia,
> And put it in my Letania.

This is suspect: the lines themselves indicate that the rime may be a bad one. The other rime is from "Satyr Unmuzzled," published in *State-Poems Continued* (London, 1702), a collection of salacious and political poetry from the period of the Restoration: *Thomas* and *Mandamus* are in rime (p. 63). In the light of all the other evidence, I do not think that the use of a continental pronunciation in England could have been anything more than a rapidly passing vogue confined to a very small circle of English cosmopolites. Lord Rochester, who should belong to such a group, always indicates the English pronunciation by his rimes of Latin words with English. Samuel Butler's *Hudibras* contains the following rimes, chosen almost at random: *satis* – hate us, *juvare* – miscarry, twice I – *vici*, *phenomenas* – case.

Milton's demand that Ellwood learn the Italian pronunciation roused all the sturdy insularity of Dr. Samuel Johnson, who writes of it in his *Life of Milton:*

> This seems to have been a task troublesome without use. There is little reason for preferring the Italian pronunciation to our own, except that it is more general: and to teach it to an Englishman is only to make him a foreigner at home. He who travels, if he speaks Latin, may so soon learn the sounds which every native gives it, that he need make no provision before his journey; and if strangers visit us, it is their business to practice such conformity to our modes as they expect of us in their own countries.[18]

Furthermore, the Doctor stuck to his guns: though he undoubtedly could use a continental pronunciation, he would not do so in London, for Boswell

17. *Diary*, ed. W. Bray (London, 1872), 1:372.
18. *Lives of the English Poets*, ed. G. B. Hill (Oxford, 1905), 1:133.

tells us that "when Sir Joshua Reynolds, at one of the dinners of the Royal Academy, presented him to a Frenchman of great distinction, he would not deign to speak French, but talked Latin though his Excellency did not understand it, owing, perhaps, to Johnson's English pronunciation."[19] He was of the opinion, however, that the Italian pronunciation was historically more "correct," for an acquaintance reports a conversation with him in which he said:

> It is probable that the immediate descendants of the Romans would be more likely to pronounce the Roman language with propriety, than foreign nations. It is probable that persons living in the same climate, and on the same spot, would be more apt to fall into the pronunciation which a Roman would adopt, than any foreigner: for the natural causes that affect pronunciation, would be common to the ancient and the modern inhabitant of the place. For these reasons I incline to think that the Italians have the chance of being more correct than any other nation.[20]

Then, to illustrate, he quoted a passage of Virgil (obviously with the Italian pronunciation), saying, "Pronounce this passage like an Englishman, and the beauty almost vanishes: pronounce it like an Italian, and it must be felt."

Among dissenting voices of the eighteenth century must be mentioned Jenkin Thomas Philipps, translator and linguist, who has a great deal to say of the faulty way in which the English pronounce Latin in his *Compendious Way of Teaching Antient and Modern Languages* (London, 1750). William Mitford, in his *Essay upon the Harmony of Language* (London, 1774), realizes the inadequacy of the English pronunciation (pp. 224 ff.), but, since "to imagine it possible to recover within many degrees the true pronunciation of the Greek and Latin languages were preposterous" (p. 213), feels that "what we should endeavor to acquire is not the particular sound of the letters, so much as the general harmony of the language" (p. 228); however, "the difficulty, or rather the awkwardness of altering our usual pronunciation of the Latin vowels, so as to give the proper quantities to all syllables, were perhaps most easily overcome by adopting the Italian sound of all the vowels" (p. 229).

To list rimes from the poets showing the English pronunciation of Latin would be an almost endless task; furthermore, it would only serve to support

19. *Boswell's Life of Johnson*, ed. G. B. Hill (Oxford, 1887), 2:404.
20. In Joseph Priestley, *Theological and Miscellaneous Works*, ed. J. T. Rutt (Hackney, 1817–32), 23:233, note.

what we already know. The poems of Swift and Byron, to mention only two outstanding figures, abound in such rimes: Swift has, e.g., fallow—*Gallo*, *praeditum*—credit 'em, abomine 'em—*ad hominem*, *ecclesiae*—please ye, penn'd 'em—*commendam*, bite 'em—*infinitum*, undermine 'em—*jus divinum*, vary—*episcopari*, jaws trow—*plaustro*, *imprimis*—rhyme is; Byron has *niger*—oblige 'er—*bos piger*, *Davus sum*—hum—dumb, *nil admirari*—vary—wary, *quarum*—harem—spare 'em, *vulgarit*—share it, *mores*—stories, *negotiis*—*sociis*—ferocious, *male*—gayly—daily, way—*sine qua*, quibble he—*impossibile*, *desideratum*—*substratum*—relate 'em, great as—*Cincinnatus*—potatoes, question—*Hephaestion*—digestion, *belli*—well I—fell I, can be—*de se*.[21]

Despite occasional signs of preference, in England and elsewhere, for an Italian pronunciation of Latin as being historically more "pure" than any other—an utterly mistaken notion advanced even by that superb pillar of common sense, Dr. Johnson—there are few evidences of real discontent with the "old" pronunciation, which seems to have served well enough for all practical purposes, until the nineteenth century, which brought with it the rise of linguistic scholarship.

As early as 1846, Charles Kraitsir, M.D., advocated what he believed to be the Roman pronunciation of Latin in his *Significance of the Alphabet* (Boston), and Mrs. M. L. Putnam, writing in the *North American Review* in 1849,[22] gives the full sanction of her authority to Kraitsir's book, at the same time expressing in no uncertain terms her dissatisfaction with, and her disgust for, the traditional English pronunciation. This learned lady well merits quotation on the subject, not only of Latin pronunciation, but also of refinement and propriety of diction in English. Because of the English method of pronouncing Latin, she writes,

> many coarse and unpleasant sounds are conveyed into the Latin which are wholly foreign to it, and which are plainly corruptions in our own language. Of these is the sound given to s and t before i followed by a vowel. This harsh sound—so displeasing to a refined ear, that, even in English, every elegant speaker is careful to avoid it, where this can be done without the appearance of affectation,—is strenuously insisted upon, and its use amply illustrated by examples. We even go beyond the English in this respect; for whereas they exempt from change the t preceded by s, our grammarians instruct us to

21. See also G. C. Moore Smith, "The English Language and the 'Restored' Pronunciation of Latin," *Jespersen Miscellany* (Copenhagen, 1930), pp. 171–73.
22. 68:436–65.

pronounce *Sallustius, Salluscheus; mixtio, mixcheo*, etc. Even these
preliminary rules are not deemed sufficient; but, since the unwarped
mind of a child is continually liable to err into the right, his memory
is continually refreshed by foot notes, which instruct him that *ar-
ti-um* is *arsheum*, and that the comparative of *mit-is* is not *mit-i-or*,
as he might reasonably suppose, but *misheor*. [Pp. 441–42]

Reform was definitely in the air, whether needed or not,[23] and the years
1850–80 saw the publication of the results of research into Latin pronunciation carried on in Germany, America, and England. In 1851, Samuel
Steman Haldeman, zoologist, geologist, chemist, naturalist, spelling re-
former, college professor, operator of a sawmill, and prominent Catholic
convert (*DAB*), published his *Elements of Latin Pronunciation, for the
Use of Students* (Philadelphia), in which he advocated a reformed pronunciation based upon his researches into the ancient Roman pronunciation.
Much more important is W. P. Corssen's *Über Aussprache, Vokalismus
und Betonung der lateinischen Sprache* (Leipzig, 1858–59), embodying
scholarship of a high order: it is with Corssen that the student of Latin
pronunciation must start, for all subsequent investigations of the classical
pronunciation must be based to a large extent on his work. J. F. Richardson,
in his *Roman Orthoëpy: A Plea for the Restoration of the True System of
Latin Pronunciation* (New York, 1859), was one of the first American
scholars to adopt the reformed methods of pronunciation, though some of
his views are not accepted by more recent scholarship. According to J.
E. Sandys, "it was mainly owing to a pamphlet issued in 1871 by Professor
G. M. Lane, of Harvard, that a reformed pronunciation of Latin was adopted
in all the colleges and schools of the United States."[24] Mention should

23. There was more need for it in America than in England, and the reformed pronunciation
made its way here more rapidly than in England largely because of the lack of a standard system
here. New England long continued in the English tradition; but in the Middle States the Dutch
and the Germans introduced their own methods. See W. M. Nevin, *Mercersburg Review*, 4
(1852),187–88: "As one of the fundamental maxims it was laid down to us, in the Grammar of
Dr. Ross, which we learned by heart, that an Anglicized pronunciation of Latin must be cau-
tiously avoided"; instead, the Pennsylvania schoolboys strove for a "sublime, sonorous pronunciation of the vowels *a* and *e*." In the South and West, French pronunciation was quite
frequently heard. To these must be added the Italianized Latin of the Catholic clergy taught in
parochial schools and Catholic colleges, all together forming, according to Harry Thurston Peck,
Latin Pronunciation (New York, 1894), "a picturesque confusion such as no European country
ever knew" (p. 6).
24. "Classics," *Encyclopaedia Britannica*, 11th ed., 6:461. The statement is not strictly
true, as we shall see later. W. A. Ellis states that in the Chicago high school which he attended
in 1878 the English pronunciation was in almost universal use, though "in Greek we gave the
continental sounds to the vowels" ("Those Good Old Days," *Classical Journal*, 27, 484–96).

also be made of the Tafels' (Dr. Leonard and Professor Rudolph) *Latin Pronunciation and the Latin Alphabet* (Philadelphia, 1860), G. K. Bartholomew's *Grammar of the Latin Language* (Cincinnati, 1873), and Walter Blair's *Latin Pronunciation, an Inquiry into the Proper Sounds of the Latin Language during the Classical Period* (New York and Chicago, 1873). By the time of the publication of Blair's book, Professor Haldeman was able to state that "after a struggle of twenty years, the claims of genuine Latin and Greek pronunciation have been admitted on both sides of the Atlantic, by an almost simultaneous movement, although some of the American colleges had adopted the ancient method at an earlier date."[25] Nevertheless, statistics gathered by the Bureau of Education at Washington show that in 1876, out of 237 colleges consulted, 90 used the English, 75 the continental, 72 the reformed method. Says A. G. Hopkins:

> They [these figures] seem to show . . . that there is no great clamor in America for the Roman pronunciation. . . . Public opinion seems to be far from satisfied in regard to it, and the great majority of our schools and colleges do not adopt it. Harvard and Princeton use it: on the other hand Dartmouth, Williams, Amherst, and multitudes of others do not. These statistics still further show that this attempt at reform has simply introduced a disturbing and distracting force into our education. Instead of having the English and the Continental,—two systems tolerably congenial,—we now have a third, which lays hold of many of our preparatory schools, and which introduces only confusion into our colleges. We shall not for many years recover from the demoralization which has been occasioned by this attempt to foist upon us an uncongenial and an ill-matured system of Latin pronunciation.[26]

Meanwhile, in England, Professors Munro and Palmer published their *Syllabus of Latin Pronunciation* (Cambridge and Oxford) in 1871, and the same year saw the publication of H. J. Roby's *Grammar of the Latin Language*, of which at least 150 pages are devoted to phonology. Benjamin Hall Kennedy likewise devoted at least 68 pages of his *Public School Latin Grammar* (London, 1871) to phonology and its applications. According to J. E. Sandys,[27] the reformed pronunciation was adopted at University College, London, and at Shrewsbury, Marlborough, Liverpool College, Christ's Hospital, Dulwich, and the City of London School. In 1874 A.

25. Review of Blair's *Latin Pronunciation*, in *Southern Magazine*, 6 (1873), 626.
26. "The Reform in Pronouncing Latin," *International Review*, 11 (1881), 73–74.
27. *Encyclopaedia Britannica*, 11th ed., 6:457.

J. Ellis published his *Practical Hints on the Quantitative Pronunciation of Latin* (London), expounding a system so complex that it is doubtful whether even Macaulay's schoolboy could have followed it.[28]

What was the reception recorded this first generation of reformers? Fired with missionary zeal, they seem to have overstepped themselves, making such difficult distinctions as A. J. Ellis makes when he says:

> The names of Roman writers which are anglicised, as Virgil, Horace, Ovid, receive their English sounds, and in accordance with them, we must when speaking English talk of Cicero as *Sis'ser-oh*, and Caesar as *Seize-her*, &c. just as we necessarily use Rome, Naples, Venice, and Florence as English words. . . . It is only in recently introduced names of foreign countries, towns, and people, that those who know the languages venture to introduce the native pronunciation in English sentences. We must adopt the same course with regard to Latin names and Latin words and phrases introduced into English sentences, as we now adopt for French.[29]

Who is qualified offhand to make such a distinction? Would one make it, say, between *Caesar* and *Scaliger*, *sine qua non* and *fieri facias*? Professor Lemuel S. Potwin, of Western Reserve College, was not so moderate as Ellis. He was for going the limit, even in the pronunciation of familiar names like *Cicero*, apparently out of respect for the feelings of their bearers, for he writes, "If there is any reader of this Article by the name of Cook, let him imagine himself addressed for a few days by everybody as *Soos*, and he can tell how Cicero would have felt."[30]

Furthermore, respect for the method was not likely to be engendered by continual references to the "English barbaric pronunciation" and by violent disagreement and uncertainty among the reformers themselves. A. J. Ellis, for instance, admits that the "restored" pronunciation is a

---

28. It should be mentioned in passing that some years previous to the introduction of the reform with which we are concerned, certain schoolmasters had begun to insist upon observance of the classical quantities. In his *Two Trifles* (London, 1895), Fitzedward Hall tells of being taken to task by his teacher for saying *dóctrīnal* instead of *doctrīnal*. Quick as a flash, this remarkable lad responded: "If others, in their solicitude to *propãgate* refinement, choose to be *irrĭtated* or *éxcĭted*, because of what they take to be my *genuĭne ignórance* in *oratóry*, they should at least be sure that their discomposure is not *gratuĭtous.*" (I have made Hall's method of indicating stress in this passage conform to modern practice.) Cf. also the fury of Dr. Skinner in Samuel Butler's *Way of All Flesh* (1903), because Ernest pronounced *Thalia* with a short *i*. "And this to me," he thundered, "who never made a false quantity in my life" (chap. 30).

29. *Quantitative Pronunciation*, pp. 2–3, note.

30. "Shall We Adhere to the English Method of Pronouncing Latin?" *New Englander*, 37 (1878), 822.

makeshift, but "these rough approximations will probably suffice for all school purposes" (*Quantitative Pronunciation*, p. 8). He is in disagreement with many of the reformers when he says, "The diphthongal forms *æ*, *œ*, I shall render by a broader *e*, like the German ä in spräche" (p. 5). In his proposed system, he allows *t* and *d* their English sounds, though "it scarcely admits of doubt that these were as unknown to the Latins, as they are now to most Europeans. But these sounds are most easy to English organs" (p. 7). On the other hand, English organs are disregarded in the pronunciation of consonantal *u*, to be "produced by sounding *v* without allowing the lower lip to touch the upper teeth" (p. 5). And after English organs have shaped themselves to sound *v* in this troublesome fashion, Ellis informs their owners that "it is not to be concluded that I consider these sounds to be perfectly correct or even justifiable by any authorities which can be cited" (p. 7).[31] Such indecision, even if justified, does not inspire confidence.

Then there were the proposed new sounds themselves. Englishmen (and Americans) could be expected to boggle at some of them, and boggle they did, particularly at the pronunciation of *c*, *g* before *e*, *i* as [k], [g] and at *v* as [w]. Professor Max Müller[32] attempted to come to the rescue with a rationalization, and argued that a "modified pronunciation" of *c* before *e* and *i* was "not incompatible with the evidence derived from Latin words transcribed by the Greeks, or Greek words transcribed by the Romans." He points out that "in trying to introduce a more correct pronunciation of Latin, the great stumbling block has always been the hard pronunciation of *c* before *e*, *i*, *y*, *ae*, *eu*, *oe*," that "'Are we to pronounce *Kikero*, *et ketera*, *skiskere*?' has generally been considered, if not a convincing, at all events a most telling, argument against phonetic reformers." Even scholars who are fully convinced of the "hard" sound have seldom ventured to adopt it, "whether from fear of ridicule or from a dislike of the harsh and disagreeable sound." He states that "I have never heard *c* pronounced as *k* before *e* and *i* in any school or university of Germany or France, though I believe there is hardly a scholar who has not declared his decided opinion that this is the right pronunciation." In a later article,[33] Max Müller writes that he himself is in favor of *k* for *c* before front vowels (though holding

31. Cf. J. F. Roxburgh, a proponent of the reformed pronunciation, who as recently as 1927 writes of it: "If we obeyed all these rules literally, schoolmastering would be a gay profession. There would not be a dull moment in a Lower School Form while the correct pronunciation of *zephyrus* or *occurrerat* was being taught. However, most schools are content with P for PH, and do not rise either to the French U or to the Italian double consonants" (*Spectator*, 138:795).

32. "On the Pronunciation of *C*," *Academy*, 2 (1871), 145–46.

33. "On the Pronunciation of Latin," *Academy*, 2 (1871), 565–68.

out for a labiodental *v*), and that he had merely wished, in justifying a "modified pronunciation" of *c* before front vowels, to remove a stumbling-block, declaring himself content to "leave the decision with those to whose judgment in this matter I shall most willingly bow, to Professor Munro of Cambridge and Professor E. Palmer of Oxford," who had been invited by the schoolmasters of England to issue a scheme of Latin pronunciation which would ensure uniformity in any changes contemplated.

The Syllabus drawn up by Munro and Palmer was, according to Robinson Ellis, who reviews the situation up to 1874,

> at once introduced into several of the larger schools in England, at least in the higher forms. I myself adopted it for the use of my classes in University College [London], and a very similar scheme of pronunciation was only last year printed by Professor Key for University College School. Independently of this, a reformed pronunciation has been adopted in various educational establishments in this country; and it is no uncommon occurrence in my classes to find students on their arrival already trained in the new method, with such slight differences (and they are really slight) as the divergence of opinion on particular points makes unavoidable.[34]

The experiment can, however,

> hardly be said as yet to have been adequately tried in schools, or properly seconded in the Universities. At Oxford, when I examined viva voce as Classical Moderator in 1872, I was the only examiner who used the reformed pronunciation, and those who came before me for examination did not generally seem familiar with it. Even now the old use predominates, and it is to be feared that even those trained by the Syllabus at school, *e.g.*, at Shrewsbury, Marlborough, Liverpool College, Christ's Hospital, Dulwich College and the City of London School, are induced to give it up, or at least to suppress it, when they proceed to the Universities. [P. 399]

Moreover, he feels that, if it is to be successful, the reformed pronunciation alone should be taught, instead of allowing the old pronunciation to linger on side by side with the new. However, the "lamentable fluctuation of opinion exhibited by the schoolmasters in their conference this year is a clear proof, if any proof were wanted, of the difficulties which invariably attend any real reform" (p. 399). Fourteen years later, as we shall see,

34. Report on Latin philology, *Transactions of the Philological Society*, 1873–74, p. 398.

this same Professor Robinson Ellis was to champ at the bit over the absence of "lamentable fluctuation" in the manifesto of the Cambridge Philological Society issued in 1887.[35]

By 1880, despite the efforts of the reformers, comparatively little progress had been made. D. B. King reports that "interest in the new method seems to be dying out in England, the head masters having in many cases gone back to the old method, and no serious attempt having been made to introduce the new pronunciation into Cambridge," adding that "in this country [America] its introduction has been much more general."[36] A. G. Hopkins reports that "in England, which is the home of the movement, the reform is but half-hearted and partial," and quotes the Head Master of Rugby as writing, "I think reformed Latin pronunciation a mere waste of time."[37] Professor Palmer of Oxford—himself one of the authors of the Syllabus— said of it, "I am not aware that individual professors, tutors, or lecturers venture upon it in dealing with their classes, nor have I heard that Cambridge has been more enterprising," adding, "I regard the syllabus as having fallen stillborn."[38] Professor T. A. Thatcher quotes "a fellow of one of the colleges of Oxford" to the effect that "zeal for the new pronunciation has sadly cooled"; that "it has been given up again in most schools, and may in fact be said to be extinct."[39] The plight of the scientific linguist is expressed by A. H. Sayce:

At present it is impossible for the comparative philologist in England to lecture upon Latin without the aid of blackboard and chalk. When he speaks of *i* in Sanskrit or other tongues, the ordinary student thinks of *e* (as in English); when he refers to *e* and *ai* the audience writes down *a* and *i*; and so long as *agis* and *cecidi* are pronounced

---

35. One feels from the tone of his remarks that the school spirit of an old Oxonian has been aroused at the effrontery of the "Cambridge triumvirate" (J. Peile, J. P. Postgate, J. S. Reid) in presuming to prescribe for Oxford men, rather than his scholarly acumen, when he says: "I had hoped that some other voice than mine would have given expression to the dissatisfied feeling which the recent manifesto of the Cambridge triumvirate . . . cannot fail to produce among Oxford men. . . . It is an outrage to research and to criticism alike to be told dogmatically that *u* as a consonant was always *w*. . . . Let us by all means aim to formulate our doctrine of immaculate pronunciation—I, for one, have, since 1873, invariably used the syllabus then drawn up, not without occasional protests from my friends—but let us take all possible care that our doctrine is a real expression of catholic feeling on the subject" (*Academy* 29:205). It is difficult to see what catholicity of opinion has to do with the matter.

36. *Latin Pronunciation* (Boston, 1895), p. 8 (written 1880).

37. *International Review*, 11 (1881), 73.

38. Ibid., p. 73.

39. *New Englander*, 37 (1878), 827–28.

ejis and *sesīdai*, it is impossible to show that they have any connection with *ago* and *cadere*.[40]

Meanwhile, on this side of the Atlantic, the reformed pronunciation, though received somewhat more generally than in England, was coming in for a goodly share of lambasting. T. A. Thatcher of Yale was one of its staunchest opponents. In an article in the *New Englander*,[41] he makes much of our ignorance of the true Roman pronunciation (a favorite argument of the conservatives), expresses alarm over what may happen to proper names and Latin phrases in English in the event that Corssen's and Richardson's "theories" are put into general practice, but is consoled by the fact that "these reforms have not thus far commended themselves to general acceptance."[42] Eleven years later, N. W. Benedict, Principal of the Rochester Free Academy, takes a cautious view, feels that a "concord of utterance, a harmony of diction," though highly desirable, is impossible of achievement.[43] In 1878 E. H. Twining alludes to a brochure of thirty pages by Professor M. M. Fisher appearing early in April of that year, in which Professor Fisher gives his views upon the pronunciation of Latin, in the form of an attack upon the Roman system and a defense of the English method. Twining's article attempts to answer Fisher's strictures, and is vigorously in favor of the reformed system.[44]

One of the most amusing blasts against the newfangled pronunciation appeared in 1879 in the *American Church Review* (31:102–18) under the title "The 'Roman Method' of Pronouncing Latin a Mischievous Mistake." The author, N. E. Cornwall, simply cannot swallow the [k] for *c* and [g] for *g* before front vowels; but even more loathsome, in his opinion, is [w] for *v*. He writes, and one can almost see his lip curling with scorn as he does so:

> What an exhibition American boys would make of themselves, repeating the Latin words *vivo, vivis, vivit, vivimus, vivitis, vivunt* with this pronunciation, *wee-wo, wee-wees, wee-weet, wee-wee-moos, wee-wee-tees, wee-woont.* . . . Many boys and girls, as well as men

40. *Introduction to the Science of Language* (London, 1880), 2:342–43.

41. 19 (1861), 102–25.

42. In 1878 Professor Thatcher had not shifted his position an inch. Despite the obvious fact that the traditional pronunciation had been supplanted almost everywhere in America by that time by the reformed method, he still thought the reform a failure. See his article in the *New Englander*, 37:827–34.

43. *Eighty-fifth Annual Report of the Regents of the University* [of the State of New York] (Albany, 1872), pp. 485–96.

44. *Western*, 4:413–26.

and women, in America, have great power of endurance. But any *lingo* so barbarous would soon prove intolerable to all. . . . And it is a happy circumstance for the cause of high rhetoric, that one of its finest specimens, in the famous dispatch of that great general and orator, Julius Caesar, "*veni, vidi, vici,*" was committed to written characters, and not handed down orally, in such childish utterances as these: *way-nee, wee-dee, wee-kee.* . . . It is to be hoped that such a barbarous pronunciation, whatever it may be called, will be henceforth regarded, not only by thorough scholars, but also by young students, at least in England and America, as a thoroughly punctured and exploded bubble. For it is, at the best, an empty and puerile conceit, especially adapted, and apparently, in part, designed, for the amusement of young students, in all nations, except, possibly, Germans. To thorough scholars whose knowledge of Latin is verified and established by the constant perusal of ancient writings of every period, and to diligent students of those languages which are most directly descended from the Latin, that whimsical conceit is sheer nonsense. [Pp. 116–17][45]

Evidently the American character has undergone a process of steady deterioration since Mr. Cornwall's day, for American schoolboys do meekly say "wee-wees" and make Julius Caesar talk like the emasculated Sam Weller of Mr. Cornwall's imagination, and there are no signs of a revolutionary war in the offing. The best that E. H. Smith could do in answer to Mr. Cornwall's invective was to point out that "the mere fact that this [reformed] method has been adopted by the Professors in Oxford and Cambridge, and by a majority of the head masters of public schools in England, and in this country by Harvard and many other colleges, entitles it at least, to consideration and careful attention."[46]

We have seen that the first attempt at reform in England, as a result of the Munro and Palmer Syllabus in 1871, was none too successful. The

45. See also "Sauce for the Latin Goose and English Gander," *Atlantic Monthly,* 61 (1888), 281–82, in which an old-fashioned man complains: "When my latest born comes home from school, and quotes an ancient warrior (whom he indicates as Yulius Keyser) to the effect that 'Wayny, Weedy, Weeky,' I try to persuade myself that my ear rather than his tongue is at fault, as regards an apparent loss of virility in the once familiar utterance." A somewhat different view is held by Walter Sellar and Robert J. Yeatman in their humorous history, *1066 and All That* (New York, 1931). They explain: "Julius Caesar . . . set the memorable Latin sentence, 'Veni, Vidi, Vici,' which the Romans, who were all very well educated, construed correctly. The Britons, however, who of course still used the old pronunciation, understanding him to have called them 'Weeny, Weedy and Weaky,' lost heart and gave up the struggle, thinking that he had already divided them All into Three Parts" (p. 2).

46. "The 'Roman Method' of Pronouncing Latin—Is It a Mistake?" *American Church Review,* 31 (1879), 377.

battle was renewed by the Cambridge Philological Society in 1886, when a committee was appointed to draw up a scheme for the reformed pronunciation. This committee's preliminary report was published in March, 1886, in the *Academy* (29:170–71),[47] to be issued with some revisions the following year under the title *The Pronunciation of Latin in the Augustan Period* (London). The committee explain their method in a foreword:

> It having been felt by some teachers at Cambridge that the time had come to make a further attempt to correct the errors of the ordinary English pronunciation of Latin, a letter of enquiry was sent out to ascertain the amount of support which such an attempt would receive. This called forth very encouraging answers from lecturers in almost every college in Cambridge and not a few schoolmasters. The following statement was therefore drawn up by a small committee: it has been fully discussed at two meetings of the Society as an approximate statement of the pronunciation of Latin by the educated classes in the Augustan period.

An anonymous writer in the *Saturday Review*,[48] exasperated by the Cambridge manifesto, sums up the situation prior to 1887. He regrets very deeply that such a thing as pronunciation reform was ever started, indeed, seems to be a man who is constitutionally "agin" all change:

> For a good many years past various systems of the kind have been put forward at headmaster's [*sic*] conferences and similar meetings, but the Universities have hitherto been indocile to change, and as long as they did not move, it was practically impossible for schools to do anything. . . . The Cambridge circular . . . changes the plaything into a "sealed pattern." If Oxford were to follow suit, there can be little doubt that the system would become almost universal—till another rose. . . . Why, then, with nothing (or *Si Peu Que Rien*) to gain, with a great deal to lose, and with no discoverable motive except the desire of innovation, should we cut ourselves off from the traditions of English scholarship, confuse and muddle the whole system of training, and install upon the ruins of the old something which will last—how long?

An American writer in the Syracuse *Academy* ("A Journal of Secondary Education")[49] states that "the advantages of this [reformed] pronunciation

47. For dissenting opinions see H. J. Roby and R. Ellis, *Academy*, 29 (1886), 187, 205.
48. 64 (15 October 1887), 513–14.
49. "Good Form in Latin Pronunciation," 4 (1889), 348–50.

are wholly confined to the business of instruction, and even within these limits are not very great." Already, apparently, people had begun to pronounce familiar Latin words and phrases in English context (such as *principia*, *sine qua non*, etc.) with the new pronunciation, and the writer, quite reasonably I should say, deplores this as "bad form":

> What we here wish to insist upon is that it betrays a lack of respect for the amenities and proprieties of social intercourse,—in short that it is in *bad form*—to speak Latin words or phrases outside the classroom, otherwise than in the traditional English manner. . . . There is a very large class of young persons "graduating" from schools and colleges who are apt to carry with them into social life the conception that the pronunciation they have been taught is the *right pronunciation*, and that they must continue to use it whenever they have occasion to utter a Latin word or phrase just as they would try to speak by the dictionary in their own language or in French or German. . . . Outside the walls [of the classroom] exists a great tradition of Latin pronunciation, to ignore which betrays an abysmal lack of *savoir faire*, a disloyalty to the decencies of life, an unfamiliarity with the code of polite intercourse. *Good form* in Latin pronunciation means pronunciation according to the ancient custom of English and American scholars. This alone is unobtrusive, quiet and gentlemanly.

The editor of *Scribner's Magazine*[50] tells of hearing Terence's *Phormio* in the original Latin given by Harvard students in the Sanders Theatre in Cambridge. "Of course," he tells us, "the now current 'classical' pronunciation of Latin was in full blast, and I, whose classical studies date back to the days of the old 'Oxford' pronunciation, looked forward to a new sensation." He began to feel, however, that something was wrong, and soon saw clearly enough that what he was hearing was no more like the Roman speech of Terence's time (one wonders how he knew so precisely what the speech of Terence's time was like) than an American schoolboy's pronunciation of French is like French. "Realizing this, I began also to see that the now current 'classical' pronunciation of Greek must be in precisely the same evil case: resulting in a gibberish no whit better." He proceeds, with some heat, "Yet these twin jargons pretend to be classically spoken Greek and Latin. *Proh pudor!* One blushes at the effrontery of our universities." His expectations of the reformed pronunciation seem rather unreasonable, however, for he declares, "It seems to me unquestionable

50. 24 (1898), 506–7.

that our university professors have by no means given us the authentic
vowel and consonant sounds—let alone the characteristic vocal inflection
and accent—of classic Greek and Roman speech, but have only taken certain
entirely English (or American) sounds and distributed them afresh over
the alphabet, thus giving the alphabet a phonetic interpretation quite new
to us.'' However, if the reformed pronunciation of Latin seems a sorry
thing, the introduction of ''the so-called 'classical' pronunciation of Greek
appears simply impudent.'' Greek is not a dead language, the writer
declares—amazingly enough, ancient and modern Greek are ''really one
and the same.'' Therefore we can learn Greek from a native; but we cannot
do so with Latin. ''What best substitute, then, can we find for a Latin
vox viva? It seems to me that the old, now abandoned 'Oxford' pronunciation
gives us this best substitute. It is admittedly not classical . . . but it is at
least English and therefore alive.''

Despite occasional opposition, however, in 1901 it was estimated that
the reformed pronunciation was in use by more than 96 percent of the
students of Latin in American secondary schools.[51] The most important
of the die-hards seems to have been Professor Charles E. Bennett of Cornell,
who was still against the reformed pronunciation in 1917, and presumably
until his death in 1921. Professor Bennett was forced to admit that, though
the English and continental methods survived in America in 1901, ''probably the two together are not represented by five per cent. of the Latin
pupils of the secondary schools; in the colleges the percentage must be
lower still.''[52] He was still saying in 1917, after enumerating the difficulties
and disadvantages of the reformed pronunciation:

The foregoing practical considerations . . . coupled with the practically universal failure to adhere to its principles, have long seemed
to my mind valid grounds for its abandonment. . . . Certainly it can
no longer be held to be a moral duty to maintain a system of
pronunciation which the experience of twenty years has shown to
result in miserable failure, and the intrinsic difficulties of whose accurate
application are so evident. . . . The foregoing are the considerations
which have for years weighed with me, and which have finally
compelled me to believe that the retention of our present unmethodical
'method' of pronouncing Latin has proved itself a serious mistake.
. . . Certain educators advocate the employment of the Roman pronunciation on moral grounds, urging that it is our bounden duty to

51. See J. E. Sandys, p. 461.
52. *The Teaching of Latin and Greek in the Secondary School* (New York, 1906),
p. 66.

apply what we know to be true. It is equally on moral grounds (among others) that I would urge the immediate abandonment of the Roman pronunciation. . . . The English pronunciation is at least honest. It confessedly violates vowel quantity, though I doubt whether it actually does so any more than the Roman method as actually employed. . . . The sober conservative sense of German and English educators has thus far resisted . . . this unwise spirit of innovation. In America we are unfortunately too prone to view with favour any new idea, educational or other, and to embark precipitately in experiments which involve serious consequences.[53]

Professor Bennett is quite correct in his remark anent the wariness of English educators. English acceptance of the reformed pronunciation was not so eager as in America, despite the authority of the Cambridge Philological Society. There was so much backsliding that the fight had to be taken up anew by the Modern Languages Association in 1901, by the Classical Association in 1904–5, and by the Philological Societies of Oxford and Cambridge in 1906. The reform was ultimately accepted by the various groups of headmasters in December 1906–January 1907, and the proposed scheme formally approved by the Board of Education in February 1907. However, as an anonymous writer in the *Spectator*[54] put it, the matter was still far from settled: "Of the public schools, Eton and Westminster are understood to hold aloof, partially or entirely." Westminster, the writer points out, would no doubt find herself in difficulties as regards the annual Latin play, "which would become unintelligible to old Westminster boys for a generation unless they chose to put themselves to school again." "Sentiment," he tells us, "or, as some people prefer to call it, taste, is in very many cases, perhaps in most, the decisive factor in the refusal of the 'restored' pronunciation." Everything was to this writer fairly easy to accept save [w] for *v*:

Read the virile phrase 'vivida vis animi' to him [the senior classic] in the English way, and then ask him to find anything virile, or rather *wereel*, in *weewida weese animi*, and he will writhe in agony. In truth, to be told that the satisfactory mouthing out of such words as 'vilis,' 'vigor,' 'vindex,' and other vital and vituperative words must give place to the weak wailings of the 'w's' is a hard saying.

However, to this writer "it is difficult to regard the whole movement . . . as a matter of supreme importance," and it is his belief that "the

53. Ibid., 1917 ed., pp. 76–80.
54. 98 (1907), 526–27.

national clock is not being put very far back every day because a large number of thinking persons still prefer 'v' to 'w,' and cannot put up with 'weekee' as the final word of Caesar's message to the Senate.''

The English are apparently more tenacious than Americans, for usage is still far from uniform in England, though Henry Bradley could quite correctly state in 1920 that the "traditional system of pronunciation is rapidly becoming obsolete,"[55] whereas I should think it perfectly safe to say that the reformers have had a complete victory in America. On the other hand, a committee appointed by the Prime Minister in England in 1921 could only state that the reformed way "has established itself without any difficulty in the Secondary Schools and the Girls' Schools. It has been officially adopted in most of the Public Schools, but in only a few of them is it consistently and uniformly used."[56] Dissenting voices in this country have been few. S. I. Lex in 1908 thought the Roman method sheer folly, rising to heights of patriotic emotion when he writes, "As lovers of our own country, as lovers of our own language, the richest and best language on the globe we inhabit, let us rise in our intellectual independence, and throw off this foreign yoke, and be no longer 'slaves to a horde of petty tyrants.' ''[57] Professor A. W. Anthony's statement in 1909 that there was "no present warrant for a standard pronunciation in present or prospective conversational uses," his question "Why perpetuate longer a custom of less than thirty years' duration, which has naught but a worn-out theory to commend it?"[58] brought forth a storm of protest in the *Nation*.[59] However, as lately as 1927, Professor B. L. Ullman of the University of Chicago expressed his belief that the present emphasis on the correlation of Latin and English vocabulary might suggest to some that the advantages of the English pronunciation are perhaps greater than was realized at the time of the adoption of the reformed method and referred to "meticulous accuracy . . . an exemplification of that pedantry which is due to our youthfulness in research."[60]

55. Introduction to Sargeaunt's *Pronunciation of English Words Derived from the Latin*, p. 5.

56. Quoted by Vernon Rendall,"The Pronunciation of Latin," *Saturday Review*, 143 (1927), 40.

57. "The Roman Method," *Journal of Education*, 68:709.

58. "Pronunciation of the Classics," *Nation* (New York), 18 March 1909, p. 276. Reprinted in *Journal of Education*, 69 (1909), 657–58.

59. See especially the letters of R. K. Hack, W. H. Alexander, C. H. Dickerman, and H. H. Yeames (1 April 1909, pp. 330–31). Remarks Professor Yeames, with admirable condescension and serene disregard of fact: "It is needless to say that our English cousins, after these centuries of insular absurdity, are now engaged in the process of wholesale reform in the pronunciation of the classical languages, and are fast conforming to the usage of the rest of the world."

60. "The Teaching of the Pronunciation of Latin," *Classical Journal*, 23: 24–32.

In 1927 the old controversy was revived in England, if, indeed, it can be said ever to have died down. Vernon Rendall points out in the *Saturday Review*[61] that "in *The Times* of late letters have been thick about pronunciation of Latin, and a leading article[62] has pleaded for the retrieval of the old system, which our grandchildren may again enjoy, talking Latin as easily as English." J. F. Roxburgh reports in the same year that "Eton has recently announced that it prefers boys to come with the old pronunciation, while most of the other schools ask for the reformed."[63] In 1932, H. K. Baker refers to "a recent pronouncement" by the Head Master of Eton that "he regarded as disastrous the recent [!] change in Latin pronunciation, which put a serious stumbling-block in the way of the average boy."[64]

We may conclude, I think, that in England the triumph of scholarship (or pedantry, as the staunch traditionalists would call it) over tradition has been gradual, and is not yet complete. The clash of the old and the new is well exemplified by Mr. Chips and Mr. Ralston in James Hilton's popular novel, *Good-bye, Mr. Chips* (Boston, 1934). Mr. Ralston accuses Chips of slackness and obstinacy:

"This question of Latin pronunciation, for instance—I think I told you years ago that I wanted the new style used throughout the school. The other masters obeyed me; you prefer to stick to your old methods, and the result is simply chaos and inefficiency."

Chips replies:

"Well, I—umph—I admit that I don't agree with the new pronunciation. I never did. Umph—a lot of nonsense, in my opinion. Making boys say 'Kickero' at school when—umph—for the rest of their lives they'll say 'Cicero.'. . . And instead of 'vicissim'—God bless my soul—you'd make them say 'We kiss 'im'!"[65]

G. C. Moore Smith, writing in 1930, expresses concern over what the reformed pronunciation of Latin may do to the English language, and reports

61. "The Pronunciation of Latin," 143:39.

62. Occasioned by a Latin play performed at Westminster and a resolution proposed at the Headmasters' Conference at Brighton, to the effect that the reformed pronunciation had failed after trial to justify itself and should be given up. The action was, however, heartily defeated.

63. "The Pronunciation of Latin," *Spectator*, 138:796.

64. *Notes and Queries*, 2 April 1932, p. 248.

65. Chap. 11. See also John Galsworthy's *Old English*, in which old Sylvanus Heythorp, the representative of the old order, just after remarking to a business associate, "Pronounce Horace like foreigners now, don't they?" is obliged to correct his granddaughter for her "reformed" pronunciation of *lares* and *penates* (3:1).

having heard *orgy* and *plagiarism* with [g] and *sociological* with [k].[66] To
these I can add from my own notes, taken at the time of hearing or as
shortly thereafter as decorum would permit, such completely "Romanized"
or hybrid pronunciations as the following:

Aesculapius [ˌɛskə'lɑpɪəs]
Africanus [ˌæfrɪ'kanəs] (preceded by Scipio ['sɪpɪo])
Agamemnon [ˌægə'mɛmnon]
alma mater ['ælmə 'mɑtər]
alumnae [ə'lʌmnaɪ]
alumni[67] [ə'lʌmni]
a priori ['ɑ prɪ'ɔrɪ]
casus belli ['kasəs 'bɛli]
caveat ['kɑwɪˌɑt]
certiorari [ˌsɜšə'rɑrɪ]
Cleopatra [ˌkliə'pɑtrə]
contemptus mundi [kən'tɛmptəs 'mundaɪ]
credo ['kredo]
cum laude ['kum 'laudɪ]
data ['dɑtə]
deus ex machina ['deəs ˌɛks 'mɑkɪnɑ] and [mə'kinə] and [mə'šinə]
dies irae ['daɪiz 'iraɪ] (also completely "Romanized")
foedera ['fɔɪdərɑ]
fungi ['fʌŋgaɪ] and ['fʌŋgi]
genus ['ǰenəs]
Gesta (Romanorum) ['gɛstə]
hic jacet ['hɪk 'jɑkɪt]
ignoramus [ˌɪgnə'rɑməs]
in medias res [ɪn 'medɪəs 'res]
lucus a non lucendo ['ljukəs ɑ non lju'kendo]
Meleager [68] [ˌmɛlɪ'ægər]
ne plus ultra ['ne 'plʌs 'ultrə]
Palladis Tamia ['pælədɪs 'tamɪə]
Phi Beta Kappa[69] ['faɪ 'betə 'kæpə]

66. "The English Language and the 'Restored' Pronunciation of Latin," pp. 177–78.

67. Note that the reformed pronunciation completely reverses the traditional pronunciation
of *alumnae* and *alumni*.

68. Sally B. Kinsolving, *Grey Heather* (Portland, Me., 1930), p. 84, rimes this name with
lagger and *stagger*.

69. The pronunciation indicated is official for the fraternity. According to the *Key Reporter*,
3 (1938), 8: "Of 276 members in attendance at the 19th Triennial Council in Atlanta in September,

principio [prɪnˈkɪpɪo]
regina[70] [rəˈginə]
sarcophagi [sɑrˈkɑfə,gaɪ]
scaena prima [ˈsinə ˈprimə]
sine qua non [ˈsine ˌkwɑ ˈnon]
status [ˈstatəs]
streptococci [ˌstrɛptəˈkɑki]
thesaurus [θɪˈsaurəs]
ultimatum [ˌʌltɪˈmɑtəm]
via [ˈviə]

These pronunciations indicate at least that there is a great deal of hesitation and confusion about the pronunciation of foreign words from Latin in English, a confusion which obviously did not exist before the introduction of the reformed pronunciation. The fact that no dictionary has given its full sanction to the use of the reformed pronunciation in such words and phrases indicates that the dictionaries, in this as in other respects, have not taken account of a definite trend of the times, a trend which has gone so far that most educated people, in America at least, look upon the traditional pronunciations of such expressions as uncouth, and would hesitate to use them even with the sanction of the lexicographer; on the other hand, as the examples show, there is much wavering in such words as *genus* [ˈjenəs], [ˈjinəs], a wavering which is due entirely, I think, to the influence of the reformed pronunciation. The pronunciations I have recorded have naturally all come from the mouths of learned men, usually from men who do not "look up" a word in the dictionary for its pronunciation, but only for its meaning. The fact that such wavering exists between "reformed" and English sounds is surely not without significance: we are witnessing in the making a definite change in the pronunciation of a largish body of words, many of them long a part of the vocabulary of the cultured speaker of English, a change that can hardly be ignored much longer by the lexicographers and the grammarians.[71]

---

123 expressed preference for Phy Bayta Kappa, 31 for Phy Beeta Kappa, and 11 for Phee Bayta Kappa. None demanded Phee Bayta Kahppa. . . . One ballot was marked 'All d——— [*sic*] foolishness.' "

70. In the phrase "Victoria Regina." "Victoria" did not, however, begin with [w]!

71. *Webster's New International Dictionary* (Springfield, Mass., 1937) recognizes the situation, but informs us that the English method is "still used . . . almost exclusively in the pronunciation of Latin scientific words in English context, for Latin legal phrases, and for familiar phrases and quotations from Latin in English context, though with many variations, especially since the English method of pronunciation ceased to be widely taught in the schools," adding that "since most of the Latin words and phrases contained in the Dictionary fall in one or another

[Addendum, 1973: By about 1955, most of the pronunciations recorded in this paper had become usual, and were soon to be recorded in the dictionaries. "Tempest in Teapot: Reform in Latin Pronunciation" and the following "The Pronunciation of Latin in English: A Lexicographical Dilemma" thus have a primarily historical interest today. The tempest has subsided; the pedants alone survive, but a state of confusion continues to prevail. T. P.]

---

of these categories, their pronunciation is indicated according to the English method" (p. liv). The Funk and Wagnalls *New Standard Dictionary* (New York, 1925) hedges likewise, pointing out that though popular usage is divided between the old and the new, "it is probable that with the lapse of time the Roman pronunciation will prevail more and more, since modern scholarship is overwhelmingly in its favor"; however, pronunciations are given according to the English method, though the editors explain that their practice by no means indicates that "a preference for that method is thereby expressed" (p. xxviii).

3

The Pronunciation of Latin in English: A Lexicographical Dilemma

SOME time ago I pointed out that, as a result of the teaching of the "reformed" (or "classical," or "Roman") pronunciation of Latin, there prevails an uncertainty, a timidity, a wavering, in the pronunciation of Latin learned loanwords, phrases, and proper names;[1] so that it may almost be said that Latin is becoming a dead language even among the learned, who now hesitate to use a Latin word or phrase, even a proper name, because they are not sure how to pronounce it. At present one hears many hybrid pronunciations, like Mr. Kaltenborn's familiar [ˌʌltəˈmatəm] for *ultimatum* and the well-nigh universal [ˈælmə ˈmatər] for *alma mater*; and I am convinced that confusion is multiplying upon confusion, for there would seem to be no longer any consistent principles underlying the pronunciation of Latin in English context.

I know of few American teachers of Latin who take the time or the trouble to teach the English pronunciation of Latin, hallowed though it is by centuries of tradition, and still (somewhat inconsistently, as I shall show) recorded, and presumably "recommended," in an overwhelming majority of words and phrases by our dictionaries. I have, in fact, heard the "reformed" pronunciation referred to by an eminent classical scholar simply as the "correct" pronunciation—that was all there was to it. After he had been reminded of the multiplicity of national pronunciations established by generations of cultured usage (a fact well known to him, of course, inasmuch as he had studied abroad), this gentleman said, somewhat belligerently, for the classical pronunciation is dear to the hearts of classicists,

---

1. "Tempest in Teapot: The Reform in Latin Pronunciation," *ELH*, 6 (1939), 138–64 [Selection 2 in this volume].

"You wouldn't read Chaucer with the pronunciation of Carl Sandburg, would you?" The question was, incidentally, quite irrelevant, since we were discussing Latin words and phrases in English context only. Somewhat later in our talk, however, he had occasion to quote the famous medieval hymn, "Dies irae, dies illa / Solvet saeclum in favilla." *Solvet* and *favilla* were pronounced with classical [w] for the *v*'s, and *saeclum* had the diphthong [aɪ]—roughly the equivalent, one might suppose, of Sandburg with a Chaucerian or even a Beowulfian pronunciation! So "correct" was this scholar's pronunciation of Latin that the *-a* in *favillā* was carefully distinguished in length from the *-a* in *illā*—a refinement which destroyed the rime of the medieval author, an uncouth fellow no doubt blissfully unaware that he was riming according to an "incorrect" national and contemporary pronunciation.[2] It should be stated, however, that this observance of classical quantity is seldom thought necessary in the "new" (or "old," according to the point of view) pronunciation of Latin, in which the vowel of *māter* is in no wise distinguished from that of *păter*; the only requirement would seem to be the value [ɑ].

I am, as I have stated, more than ever convinced that among those who have the courage to use Latin in English context at all, the hybrid pronunciations to which I have referred, as well as a number of completely "Romanized" pronunciations, are rapidly gaining ground, and that the dictionaries, if they are to be regarded as representing contemporary "good" usage, should get around to recording them. The words and phrases in question would be used in the main only by educated men and women; some are exclusively the property of the learned. If such usage be not standard, at least in American English, one wonders what indeed are the criteria of lexicographers. The same is, of course, true of British English usage, though to a lesser extent; the presence of a somewhat better established tradition for the English pronunciation of Latin in England has made for a degree less of confusion there, although most of my observations hold true of British usage, and the difference is only one of degree.[3] Daniel

2. "Dies Irae, Dies Illa" is said to have brought tears to the eyes of Dr. Johnson every time he tried to repeat it, though probably not because of its "false" quantities (*Johnsonian Miscellanies*, ed. G. Birkbeck Hill, Oxford, 1897, 1:284).
3. See, for example, G. C. Moore Smith, "The English Language and the 'Restored' Pronunciation of Latin," *Jespersen Miscellany* (Copenhagen, 1930). Henry Bradley could report as long ago as 1920 that in England "the traditional pronunciation is rapidly becoming obsolete" (Introduction to J. Sargeaunt's *Pronunciation of English Words Derived from Latin*, SPE Tract 4, Oxford, 1920). A committee appointed by the Prime Minister in 1921 observed, however, that although officially adopted in most of the public schools, the "reformed" pronunciation was consistently and uniformly used in only a few of them (Vernon Rendall, "The Pronunciation of Latin," *Saturday Review*, 143, 1927, 40). The late Professor Moore

Jones's *English Pronouncing Dictionary*, 5th ed. (New York, 1943), as a matter of fact, records more hybrid and "Romanized" pronunciations than any American dictionary that I have consulted; this fact is to be interpreted, however, merely as indicative of Jones's concern with what well-bred, educated people actually say, not as evidence that the "reformed" pronunciation has made more headway in British than in American English. There are, as my illustrations will show (and the reader's familiarity with them, perhaps his own usage, will attest to their frequency), a host of Latin words and phrases seldom if ever pronounced as our American dictionaries record them. Even Kenyon and Knott's *Pronouncing Dictionary of American English* (Springfield, Mass., 1944), enlightened though it is, fails to record the very common [ˌʌltəˈmatəm] for *ultimatum*.

Although a few ultrafastidious speakers fond of the old ways will doubtless continue to use the traditional English pronunciation, there can be no doubt whatever that hybrid or completely "Romanized" pronunciations must not be considered "bad" usage, as the neglect of the dictionaries to record them would seem to indicate; for the unlettered would not use the words in question at all. As a matter of fact, only an educated (if phonologically bemuddled) speaker could be guilty of pronouncing *Plautus* as [ˈplautəs]; the unschooled have never even heard of the Roman comedian.[4]

Particularly noticeable as hybrids are Latin plurals in *-i* and *-ae*, because in common educated usage, i.e., in the usage of those who in one way or another have been exposed to the teaching of Latin, the traditional pronunciation is completely reversed: *-i* [aɪ] > [i] and *-ae* [i] > [aɪ]. In *alumni* and *alumnae* ambiguity may result until the listener has assured himself *which* pronunciation of Latin the speaker is using—the hybrid (for the vowel of the stressed syllable is usually English [ʌ] rather than Latin [u]) or the traditional. In my observation about eight out of ten speakers, conscious of their high school and college Latin classes, would use the hybrid pronunciation.[5] At a recent commencement program yet another

---

Smith wrote me (11 June 1939): "You will have gathered that I regret the course things have taken, especially as English is made up so largely of Latin words, and it is certain that the pronunciation of these English words will be affected by the pupil's familiarity with a supposed more correct pronunciation of the Latin originals. . . . It is too late to go back in England, and I gather in the States still more so, but the results seem to me deplorable. . . . I think it was so important to do nothing to affect the natural pronunciation of English, that the introduction of the 'reform' in schools was a regrettable mistake."

4. The name was, as it frequently is, coupled with that of Terence, which was *not* pronounced [təˈrɛntɪəs].

5. In a freshman spelling examination, in which I pronounced the words in the traditional manner, with the warning that I was so pronouncing them, more than seventy per cent of those tested made the reversal, writing *alumnae* for [əˈlʌmnaɪ] and *alumni* for [əˈlʌmni].

possibility—reduction of -*i* to [ə]—suggested itself when both the secretary of the alumni association, an experienced public speaker who has occasion to use the word in his official capacity many times in the course of a year, and the young graduate accepting alumni membership for the current graduating class, pronounced the plural masculine form [ə'lʌmnə]—thereby beginning further confusion of *alumni* and *alumna*. Perhaps both were uncertain what to say and thought it "safe" to reduce the final vowel (they would think of it, if they thought of it at all, as "slurring over"). While this reduction may be regarded as rare, it suggests a very natural phonetic possibility; thus, in its two hybrid pronunciations, *alumni* may come to be equated with *alumna* as well as *alumnae*, and further confusion begotten.

It is safe to say that [-aɪ] is coming to be much more frequently heard than traditional [-i] in such words as *antennae*, *differentiae* (with [-šɪaɪ] or [-šaɪ]), *formulae*, *minutiae* (which I have heard a professor of Latin pronounce [mɪn'jušɪaɪ]), *vertebrae*, etc.; conversely, [-i] or [-ɪ] is frequently, if not indeed usually, heard in such words as *bacilli*, *calculi*, *foci*, *fungi*, *loci*, *stimuli*, *streptococci*, even in the pronunciation of physicians, whose usage would be expected here to set a standard. I can, however, find no dictionary which records the shifted pronunciations of -*i* and -*ae*, save for the very few examples noted below in the sections "Restoration of Latin [aɪ] (ae), [aʊ], [ɔɪ] (oe)" and "Restoration of Latin [i]."[6] Most recognize the fact that the "Roman" pronunciation has affected the pronunciation of loanwords and foreign words and phrases, but few record hybrid and "Romanized" pronunciations.

Webster's *New International Dictionary*, 2d ed. (Springfield, Mass., 1943) states that, since most of the Latin words and phrases listed are scientific words, proper names, legal phrases, and familiar phrases and quotations from Latin in English context, their pronunciation is indicated according to the English method (p. liv). This dictionary is, however, better than its word, for a number of completely "Romanized" pronunciations are recorded, e.g., for *cum laude*, *magna cum laude*, and *summa cum laude*, as well as for *alma mater*, though the hybrids with [kʌm] and [ælmə] are not recorded. Webster's *Collegiate Dictionary*, 5th ed.

6. C. R. Ball, "English and Latin Plurals," *American Speech*, 3 (1928), 316, speaks of the uncertainty of pronunciation of -*i*, but is apparently referring only to "whether the final -*i* should be long or short." His statement, "in practice, the -*i*'s have it," seems to indicate a wavering between [-aɪ] and [-ɪ], and not to refer to the shift to [-i]. However, when he refers on p. 295 to "two recognized pronunciations [of -*ae*], namely, long -*e* and long -*i*," he is presumably referring to [-i] and [-aɪ]. One wonders, incidentally, what confers recognition, since, as I later point out, the dictionaries, with the exception of two examples in Jones's *English Pronouncing Dictionary*, do not record [-aɪ] for -*ae*.

(Springfield, 1941) states: "For those who prefer to pronounce Latin entries according to the 'Roman' method, the syllabification as indicated, together with the rules for such pronunciation as set forth in the Latin grammars, will be a sufficient guide" (p. xix). The implication is that the traditional pronunciation only is recorded, although the shorter dictionary likewise records "Romanized" pronunciations for *alma mater* and *cum laude*. The Funk and Wagnalls *New Standard Dictionary* (New York, 1940) points out that popular usage is divided, and that it "is probable that with the lapse of time the Roman pronunciation will prevail more and more." Although most pronunciations are according to the English method, the editors explain that "this practice does not indicate a preference for that method" (p. xxviii), at the same time recognizing that the English method of pronouncing many phrases has been so long fixed in the vocabularies of philosophy, law, medicine, etc., "that a public lecturer, a lawyer, or other professional man, quoting these familiar phrases, will usually pronounce them by the English method" (p. xxxiv).[7] *The Winston Simplified Dictionary*, Encyclopedic Edition (Philadelphia, 1927), mentions two methods of pronouncing Latin, the English and "the so-called Roman, or Continental method,"[8] and states that "the English pronunciation is still generally used [*dubito*] for Latin scientific terms, and for names, phrases, and quotations in English context. . . . in the case of Latin words and phrases, the pronunciation is given according to the English method" (p. 1182). Nevertheless, in the main body of this dictionary ['kʊm 'laʊde] and ['ælmə 'mɑtər][9] are recorded. *The New Century Dictionary* (New York, 1936) does not indicate pronunciation of foreign words and phrases listed in its supplement. The main body of the dictionary lists no "Romanized" pronunciations so far as I can discover. *The Universal Dictionary* (New York, 1897),[10] after recommending for Greek words and phrases a Graecized pronunciation (one which is somewhat at variance with present scholarly practice) because the traditional pronunciation of Greek, "although it is universally adopted in England, is absolutely indefensible from the point

---

7. This is certainly truer of lawyers than of other professional men. Legal words and phrases have acquired a traditional pronunciation not likely to be shaken for many years to come. The same cannot be said for medical Latin. The Latin of Protestant ministers is likely to be "Romanized" (i.e. "reformed"), and that of the Roman Catholic clergy is pronounced as modern Italian. As for professors of the humanities, the great majority of my hybrid and completely "Romanized" pronunciations have been supplied by them.

8. These are by no means the same: cf., for instance, treatment of classical *ae*, *oe*; *c*, *sc*, and *g* before *e*, *i*, *ae*, *oe*.

9. Presumably ['ælmə], since only ['mɑtər] is given in the second pronunciation: the ['ælmə] of the first (and traditional English) pronunciation is not repeated.

10. This is *Hunter's Dictionary* "adapted for the American public."

of view of accuracy," says of Latin: "At the outset it must be explained that the custom in English has been to disregard the obvious facts of the case, and pronounce Latin as though it were English. There is, however, in the present day a consensus of opinion against this practice, and the conclusions to which modern scholars have come as to the pronunciation of Latin are briefly stated" (4:5309)—and by implication specifically recommended. These rules are those generally followed by present-day teachers of Latin, except that *ae* is "as the ä in German." *C* is "always hard in Latin, never soft . . . ; *e.g.*, Cicero should be pronounced *Kikero*"; *g* is also "always hard"; and *r* "must always be trilled." The Roman pronunciation was apparently like a new toy at this time. Nevertheless, I have been unable to find a single "Romanized" or hybrid pronunciation recorded in the main body of this dictionary. Kenyon and Knott's *Pronouncing Dictionary of American English* points out that the "so-called Roman pronunciation is very inconsistent in actual practice" and records a few hybrid or "Romanized" pronunciations, though only the traditional pronunciations of -*ae* and -*i* are recorded. We are promised, however, that some form of the Roman pronunciation is sometimes added "if it has become widely current in actual use" (p. xlviii). The reader may judge for himself from the examples given below whether this promise has been made good; actually, many forms in common educated use are not recorded. The *OED* has no general statement on the pronunciation of Latin words and phrases, nor has the *Shorter Oxford*; the latter work records a few "Romanized" pronunciations not recorded in the more old-fashioned longer work. Jones's *English Pronouncing Dictionary* likewise has no general statement, but the editions of 1937 and 1943 label "old-fashioned" a good many pronunciations given first place in previous editions. H. C. Wyld's *Universal Dictionary* (London, 1932) records a few "Romanized" pronunciations, one of them (*genius loci*) quite startling. As a matter of fact, Wyld and Jones are both somewhat more realistic than any of the American dictionaries in this respect. Although my concern has been mainly with American dictionaries and American usage, I have consulted the English dictionaries mentioned above for purposes of comparison.

My lists are not exhaustive, and other, perhaps better, examples will probably occur to the reader. I have selected, more or less at random, likely words, names, and phrases which I have heard over a longish period of time. They will suffice to illustrate my contention.

Variants having no bearing upon "Romanization" have been normalized according to the type of American pronunciation with which I am most familiar. I have not been concerned with the reduction of Latin -*as* [æs] to [əs] or of *-a* [e] to [ə] or of *-i* [aɪ] to [ɪ], inasmuch as these have occurred within the English pronunciation of Latin. For the sake of uniformity, I have indicated all pronunciations by the phonetic notation used by Kenyon and Knott [except that š, ǰ, and ər have been substituted for their symbols]. When a dictionary is not mentioned, it will usually be understood that the only pronunciation recorded therein is the traditional English, or that the word or phrase is either not listed or its pronunciation not recorded. The numbers indicate order among variants; in the case of the more scientifically prepared dictionaries, such as Jones or Kenyon and Knott, a first recording does not necessarily indicate a "preferred" pronunciation, though it frequently indicates a more usual pronunciation. Where no number appears, the pronunciation given is the only one recorded.

The following abbreviations are used:

Cent.:   *The New Century Dictionary*, ed. cit.
C.O.:   *The Concise Oxford Dictionary* (Oxford, 1928).
F.W.:   *Funk and Wagnalls New Standard Dictionary*, ed. cit.
J.:   Daniel Jones, *English Pronouncing Dictionary*, 5th ed. (New York, 1943), except where otherwise noted.
KK.:   J. S. Kenyon and T. A. Knott, *A Pronouncing Dictionary of American English*, ed. cit.
Mac.:   *Macmillan's Modern Dictionary*, revised ed. (New York, 1944).
OED.:   *The Oxford English Dictionary* (Oxford, 1884–1928).
S.O.:   *The Shorter Oxford Dictionary* (Oxford, 1933).
T.C.:   *The Thorndike-Century Senior Dictionary* (Chicago, 1941).
Web.:   *Webster's New International Dictionary*, ed. cit.
Win.:   *The Winston Simplified Dictionary*, ed. cit.
Wy.:   H. C. Wyld, *The Universal Dictionary of the English Language*, ed. cit.

RESTORATION OF LATIN [ɑ]

With Dictionary Sanction

A (fortiori).[11] J. (4th and 5th eds., 1937 and 1943) 2: [ˈɑ (ˌfɔtɪˈɔri)]. Previous eds. record only [ˈe (ˌfɔšɪˈɔraɪ)].
*A*GNUS (Dei). J. 2; S.O. 2. Both words are of course "Romanized."
*A*LMA M*A*TER. K.K. 2 ("The hybrid ˈælmə ˈmɑtər is frequently heard"); Web. 2; Win. 2 ([ˈælmə ˈmɑtər], presumably); T.C. 2. Despite the weight

---

11. In these forms, the letter which is under discussion at the moment is italicized.

of educated usage, F.W. and Cent. fail to record either the hybrid or the completely "Romanized" form.[12] Of the dictionaries of British English, none records any pronunciation save the traditional English, which also is the first given in all American dictionaries. The phrase is, of course, not so frequent of occurrence in England as in America, where it appears in the "chants" and organized cheers of many a college and university, as well as in the sentimentalities of bibulous alumni on Homecoming Day.

*A*NA, -*A*NA (sb. and suffix). Web. 2; K.K. 2 (sb.), 3 (suffix); J. (sb., J. does not list the suffix separately, but *Americana* has [-'ɑnə]); OED. 2; S.O. 2; Wy. 2.

A (posteriori). Cent. 2; J. 2; OED. 2; S.O. 2. The final *-i* of the second word is also "Romanized."

APPAR*A*TUS. F.W. 2: [ˌæpə'rɑtəs].

A (priori). Cent. 2; Mac. 2; T.C. 2; Web. 2; Win. 2; J. 2; S.O. 2.

*A*VE. Cent. 2; F.W. 2; K.K. 2; Mac. 2; T.C. 2; Web. 2; Win. 2; J. 1 (beginning with 1937 ed., J. reverses order of recordings for this word); Wy. In *Ave Maria* the Roman Catholic pronunciation of both words seems to prevail (with Italian [v], of course, not classical [w]). But the English *Ave Maria Lane* is ['evɪmə'raɪə'len].

CANDEL*A*BRUM. T.C. 1; Web. 1; J. 1; Wy. 2.

C*A*SUS BELLI. J. (4th and 5th eds.) 2: ['kɑsus 'bɛli].

CERTIOR*A*RI. Wy. gives only the hybrid [ˌsəšɪɔ'rɑrɪ].

CIC*A*DA. K.K. 2; Web. 2; J. 1 (J. changes order of pronunciations in 5th ed.).

CLEOP*A*TRA. K.K. 2; Web. 2; J. 1 (note that [i] in the first syllable makes this a hybrid).

COLLECT*A*NEA. Wy. 1.

D*A*TUM, -A. Web. 2; K.K. ['detəm] only, but ['dɑtə] as alternative for the plural.

ERR*A*TUM, -A. K.K. 2; T.C. 2. A. G. Kennedy, *Current English* (N.Y., 1935) lists *errata* among words which "have, usually, [ɑ]" (p. 168). Despite the fact that only two dictionaries even record the pronunciation, few observers would doubt the correctness of Kennedy's statement.

GLORI*A*NA. J.

---

12. When I say "completely Romanized," I am referring only to vowel quality. The words in question receive the Germanic stress-accent, and classical quantities are seldom observed save by the extremely pedantic: thus, *mater* and *pater* rime in this supposedly "correct" pronunciation, and no distinction is made between *alma mater* and the general American pronunciation of the name *Alma Motter*.

(Gloria) P*A*TRI. Mac.; K.K. 1; Web. 2.

JUBIL*A*TE. Mac. 2; Web. 2; Win. 2; C.O. 1, 2: ([ǰu-] or [ju-]); J. (4th ed. drops [-ˈletɪ] as second pronunciation); S.O. 2: [ju-]; Wy.

LITER*A*TI. K.K. 2; T.C. 2; J. 1. All dictionaries consulted give only the traditional [lɪtəˈretɪm] for the more firmly entrenched *literatim*.

M*A*GNA. Web. 2 (in "Romanized" *magna cum laude*).

M*A*NES. J. 2: [ˈmɑnez].

MUT*A*TIS (mutandis). J. (4th and 5th eds.) 2: [mjuˈtɑtɪs (mjuˈtændɪs)]. Previous eds. have only [mjuˈtetɪs].

OR*A*TIO (obliqua). J. 1: [oˈrɑtɪo (oˈbłɪkwə)]. The traditional [əˈrešɪo (əˈblaɪkwə)] is labeled "old-fashioned."

P*A*TER. Web. 2, but only [ˈpetər-] in *pater-familias*, [ˈpetər-] and [ˈpætər-] in *pater-noster*.

PECC*A*VI. Mac. 2; Web. 2; Win. 2; J. (4th and 5th eds.) 1, with first pronunciation of 1927 ed. [pɛˈkevaɪ] labeled "old-fashioned."

(Persona) GR*A*TA. K.K. 2. It would seem that, on the basis of actual usage, the alternative pronunciation recorded by K.K. should be listed first in any dictionary. It is noteworthy that K.K. is alone in listing the usual pronunciation at all.

QU*A*SI. K.K. 3; Web. 2; T.C. 2.

(Quo) V*A*DIS. F.W. 1; Web. 2.

STR*A*TUM. J. (4th and 5th eds.) 2.

TIT*A*NIA. F.W. 2; Win. 2; J. 2.

(Vox) HUM*A*NA. J.

Without Dictionary Sanction

I have heard [ɑ] from educated speakers in all the following words and phrases. Such pronunciation is not recorded in any dictionary which I have consulted.

*A*D (— eundem, — hoc, — hominem, — infinitum, — nauseam, reductio — absurdum).

AESCUL*A*PIUS.

CASS*A*NDRA.

C*A*VE*A*T.

CINCINN*A*TUS.

CLO*A*CA.

COMIT*A*TUS. (I have never heard the dictionary pronunciation of this word.)

DESIDERATUM, -A.

(Deus ex) MACHINA.

(Exempli) GRATIA (with [-trə] and [-tɪɑ]).

GRATIS.

(Hic) JACET.

IGNORAMUS.

IMPRIMATUR.

INCUNABULA.

(In) FLAGRANTE (delicto).

(Inter) ALIA.

LARES AND PENATES (with [-ez] or [-iz]).

LITERATIM.

(Lucus) A (non lucendo).

MANDAMUS.

MANET.

(Mutatis) MUTANDIS (J. records [-'tɑt-], but not [-'tɑnd-]).

NOSTRADAMUS.

NOTANDUM.

PATERFAMILIAS.

SALVE.

SIMULACRUM.

(Sine) QUA (non) (entire phrase "Romanized").

STATUS.

ULTIMATUM. Usually [ˌʌltə'mɑtəm], but I have heard a news commentator (Henry Cassidy) pronounce [ˌultɪ'mɑtəm] (13 August 1945). A.
G. Kennedy, *Current English:* "Likewise both long [e] and the Latin
[ɑ] are to be heard in . . . *ultimatum"* (p. 174). But no dictionary has
"approved" (i.e., recorded) the pronunciation with [ɑ].

VALE ['vɑle], ['vɑlɪ], ['wɑle].

VERBATIM.

RESTORATION OF LATIN [e]

Speakers who are conscious of their training in Latin are of course likely
to pronounce an unstressed final *-e* as [-e]: *vale* ['vɑle], *salve* ['sɑlve],
etc.; though the unstressed syllable tends, because of English speech habits,
to become [·ɪ] even when the vowel of the stressed syllable is "Romanized." In stressed syllables the restoration of [e] is much less common
than the restoration of [ɑ], and comparatively few such pronunciations
have dictionary sanction. Thus, as has been pointed out, K.K., Web., and

J. record for *Cleopatra* [klɪə'pɑtrə] or [klɪə-]; none records [kleə'pɑtrə], which, though I have not heard it, is entirely within the realm of possibility.[13]

With Dictionary Sanction

(Agnus) D*E*I. J. 2.

A*VE*. See above, under "Restoration of Latin [ɑ]."

COM*E*NIUS. F.W. 1; Web. 1; Win. 1; J. *Webster's Biographical Dictionary* (Springfield, Mass., 1943) records only [kə'minɪəs].

CR*E*DO. Web. 2; J. 2.

MAN*E*S. J. 2: ['mɑnez].

N*E* (plus ultra). J. (4th and 5th eds.) 2: ['ne (plus 'ultrɑ)].

V*E*NI (vidi vici). Web. 2; J. (4th and 5th eds.) 1. In 1927 ed. J. has ['veni ('vidi 'viki)] 2, with note that this pronunciation "is now generally taught in schools, and is therefore likely to supplant the former traditional English pronunciation before long. The former pronunciation, however, still seems, on the whole, the more frequent among grown-up people." Time flies, alas, and those who were learning the "Romanized" vowels in school are now grown-up people, whereas those who say ['vinaɪ'vaɪdaɪ 'vaɪsaɪ] are presumably in second childhood; for in the two latest eds. J. labels "old-fashioned" the traditional English pronunciation listed first in preceding eds. One wonders how long it will take for the pronunciation with initial [w] to "make the grade." As a matter of fact, Web. does record this pronunciation.

Without Dictionary Sanction

A*VE* ATQU*E* VAL*E* ['ɑve 'ɑtkwe 'vɑle]. Restoration of Latin [w] is also conceivable here.

D*E* (profundis).

D*E*US (ex machina).

DI*E*S (irae) ['dies ('ɪraɪ)].

M*E*DIAS R*E*S.

MOR*E*S.

P*E*R S*E*.

SIN*E* DI*E*, SIN*E* (qua non) (completely "Romanized").

(Sub) JUDIC*E*. Chief Inspector Masters in Carter Dickson's *The Reader*

---

13. The hybrid [kleo'pætrə] was the stage pronunciation of Forbes-Robertson, Richard Mansfield, and Ada Rehan, according to Theodora Irvine's *Pronouncing Dictionary of Shakespearean Proper Names* (New York, 1944).

Is Warned (Pocket Book reprint, N.Y., 1945, p. 59) says "sub-ju-de-cay."

VAD*E* M*E*CUM.

(Via) M*E*DIA [('viə) 'medɪə].

RESTORATION OF LATIN [i][14]

Restoration of Latin [i], while not so common as restoration of [ɑ], is much more frequent than restoration of [e]. Final *-i* [aɪ] in foreign words is frequently reduced to [-ɪ], or even to [-ə], as in *semi-* (K.K.), but more frequently the Latin [-i] is fully restored, sometimes engendering confusion as in *alumni, alumnae* (see above). Perversely, *anti* and less frequently *semi*, which the dictionaries record with reduced vowels, are sometimes heard with [-aɪ] when analysis occurs (particularly when the following sound is a vowel), as in *anti-intellectual(ism), anti-everything, semiannual* (but not, of course, in compounds like *semicircle, semicolon*).

With Dictionary Sanction

(A) FORTIOR*I*. J. 2.

(Agnus) DE*I*. J. 2 (completely "Romanized" in eds. of 1927, 1937, 1943).

(A) POSTERIOR*I*. Cent. 2; J. 2.

(A) PR*I*OR*I*. Cent. 2: [-ɪ]; Mac. 2: [-ɪ]; T.C. 2: [-ɪ]; Win. 2: [-ɪ]; Web. 2: [-ɪ]; J. 2: [-i].

(Casus) BELL*I*. J. 2 (completely "Romanized").

CERTIORAR*I*. Wy.: [sɜšɪɔ'rɑrɪ]. The presence of [ɑ] in the stressed syllable would indicate that [-ɪ] is a reduction of [-i] rather than of [-aɪ].

CU*I* (bono). Web. 2; J. (J. labels the traditional [kaɪ] "old-fashioned" in eds. of 1937 and 1943. Previous eds. reverse the order.)

(Cursor) MUND*I*. J. 2: [-'mundi].

(Gloria) PATR*I*. Mac.; K.K. 1; Web. 2.

LIB*I*DO. Cent. 2; F.W. 2; Win. 1; Wy. (Appendix) 2. (Restoration is not exceptional in recent borrowings.)

LITERAT*I*. K.K. 2; J. 1 ([ɑ] in stressed syllable).

(Oratio) OBL*I*QUA. J. 1 (completely "Romanized").

PECCAV*I*. Mac. 2; Web. 2; Win. 2; J. (4th and 5th eds.) 1 ([ɑ] in stressed syllable).

PISC*I*NA. Cent. 2; F.W. 2; Mac. 2; Web. 2; J. (4th and 5th eds.) 1; Wy. 1 (all [pɪ'sinə]). The next "improvement" will no doubt be [pɪs'kinə].

---

14. Including [-ɪ] when it is presumably a reduction of [-i].

QUAS*I*. K.K. 2; T.C. 2; Web. [-ɪ] 2 ([ɑ] in stressed syllable).
TR*I*UMVIR*I*. J. (4th and 5th eds.) 1: [trɪ'ʌmvɪri]. Previous eds. have
 only [traɪ'ʌmvɪraɪ].
VEN*I* VID*I* VIC*I*. J. (4th and 5th eds.) 1; Web. 2.

Without Dictionary Sanction

ALUMN*I*.
BACILL*I*.
COCC*I* [-ki], [-kɪ], [-si], [-sɪ]. Also staphylo-, strepto-, pneumo-.
COLOSS*I*.
(Contemptus, Sic transit gloria) MUND*I*.
D*I*ES *I*RAE [-ɪraɪ].
FOC*I*. (Cf. *cocci*, above.)
FUNG*I*.
GLADIOL*I* (with stress on any of the first three syllables); also [glæ'diəli].
LOC*I*. (Cf. *cocci*, above.)
NARCISS*I*.
N*I*S*I* PR*I*US (from a cultivated layman).
(Per) D*I*EM.
P*I*A (mater). (Cf. Denham's rime "Mater pia . . . Gonorrheia . . . Letania"
 in "A Dialogue between Sir John Pooley and Mr. Thomas Killigrew.")
REG*I*NA [rə'jinə], [rə'ginə] (in the title of Housman's *Victoria Regina*).
(Religio) MEDIC*I*, LAIC*I*.
S*I*NE D*I*E.
S*I*NE (qua non) (completely "Romanized").

RESTORATION OF LATIN [o]

As taught in the schools, the pronunciation of Latin *o* coincides with that
of English *o* in open syllables. It is therefore only in closed syllables that
the tendency to restoration would be evident. It may be observed occasionally in *ad hoc* from those who have learned to say "correctly" [hik
haɪk hok], as well as in *non* (sine qua —, lucus a — lucendo, persona
— grata, — sequitur). I have also heard *Agamemnon* as [ˌægə'mɛmnon].

RESTORATION OF LATIN [u], [ʊ]

Latin *ū* coincides with English *u* in open syllables, and becomes [ju] under
the same circumstances as in English: a speaker who pronounces *Luke* as
[ljuk] would be likely to pronounce Latin *lucus* as ['ljukəs], even when
consciously "Romanizing," as in *lucus a non lucendo* ['ljukəs ɑ ˌnon
lju'kɛndo]. Such a speaker might conceivably, however, under the influence

of his Latin instruction, make the simplification to [u]. No examples of this simplification are given below. Most speakers of American English would pronounce a simple vowel in accordance with native speech habits, thereby unconsciously reproducing the Latin quality.

Latin *ŭ* in closed stressed syllables becomes [ʌ] in the traditional English pronunciation; it is reduced to [ə] in unstressed syllables. Frequently, however, the Latin value is restored as supposedly more "correct."

With Dictionary Sanction

AGN*U*S (Dei). J. 2: ['ɑgnʊs ('dei)].

CAS*U*S (belli). J. 2: ['kɑsʊs ('bɛli)].

C*U*M (laude). K.K. 2: ['kʊm ('laʊdɪ)]; T.C. 2; Web. 2: ['kʊm ('laʊdɛ)]; Win. 2: [kʊm ('laʊde)]. The hybrid ['kʌm 'laʊdɪ], frequently heard at commencement exercises, is nowhere recorded.

(Cursor) M*U*NDI. J. 2: ['mʊndi].

PL*U*S *U*LTRA. J. 2.

S*U*MMA C*U*M (laude). Web. 2.

Without Dictionary Sanction

AL*U*MNUS, -AE, -I (rare, but heard).

(De) PROF*U*NDIS.

*U*LTIMAT*U*M (rare, but heard. The stressed syllable would of course be [ɑ]).

RESTORATION OF LATIN [aɪ] (AE), [aʊ] (AU), [ɔɪ] (OE)

F.W. misinterprets the statement of the *OED* that classical scholars tend to make Latin *ae* "long (ī) in all positions." The symbol used by the *OED* stands of course for [i]. F.W. misquotes as "long (aɪ or ī)"—an amazing example of misunderstanding. No pronunciations of *ae* as [aɪ] are, however, recorded by F.W.

I have been able to discover only two recordings of *ae* with classical value, both of them in J. They occur in *lapsus linguae* ['læpsəs 'lɪŋgwaɪ], with traditional [-gwɪ], [-gwi] labeled "old-fashioned," and in the phonetic term (pl.) *mediae* as a second pronunciation ['mɛdɪaɪ]. The restoration is, however, likely to occur wherever *ae* appears. I have heard it in *aes* (*triplex*) [aɪs], *coronae*, (*dies*) *irae*, *differentiae*, *ferae naturae*, *formulae*, *Getae* ['getaɪ], *literae* (*humaniores*), *lacunae*, *minutiae*,[15] *morae*, *Tenebrae*, *vae*

---

15. See "Professors Like Minutiae" by Helen Bevington in the *New Yorker* for 9 February 1946, with the final couplet "With whom how friskily did I pass by / The literature for the minutiae."

(*victis*), *vertebrae*. *Alumnae* has already been discussed at some length.

K.K., Web., and Win., as has been seen, record (*cum*) *laude* with [aʊ]. The Latin diphthong is almost as frequently heard in (*honoris*) *causa*, though nowhere recorded. I have also heard the diphthong in the following: *Au*rex (name of a hearing device, so pronounced by a classical scholar), *Au*sonia, *Au*lis, *au*rist, *au*rum (potabile), B*au*cis, f*au*ces, thes*au*rus.

Oe is of comparatively rare occurrence. I have heard an approximation of the Latin diphthong in a well-known scholar's pronunciation of Thomas Rymer's collection, *Foedera*, as ['fɔɪdərɑ]. The title is obviously one that would be known only to the learned. It is very doubtful that Rymer would have recognized the "improved" pronunciation.

RESTORATION OF LATIN [k]

The only dictionary recognition that I have found for Latin *c* as [k] preceding *e*, *i*, *ae*, *eu*, *oe* is Wy.: (*genius*) *loci* ['lokaɪ]. The velar stop is, however, to be heard frequently in *foci* ['fokaɪ, -i, -ɪ], and even physicians have been heard to pronounce plurals such as *streptococci* and *staphylococci* with [-kɪ]. Similarly, *coccyx* may be heard as ['kɑkɪks]. In actual usage, the traditional English pronunciation of Latin *c* would seem to be pretty completely lost. I have heard [k] in the following also: B*au*cis ['bɔkɪs, 'baʊkɪs], (hic) j*a*cet ['jɑkɪt], (Religio) Lai*c*i, – Medi*c*i ['laɪki, 'mɛdɪki], (Newton's) Prin*c*ipia, (lucus a non) lu*c*endo.

RESTORATION OF LATIN [g]

Restoration of Latin [g] is especially likely in words ultimately of Greek origin, transmitted by way of Latin. H. W. Fowler liked the "hard sound" in such Greek-derived words as are "not in popular but only in learned, technical, or literary use," such as pedago*g*y, menin*g*itis, anthropopha*g*i (his list of "deserving cases" includes some words of Latin transmission)— "a harmless pedantry that affects after all but a few words."[16] It is greatly to be doubted that Fowler would have cared for the velar stop in such Latin-derived words as *regicide*, which I have heard, and which is perfectly natural for a student who has learned [reks, 'regɪs] instead of [rɛks, 'riʝɪs].[17]

---

16. "Greek G," *A Dictionary of Modern English Usage* (Oxford, 1940), p. 221.

17. G. C. Moore Smith, *Jespersen Miscellany*, pp. 177–78, reports having heard *orgy* and *plagiarism* with [g]. The first, I should say, is quite common, particularly in these days, when "schooling" has become more important than a cultural tradition not to be easily acquired in the schools.

Were it not for the analogy of the familiar *suicide*, one might even expect [-kɪd] in the final syllable, for the bright student, coming upon *regicide* first in a book, might very well connect *-cide* with a Latin verb which he has learned as ['kido].[18]

With Dictionary Sanction

AREOPAG ITE. Cent. 1; C.O. 1; F.W. 2; J. 1 (but only [-ǰ-] in *Areopagitica*); K.K. 2; S.O.; Win. 1; Web. 2; Wy.

AREOPAG ITIC(A). Cent. 1; F.W. 2; Web. 2.

FUNG I. J. (1927): ['fʌŋgaɪ]; J. (1937, 1943): ['fʌngaɪ].

GERONTIUS. J.

GERYON. J.

MELEAG ER. J.: [ˌmɛlɪ'egə].

SARCOPHAG I. C.O. 1; J. 1; Wy. 1.

VIRG INIBUS (puerisque). J. 1.

Without Dictionary Sanction

(Fors) CLA VIG ERA.

G ESTA (Romanorum).

SCALIG ER.

(Tempus) FUG IT.

RESTORATION OF LATIN [j]

Mac. records for *jubilate* [ju-] 2, as do C.O. and S.O. also. Restoration may also be heard in *(hic) jacet* and *jus (divinum)*.

RESTORATION OF LATIN [s]

I find no examples of this restoration in the dictionaries. I have observed it in the following, all completely "Romanized": ae*s* (triplex), ar*s* (longa), die*s* (irae), For*s* (Clavigera, — fortuna), (in medias) re*s*.

RESTORATION OF LATIN [t] (TH) < GREEK θ

The [t] is restored in *(ex) cathedra* by J. 2 and J. 4: [kæ'tɛdrɑ, kə'tɛdrɑ].[19]

---

18. It may be suggested that we have, in the interest of an intransigent conception of "correctness," sacrificed some of the effectiveness of integrating Latin and English when we insist that students connect *suicide* with Latin ['kido] instead of with ['saɪdo].

19. It is of interest that J. records no pronunciation of this word with classical initial stress, though such stress would seem to be gaining ground, as also in *éczema* and *ángina*. ['kæθ-] is the only pronunciation given in F.W. and Wy. All the other dictionaries consulted save C.O. and S.O. recorded the initial stress.

RESTORATION OF LATIN [-tɪ-]

With Dictionary Sanction

(A) FOR*TI*ORI. J. 2: [(a) fɔtɪ'ɔri]; Wy.: [(e) fɔtɪ'ɔraɪ].
CER*TI*ORARI. C.O.; J.
GERON*TI*US. K.K.; J. 1.
ORA*TI*O. J. 1.
TER*TI*UM. J. 3.
TO*TI*ES QUO*TI*ES. C.O. 1; Wy.

Without Dictionary Sanction

DIFFEREN*TI*A(E).
(Exempli) GRA*TI*A.
GRO*TI*US.
(In) ABSEN*TI*A.
MINU*TI*A(E).

RESTORATION OF LATIN [w]

The English have apparently boggled at [w] for *v*. Long ago, in 1871, Max Müller thought that "in trying to introduce a more correct pronunciation of Latin, the great stumbling block has always been the hard pronunciation of *c* before *e*, *i*, *ae*, *eu*, *oe*";[20] but the current British ['viki] for *vici*, as recorded in J. (4th and 5th eds.), would seem to indicate that *v* as [w] has been an even greater one. Americans have had no such qualms. I have heard the short biographical sketch usually appended to a doctoral dissertation referred to as the ['wita]. With a fine disregard for chronology,[21] the title of the journal *Medium Aevum* is frequently pronounced ['medɪum 'aɪwum], even by linguists and medievalists. The only dictionary recording of the Classical Latin sound, which to English and American ears of a generation ago would have seemed to deprive Caesar's famous utterance of all its vitality and virility, is, as far as I have been able to discover, that given for *veni vidi vici* in Web. 2; the first pronunciation recorded in Web. is ['vinaɪ 'vaɪdaɪ 'vaɪsaɪ] (and one wonders how many speakers nowadays would actually so pronounce it). Restoration of [w] may also

20. "On the Pronunciation of C," *Academy*, 2:145–46.
21. Latin [w] became a bilabial spirant "probably early in the Empire," the bilabial sound later becoming labiodental [v] (C. H. Grandgent, *An Introduction to Vulgar Latin*, New York, 1907, pp. 135–36).

be heard in the following: caveat, (in) vino veritas, (pax) vobiscum, peccavi, (rara) avis, vade (mecum), vae victis, vale.

It is obvious that the pronunciation of learned loanwords, foreign words, and phrases from Latin is now in a transitional stage. One hesitates, as has been pointed out, to use a Latin word or phrase for fear one's pronunciation will invite ridicule or suspicion of one's learning: the speaker is, in fact, almost forced to have *two* pronunciations of Latin, one—the "Romanized"—for the partially educated and the academically hidebound, and one—the English—for the sophisticated; though it is clear from the number of "Romanized" pronunciations recorded by Jones—and he is recording only sophisticated speech—that even on a sophisticated level there is considerable wavering. The effect upon words, names, and phrases of long residence in English is apparent. It is perhaps regrettable that the development of English has been somewhat altered; but altered it has been, and it is high time that the dictionaries record the alteration on a much wider scale than they do at present. A little learning combined with a lack of *savoir faire* was perhaps responsible in the beginning; but those who have a speech tradition by inheritance are now kowtowing to the almighty schoolmarm. Tradition has gone down before scholarship, and, whether we like it or not, as scientific students of language we must accept the facts as they present themselves.

De Temporibus et Moribus

4

That Fine Italian *A* in American English

FOR many years British observers descanted upon the ''barbarous'' qualities of American English.[1] Its slang appalled, its colloquialisms disgusted; and the English, regarding themselves as the rightful custodians of Anglistic propriety, were convinced that ''their'' language was ''going to the dogs'' on these shores.

But there is another side to American English. While we may lack a tradition for pronouncing *Derby*, *Cirencester*, *Cholmondeley*, et al., we have by this time acquired a tradition of our own—a school tradition inculcated by generations of teachers, who in this country are mahatmas of marvelous potency in matters linguistic, though, ironically enough, little regarded in other departments.[2] Knowing how the language should be spoken and written is an important part of the schoolmarm's stock in trade. She —or he—can no more afford to claim ignorance in this respect than a village GP can afford to admit his mistakes in diagnosis and therapeutics, for each is expected to be infallible—the scientific attitude is not for them.

Popular notions regarding the free-and-easy nature of American English to the contrary notwithstanding, as spoken by the educated—that is to say, by the schooled—it is if anything overcareful and precise; indeed,

1. See Mencken's *American Language* and *Supplement I*, passim.
2. As a professor of English in state universities, I have received many written requests (to put it politely, for some were in the nature of demands for the ministrations of a public hireling) for an ''authoritative'' opinion on ''correct'' usage from business and professional men whose attitude towards me in other circumstances would undoubtedly have been patronizing. (Doubtless they have by now come to think me quite incompetent, for I have frequently had to reply that I could not presume to pontifical infallibility in such delicate matters as the proper choice between ''it is I'' and ''it is me.'')

almost "prissy" in its concern for and subservience to what are thought
of as "standards." The influence of the schoolmarm (the term may be interpreted bisexually), who frequently comes to regard herself as linguistically *sine labe nota* — the distinction was in the beginning thrust upon
her, and she can hardly be blamed if it has gone to her head — must ever
be reckoned with: the layman has unadulterated confidence in her secret
sources of information as to what language ought to be — sources which
he *qua* layman is quite incapable of tapping.

Now, an attitude of mind has developed concomitantly with the teaching
of the modern foreign languages (the teaching of the "reformed," or
"classical," pronunciation of Latin, with its un-English vowels, has doubtless contributed) that words of foreign origin, when their foreign origin
is recognized — sometimes mistakenly, as indicated by pseudo-French
[ˌdɪləˈtɑnt] for Italian *dilettante* — should be pronounced according to the
phonetic system of the language from which they have been borrowed,
insofar as this system is known.[3] To do so would seem to be in the nature
of a linguistic obligation on the part of many speakers. This attitude has
been staunchly sponsored by the schools, so that by now every American
who ever went to high school has been made aware of the fact that in
languages other than English the letter *a* has typically the approximate
value that it has in Present English *father*. This is an elementary fact which
almost any linguistic booby can — and frequently does — remember.

I think there can be little doubt that such "new" pronunciations with
[ɑ] as I propose to discuss are due to the smattering of modern foreign
languages now taught in our schools, coupled with the American's over-
weening desire to be "correct." A contributing factor, no doubt, is the
widespread patronizing attitude towards our language on the part of many
who speak it: it's "good old Anglo-Saxon," true; but, after all, French
("the language of diplomacy") is capable of so many more "refinements
of meaning," Italian and Spanish are more "musical," "euphonious,"
"beautiful," etc., etc. English, though "good" and "old" and "Anglo-
Saxon," is felt to be somehow inferior to the languages of the continent
of Europe.[4]

---

3. Fortunately for the natural development of the English language, those who feel so
about the matter are usually not aware of the non-English origin of many words which came
into English, principally from French, before the Great Vowel Shift.

4. Though German is frequently denigrated because of its "gutturals." According to
Hollywood opinion, the Nazis developed a particularly offensive way of articulating these
"gutturals." I quote from a Hollywood dispatch regarding one Kurt Kreuger, a German-
born film player, printed in the Oklahoma City *Oklahoman* (30 September 1945): "He's
working hard on his accent, which is German, but not the typical Nazi guttural."

The "new" sound for earlier [æ] occurs principally in words whose foreign origin is definitely recognizable—not as a rule in the more familiar Renaissance borrowings like *balcony*, *cameo*, *stanza*—and is to be heard usually from speakers who take pride in their linguistic Americanism and who would never think of using [ɑ] in such words as *path*, *grass*, *staff*, etc., that is, words which in British English have [ɑ] instead of the earlier [æ] preserved in American English. It would seem to be used out of a quite conscious desire for "correct" pronunciation, and its origin is probably to be found, as I have stated, in the contemporary study of the modern foreign languages, with the "classical" pronunciation of Latin as now taught in the schools a contributing factor. On the public-school level, [ɑ] is likely to be the value given by students, regardless of the correctness of their teaching, to the letter *a*;[5] for the [a] of French, Spanish, and other foreign languages would seem to be practically impossible of articulation for most speakers of American English. Thus, [ɑ] tends to be used as preferable to, i.e., more "correct" than, [æ], the latter vowel being thought of, no doubt, as exclusively English—though actually about as good a compromise for French and Spanish [a] as is [ɑ]. Italian is not much taught in the secondary schools; it is ironical that the [ɑ]-sound used in the pronunciation of a good many words of Italian origin, like *Dante*, *dilettante*, *canto*, etc., should have been acquired by way of French and Spanish. (The fact that [ɑ] is also the sound used by native speakers of Italian in these words is quite irrelevant to the matter under discussion.)

This new [ɑ] is not to be confused with [ɑ] from earlier [e] or [æ] in Latin learned loanwords and foreign words like *ultimatum*, *errata*, *data*, *alma mater*, in which the Latin quality is used in the stressed syllables as supposedly more correct than the traditional English one—a direct result of the teaching of the "classical" pronunciation of Latin in the schools, with seldom a word of instruction as to the "English" method sanctioned by centuries of cultivated usage. It is instead to be heard in words which

5. Use of [ɑ] in the syllables bearing the principal stress in *mineralogy* and, even more frequently, *genealogy* is quite unconscious. As Kenyon and Knott point out (*Pronouncing Dictionary of American English*, Springfield, Mass., 1944, s.v. *genealogy*), [ɑ] appears in these words by analogy with a much larger group of *-ology* words (*geology*, *psychology*, and the like), though the more familiar word *analogy* itself has not been so influenced. I have also heard [ɑ] used quite unconsciously in the second syllable of *collaboration* (influence of *corroboration*?). Perhaps [ɑ] in the third syllable of *onomatopoea* and its derivatives is likewise unconscious (assimilation to the American [ɑ] of the first syllable?); it may also be due to the feeling that the word is of classical origin. Thanks to the relinquishment of the "English" pronunciation of Latin in the schools, everyone is now aware that *a* in words of classical origin is pronounced [ɑ], at least when one is thinking about it; the result is frequently a hybrid like *alma mater* ['ælmə 'mɑtər].

have come to us by way of the modern foreign languages, excluding recent borrowings, for which the current fashion prescribes pronunciation approximately according to the phonological principles of the language of origin[6] — words of long-established use in English, particularly borrowings which, despite comparative unfamiliarity,[7] have nevertheless a long tradition of Anglicization behind them. Thus, an Italian proper name of long standing in English is likely to undergo pseudo-Italianization, even when the form itself differs from the Italian: cf. *Milan* (It. *Milano*), a very frequent American pronunciation of which is [mɪ'lɑn], or even [mə'lɑn].[8] One would expect that a name so long used in English as that of the foremost Italian poet would be just ['dænti]—or even [dænt], which would be the normal English development of the name as it occurs in Middle English. Disyllabic pronunciation with [æ] in the first syllable is indeed the only one recorded by Daniel Jones,[9] and Kenyon and Knott record it first, with the alternative ['dɑntɪ]. If Kenyon and Knott's order indicates relative frequency, as it

---

6. When these are known. When they are not, it seems to be sufficient to pronounce in an obviously un-English fashion. I have heard radio commentators pronounce the Russian dictator's name (actually his nom de guerre) as [šta'lin], with initial consonant precisely as in German, and fancy American-school-French stress on the final syllable. I have heard from the same arbiters of linguistic elegances (for so they are indeed regarded by the common man) the names *Rommel* and *Beneš* stressed heavily on the final syllable. Perhaps the ultimate in such silliness was reached when newscasters—even highly paid network performers—pronounced General (now Lord) Wavell's name [wɑ'vel].

7. Because of this same comparative unfamiliarity, the words in question are used only by people of some learning; consequently, many of the pronunciations with which I am here concerned are "professorial." But if only professors (or their equivalents, if there are any) say the words, then the way the professors say them would seem to me to be the way they are pronounced, the recommendations of the dictionaries to the contrary notwithstanding.

8. Both the *Pronouncing Dictionary of American English* and W. Cabell Greet, *World Words* (New York, 1944), give only [mɪ'læn] and ['mɪlən] as American pronunciations of the name of the Italian city. According to my own observation the first pronunciation is considerably less frequent nowadays than the pseudo-foreign [mɪ'lɑn]—in fact, it would in many educated (not to say sophisticated) circles be considered somewhat "crude," or at least "eccentric"; and the second I have never heard save from a few elderly Englishmen. I venture the observation that the second is as rare in American usage as ['sevɪl] for Seville (a pronunciation for the name of the Spanish city recorded as American by both Greet and the *PDAE*). Incidentally, Milan when it names towns in Michigan, Missouri, and Tennessee is quite modestly pronounced ['maɪlən].

9. *An English Pronouncing Dictionary* (5th ed., New York, 1943). The Funk and Wagnalls *New College Standard Dictionary* (New York, 1947) records only ['dænti] for the single name, with Italian pronunciation for the full *Dante Alighieri*, which would seem to be quite in accord with what was the usual practice among the educated before the onset of the tendency which I am discussing: that is, Anglicization for the single form, of long standing in English, and Italianization for the full name, much less frequently used. The *American College Dictionary* (New York, 1947) records ['dænti], ['dɑnte], with the latter pronunciation labeled "Italian," but not the predominating ['dɑnti]. Incidentally, the original form of the name, *Durante*, which is not uncommon in America, always has [æ] in the stressed syllable.

need not necessarily do, it should be reversed, for ['dɑntɪ] is certainly the predominant American pronunciation, practically the only one I have heard, from professors and amateurs alike. In the pronunciation of this word, as in *dilettante*,[10] it will be observed that American pronunciation is more self-conscious, more elaborate than the "flossiest" type of British Received Standard; for the [ɑ] in these words, as also occasionally in *canto* (professorially), *andante*, and *regatta* may be fairly regarded as a self-conscious elaboration of natural English speech, born of a passionate lust for "correctness" which has here superseded long tradition.

It will be noted, of course, that the final -*e* of *Dante*, *dilettante*, *andante*, and the like in this elegant pseudo-Italian pronunciation is usually reduced to [ɪ], in accordance with English speech habits. Somehow, in the *psyche linguistica* of those who use the fancier (and, as far as Modern English is concerned, newer) [ɑ], traditional pronunciation with [æ] would seem to have become "crude" and "uneducated"; but all requirements for orthoëpic purity seem to be satisfied by the mere substitution of [ɑ] for [æ]. Italianization of the final syllable would seem not to matter—or could it be simple unawareness of the quality of Italian final -*e*?

In any case, we have in the tendency which I have here noted a further instance of the triumph of a little learning over the traditions of centuries of cultivated usage. Professor W. Cabell Greet has declared that "absurd foreignisms will be labeled pretentious and asinine, fine as the line is between what seems absurd and what seems 'correct.'"[11] In the examples which I have cited, the line seems to me to be rather fine; indeed, there are many (including most speakers of Received Standard) who would consider [ɑ] in the cited words to be pretentious. It is likely, however, as Greet has pointed out, that "our bright people are more interested in the present international world than in the traditions of English."[12] "Correct" pronunciation, even of words long established in English, has come to be "foreign" pronunciation (usually only approximately so, but any shortcomings are due to the speaker's linguistic limitations, not to any lack of desire to speak precisely according to foreign standards). This is a tendency "al of the newe jet"; the tradition for Anglicization would seem to be in large part lost, in American English at least, a loss nowhere more evident than in the replacement of older [æ] with "foreign" [ɑ] in the words which I have discussed.

10. I.e., as [ˌdɪlə'tɑntɪ, -te]. An erroneous impression that the word is French, strengthened by the analogy of *débutante*, is probably responsible for the very frequent [dɪlə'tɑnt].

11. *World Words*, p.4.

12. *World Words*, p.4.

5

Subliminal Words Are Never Finalized

THE past ten years or so have yielded an amazingly fruity crop of "vogue words," an examination of which cannot fail to throw light on the times in which we live. Just as the Renaissance rage for so-called "inkhorn termes"—words like *mendaciloquent* 'speaking lies' and *anacephalize* 'recapitulate'—indicates the tremendous prestige of classical learning in that period, so does the current vogue of words taken from psychology, medicine, and elsewhere tell much about the predilections of our own day. And perhaps the vogue of a large group of self-consciously homely expressions can be partially explained as an endeavor, hollow though it may be, to show that for all our scientific and technological lore we are still just plain folks—homespun, guileless, and democratic as all get-out.

Vogue words are words with prestige value, words whose use is intended to establish the user as belonging to a sort of verbal Ivy League. They are not necessarily new words; *automation* is new, to be sure, but *global* has pursued an even tenor for a very long time only to become voguish comparatively recently.

Many such words ultimately become the property of the common man, like *to contact*, a vogue word of a bygone day which has long been with us and is doubtless here to stay. Most of the words to be discussed here are even now in the trickling-down process. A few, though well known to us all, are still the property of those who in our democratic society constitute an élite—bureaucrats, administrators, and executives of all kinds and sizes, professional commentators on national and "global" affairs, practitioners of the so-called behavioral sciences and, to a very limited extent, popular literary critics and writers of book reviews.

Thus, from the mists of bureaucracy, the word *finalize* has descended to general voguish usage. It has not yet entered the vocabulary of simple, unpretentious people, though they all know the word—after all, Mr. Eisenhower gave it his imprimatur in his "State of the Union" message, so that it is now "President's English." The *-ize* suffix of this word is very voguish in advertising copy, a most potent disseminator of modish expressions; witness *personalize, moisturize, accessorize*, and a host of others. Its fashionableness may explain why *hospitalize,* current since the turn of the century, has recently begun to flourish.

Guilt complex, to denote nothing more than 'a feeling of guilt,' is probably the most recent scion of *complex*, a term used by psychoanalysts more than a half-century ago to refer to a type of mental aberration resulting from the unconscious suppression of more or less related ideas and attitudes. The word soon passed into voguish and subsequently into general use, to designate an obsession of any sort—a bee in the bonnet. Among its other progeny have been *Oedipus complex, sex complex, herd complex*, and the highly successful *inferiority complex*, originally a technical term for an unconscious sense of inferiority often resulting in self-assertion. *Inferiority complex* became a voguish synonym for *shyness* in the late teens of the present century and is now well established in general use. The odds on the continuing fecundity of *complex* are high.

Other voguish terms from psychoanalysis and psychology are *subliminal* (applied very recently to a sneaky kind of advertising), *sadism, compulsive, empathy, ambivalence, schizophrenia, psychosomatic, neurotic*, and *exhibitionism*. As might be expected, their voguish meanings show a considerable extension of the earlier technical meanings of these words. Thus *sadism* has come to mean simply 'cruelty,' and *exhibitionism* simply 'showing-off,' without so much as a connotation of perversion. Similarly, the word *psychology* itself may mean merely 'mental processes.' Our present-day preoccupation with what is fashionably and humanely referred to as *mental illness* must to a large extent be responsible for the use of such terms.

Physical scientists, though men of awesome prestige nowadays, as a rule tend to be rather inarticulate. This is perhaps the reason why there are fewer vogue words from physics and chemistry than from social psychology. (Another is that the concepts of the physical sciences are comparatively difficult to grasp.)

Satellite, nuclear, and *chain reaction*, although much used, are not really very choice. But *atomic* has certainly been one of the most successful of all vogue words of our day. *Atomic age, atomic warfare, atomic cocktail,* and, as the nom de guerre of a strip-tease artiste, *Atomic Bombshell* are only a few of its proliferations. It is not outside the bounds of possibility that it should become a mere superlative and ultimately supplant the already moribund *colossal*.

From medicine come *allergy* (a voguish alternative for *distaste*), *intern* (for a beginning public school teacher), and *clinic*, as in *reading clinic* (an establishment or university department for the "diagnosis" and correction of reading difficulties of those who have not hitherto learned to read without lip movement), *auto clinic* (a hospital for ailing cars), and *retail hardware salesmanship clinic* (as far as I can determine, a conference of hardware salesmen). The extension of *clinic* to humbler lines of endeavor is identical with that of *laboratory*, as in *writing laboratory* (for a classroom supplied with tables, chairs, and dictionaries, where students of composition write under supervision). This might also be called a *workshop*, which seems rather plebeian compared with *clinic* and *laboratory*, but is nonetheless quite voguish.

Dichotomy, first used as a technical term in logic in the early seventeenth century, very soon acquired a simplified popular sense, 'division into two.' Its use even in this sense, however, was restricted to scholarly writing until comparatively recently, when it achieved a considerable vogue. The current issue of *Inside the ACD*, the bulletin of the American College Dictionary staff, reports *overdichotomize*, apparently meaning to make foolishly fine distinctions, as the creation of Dr. Bernard Schwartz, former counsel of the House subcommittee investigating regulatory agencies. It is, alas, too much to expect that this fine flower of language, a veritable hot-house specimen—combining as it does a vogue word with a vogue suffix—will long survive. It is too rarefied for the popular taste.

Dilemma, sharing the prefix *di-* ('two') of *dichotomy*, was also in the beginning a technical term of logic implying a choice between two alternatives. As early as the end of the sixteenth century it acquired the meaning 'predicament,' without any necessary connotations of twoness. But, like *dichotomy*, it did not become really voguish until fairly recently.

Condition, with many different uses, is a great favorite with voguish speakers. Its verbal function, as in *conditioned to the atomic age* (*geared* might be substituted here with no loss of prestige), is doubtless an outgrowth of the technical use of the word in psychology, as in *conditioned reflex*. There are a number of very stylish compounds on the analogy of *air-conditioned*—*flight-conditioned*, *speed-conditioned*, and the like. As a noun, *condition* frequently has a dire connotation in voguish usage in such phrases as *heart condition* and *malignant condition*. This essentially euphemistic use of *condition* to mean 'bad condition,' which probably originated in the usage of medical men, is already in limited use among the folk. It is undoubtedly here to stay, though as yet neglected by the dictionaries.

Global, in its earlier sense of 'globe-shaped,' has been with us since the latter part of the seventeenth century, but its voguish use to mean 'world-wide' is comparatively recent. Mrs. Luce's *globaloney* was a happy blend, but it never really caught on, perhaps because wit cannot flourish amid such global responsibilities as we are constantly being told we must face.

In a way of life which must perforce concern itself with such phenomena as the atom and dedicate itself to such purposeful ideals as social justice and togetherness, it is not surprising that light-hearted creations like *globaloney* and, to cite another, *egghead* should have failed to achieve the success they deserve. Nor is it surprising that "earnest" words such as are used in the preceding sentence should have acquired so high a tone. Perhaps this is why *meaningful*, which made its debut in the language as early as 1852, never got around much until recently.

The current productivity of *-wise*, long established in such words as *likewise* and *sidewise*, is incapable of explanation. Almost every day brings forth new examples like *weatherwise*, *healthwise*, *budgetwise*, and *productionwise*. One would hesitate to venture any prediction as to the viability of the offspring of this rejuvenated affix, but there can be no denying their present voguishness.

A group of anemic and more or less meaningless vogue words may be considered together: *level*, *bracket*, and *media* (as in *mass media*, *advertising media*; the singular *medium* is not particularly voguish). The first two of these are practically interchangeable and are widely used by men of distinction in such locutions as *upper-age brackets*, *high-level business*, *teen-age level*, *policy level*, *income bracket*, and *top-level planning*. To be ultravoguish one might substitute *echelon* for either *bracket* or *level*, though in stodgily conservative circles that might be considered a bit on the flamboyant side.

Hassle, *clobber*, *gimmick*, and *latch on* have inexplicably emerged from underground to become very voguish in formal speech. Ironically enough, in the light of their lowly origins, their use is practically confined to sophisticated urban, suburban, and exurban groups.

In a period of widespread partial literacy such as ours, *analysis*, *examination*, and *organization* are surely perfectly familiar to everyone. We must therefore assume that the current use of such homely synonyms for these words as *breakdown*, *screening*, and *set-up* is in the nature of an affectation. Because the highest frequency of such expressions occurs among persons who work in cities and towns, regardless of where they live, the homespun quality must be regarded as deceptive. These apparent "homespunisms" are really rather elegant artificial productions. They are not used by the folk, because the folk are not aware of them.

Only the man possessed of "savvy" and "know-how" "spells out" when he explains, "briefs" when he supplies facts, and "pinpoints" when he determines something exactly. In keeping with his reputation as a "knowing" individual, he almost invariably gives a "run-down" instead of a summary, a "fill-in" instead of a background sketch, a "blueprint" instead of a plan, and an "overall" view instead of merely a comprehensive one.

He sets a "target date" for the completion of any job, he takes a "break" instead of a recess from work and when he verifies something at random he makes a "spot check." He is truly "geared," not simply adapted, to the push-button efficiency of a streamlined world. Because he is so "knowledgeable" it is but natural that he should be chosen to "spearhead" drives of one sort or another. A few years back, he gave his "reaction" when asked for his opinion, but *reaction* has become old-hat and now (or "as of now") he gives his "thought," occasionally his "thinking." He "goes along with" what he agrees with and may even say that he will "buy" it. His is not just a life, but a "way of life," and the sum of his practical observations about it is a "philosophy."

As fashions in attitudes toward life change, so do the words with which we clothe those attitudes. Inasmuch as it is in the nature of language thus to fluctuate, it is safe to predict that a new litter of vogue words is even now in gestation, and that many of those now [1958] current will be as outmoded by 1968 as *momism*, *stateside*, and the admirable *gobbledegook* are today.

6

"Task Force" Makes "Breakthrough"

TO those who help keep America great by writing its advertising copy and its industrial news releases, every development, every disclosure, every discovery is nowadays a *breakthrough*. This high-powered and extremely voguish word is even now trickling down from Madison Avenue into the provinces and will doubtless in time take its place beside the already well-established *breakdown* 'analysis,' with which it is parallel in structure. Indeed, a breakthrough may ultimately come to be the normal result of certain types of breakdown. Such is the craze for this word that it may even be used with reference to packaging, as in the following recent news release of the Scandia Packaging Machinery Company: "Scandia Reports 'Break Through' in Polyethylene Wrapping."

Breakthrough seems originally to have been a military term, though apparently not a very old one, since it is not listed in either the *Oxford English Dictionary* or *OED Supplement* of 1933. Of the dictionaries that I have consulted, only the current (1958) edition of the *American College Dictionary* gives a really satisfactory definition of the newer, nonmilitary meaning of *breakthrough*. The 1947 edition of the same work defines the word only as a military term for an advance penetrating through and beyond a defense. *Webster's New Collegiate Dictionary* (1949) recognizes a meaning which is an extension of the military meaning, as does the *Webster New World Dictionary of the American Language* (1954), but neither definition precisely fits the modern voguish usage.

All the illustrative specimens which follow save the last are news releases of 1959 which have been supplied by my friend Melvin Mandell, industrial editor of *Dun's Review* and a man with a nice sense of style in words. It will be noted that the term may be written solid, with hyphenation, or, as in the example cited in the first paragraph above, as two words:

> It [a new method of extracting sugar from cane] is a major technical breakthrough after 50 years of various attempts to adapt the diffusion technique. [Chemetron Corporation and J. B. White Engineering Corporation]

> Mr. McCleary described the new paper as "a significant breakthrough in the industry's campaign to reduce package weight and bulk." [Olin Mathieson Chemical Corporation]

> Four new "Break-Through" Awards were given for pioneering new markets for flexible packaging materials. [National Flexible Packaging Association]

> Ford Motor Co. unveiled its new economy car, the Falcon, yesterday and said it represented a "revolutionary breakthrough" in automotive design. [*New York Mirror*, 3 September 1959, p. 11]

> Helena Rubinstein Announces Sensational Break-Through in Tinting Hair at Home. [Advertisement in *New York Times Magazine*, 20 September 1959, p. 67]

> Except in the case of Arnel, Celanese has made few major breakthroughs on its own. [*Fortune*, December 1959, p. 128]

It is my impression that *breakthrough* has been the darling of the copy writers and the press agents only for the past year or so. Mr. Mandell, who notes astutely that "there are never any minor breakthroughs," has a "distinct notion" that *Fortune* was the first to use the word in the voguish, nonmilitary sense.

The dissemination of *breakthrough* into civilian usage has probably been similar to that of the slightly less popular *task force*, as in the following news releases of 1959:

> Chamber Organizes Task Force to Defend Calif. Defense Business. [Los Angeles Chamber of Commerce]

> Breaking sharply with traditions of the aviation industry, Martin-Baltimore reorganized its 2,000-man engineering organization into separate "task forces" to develop and deliver unsurpassed manned vehicles and missiles and electronic systems required for world leadership. [Martin, Baltimore Division]

Theirs [i.e., those who created Firebird III] was a task force operation in an all-out experiment in research, engineering, and styling. [General Motors]

Task force and *breakthrough* are attractive additions to the vocabulary of those who are geared to the space age, who spearhead drives, set target dates, make spot checks, give rundowns and fill-ins—in short, of those who take an overall view instead of merely a comprehensive one, and who give the rest of us the advantage of their thinking on whatever is truly meaningful in the American way of life.

7

Inkhornisms, Fustian, and Current Vogue Words

Ebuccinate 'to trumpet forth,' *direptitious* 'given to plundering,' *ineffrenate* 'unbridled,' *honorificabilitudinity* 'honor'—such lush creations of classically educated intellectuals and those who, like Shakespeare's Holofernes, aspired to be thought of as intellectuals had a considerable vogue in the early Modern English period. Words like these were in the nature of caste-designators: their use indicated that one was "in," that one knew his way about in what were conceived to be the most exalted intellectual circles. Nevertheless, they were lambasted about as vigorously by the conservative folk of the time as the considerably less colorful and less flamboyant *finalize* has been in our own day.

Such words were derisively called *inkhorn terms*. The author of *The Arte of English Poesie* (1589) tells us that "*Irreuocable, irradiation, depopulation* and such like . . . were long time despised for inkehorne termes."[1] They could not have been far removed from the so-called fustian eloquence of the time.

Education (1531), *chronology* (1593), and *contemplate* (1594),[2] however, must have seemed equally gaudy and tasteless to linguistic conservatives as those words just cited as having been "long time despised." They, like many other learned adaptations of the early Modern period, were ultimately to enter ordinary usage; yet they were just as vulnerable as the archaisms cited at the very beginning of this paper, and must have been regarded with like abhorrence by those who wished above all things to keep the

1. Cited in the *OED*, s.v. *ink-horn*. *Inkhornism, inkhornist,* and *inkhornize* are also listed as from this period.
2. The dates of earliest known occurrences are those given in the *OED*.

English language "pure," whatever that may mean. The conclusion is obvious: there is no way of predicting which words will catch on, which will die.

It is just as impossible to predict which of those words which have long been a part of our word stock will suddenly become vogue words. *Activate* and *priority* have been with us in an unobtrusive way for a very long time, only to become voguish in our own day. *Automation* has been with us for less than two decades, but it is likely to stay with us for a long time to come. In the history of vogue words, however, no man dare prophesy. On the other hand, fashion, to some extent governed (the voguish word here would be *conditioned*) by the political, economic, intellectual, and religious life of a people, to some extent purely whimsical, has driven out of use such mellifluous American words as *conbobberation*, *absquatulate*, *peedoodles*, and *hornswoggle*, all of which enjoyed a considerable vogue on the frontier in the more innocent days of our country; nowadays they are not heard even in the "Westerns."

As I have pointed out elsewhere,[3] vogue words are, to use a voguish phrase in defining them, words which have prestige value. They invariably have a flavor of bright sophistication, of urbanity, of ultramodernity—in short, of know-how—and they are in the beginning employed for this very reason. Many in due time enter the general word stock, like *to contact*, which has survived the belaboring of teachers, who objected to it on the grounds that *contact* was "properly" a noun, despite the fact that there are many instances of such conversion of noun into verb in English. No really up-to-date purist winces at it nowadays; those who conceive it to be their mission to police the language have other supposed offenders against linguistic propriety to bludgeon. Some such words, as we have seen, disappear altogether. By the time either of these possibilities occurs, there is bound to be a new flowering among those who set the pace.

In the mid-teens of the present century, according to Sir Arthur Quiller-Couch in his chapter "On Jargon" in *The Art of Writing* (1916), English newspaper writers were excessively fond of such locutions as *psychological moment*, *obsess*, *recrudesce*, *envisage*, and *adumbrate*. Today not one of these is really fashionable, and only one calls for comment—*psychological moment*, used then as now in the sense 'most favorable time,' though this was not the meaning of the German *das psychologische Moment*, its ultimate

3. "Subliminal Words Are Never Finalized," *New York Times Magazine*, 15 June 1958, pp. 16, 55, 57, 58 [Selection 5 of this volume]. Some of the examples to be cited subsequently also occur in this article.

source.[4] The mistranslation has been so long established and so freely used as to have become a mere cliché, though it is rapidly being supplanted by *moment of truth*.

An examination of the vogue words of the middle years of our century must inevitably tell us a great deal of the concerns and the mores of the period—its spiritual, intellectual, and social aspirations and predilections. Just as the Renaissance rage for inkhornisms indicates the tremendous enthusiasm in those days for classical values—misguided though it certainly sometimes was—so does the current rash of vogue words taken from psychiatry and the so-called behavioral sciences indicate the values of our own world, ignoble as some of these may seem to those who live in ivory towers. It is likely that many of these words would be incomprehensible to one who died so recently as Franklin Delano Roosevelt, if we were able to resurrect him; and it is certain that under the same happy circumstances Calvin Coolidge would be completely in the dark as to the meaning of, say, *name-dropping*, *psychosomatic*, *isometric*, and *moisturize*.

Just as *disposition*, *complexion*, *temper(ament)*, *humor*, *choleric*, *melancholy*, *sanguine*, *phlegmatic*, and a number of other words taken from the voguish scientific and pseudoscientific parlance of an earlier day indicate to us an intense concern with astrology and physiology, so future commentators on our own era will certainly note our vast preoccupation with mental aberration of one sort or another as this is reflected in our voguish use of the terminology of psychoanalysis and psychology. Practically always these lose any sharpness of definition when they pass into popular use and are employed in reference to widespread and more or less vaguely delimited traits of character. This has happened, for instance, to the psychoanalyst's *complex*, which in voguish use has come to designate little more than the sort of obsessing idea which has temporarily taken hold of many of us at some time or other in our lives without in the least upsetting the mental balance. The word has been highly progenitive; there are nowadays many complexes which Freud never dreamed of. It is similar with the word *psychology* itself, as in *sales psychology*, which apparently means some-

---

4. The French misunderstood it first, at the time of the Siege of Paris in 1870, when they encountered the phrase in a German journal in reference to the bombardment. In German *Moment* means 'momentum, impetus' when used as a neuter noun; only as a masculine does it mean 'moment of time.' According to the *OED*, the French mistranslation of *das psychologische Moment* as *moment psychologique* "has passed equally nonsensically into English journalese." (The relevant section of the *OED* was issued in 1909, a date which accords well with Quiller-Couch's statement.) This example I have used in a somewhat different connection in *The Origins and Development of the English Language* (New York, 1964), p. 311 [2d edition, 1971, pp. 351–52].

thing like 'ability to discern the mental processes of one's "prospects" in such a way as to persuade them to purchase from one what they have no need for and frequently cannot afford.'

As E. E. Ericson has shown, with many citations, *sadism* has come to mean simply cruelty, with no connotations of *psychopathia sexualis*, and *moron*, at least in the Chicago area in the 1930s and 1940s, was used, perhaps euphemistically, in the specialized sense 'sex degenerate'[5]—a usage most unfair to those actual morons whose name is legion and who do much of the uninspiring but nonetheless useful work of the world. It is doubtful that calling a person an *exhibitionist* is any longer actionable, inasmuch as the word has come to refer to a comparatively harmless human failing referred to less pretentiously as "showing off," and is so defined in recent dictionaries[6]—a far cry indeed from the Baron von Krafft-Ebing and Havelock Ellis. Other terms from psychiatry and social psychology which have passed into voguish usage include *behavior pattern* 'behavior,' *neurotic* 'nervous, worrisome,' *ambivalent* 'ambiguous, two-sided' (like *empathy*, a great favorite nowadays with literary critics), and *compulsive* 'habitual.' The last-cited word is doubtless used out of humanitarianism, as in *compulsive drinker*, with much the same sense as *alcoholic* 'one who likes to drink, does so habitually and usually over his capacity.' On the other hand, *insanity*, a more or less technical term, has come to be replaced by *mental illness*, but this is doubtless to be attributed to the same sort of tender feeling which calls a drunkard a compulsive drinker or an alcoholic. (It should be noted also that *sick* has acquired a specialized meaning 'insane,' so that one can tell only from the context whether a *sick man* is crazy or merely dyspeptic.) It is similar with sociological *senior citizen*, beloved of politicians for 'aging and decrepit person,' and *juvenile delinquent* 'underbred and badly behaved adolescent.' No doubt such verbal subterfuges help to make life more bearable for decaying oldsters and the parents of naughty brats.

The voguish use of *image* seems to be an extension of its use in psychology for the phenomenon of experiencing anew some sensation with the original stimulus lacking. In really up-to-date speech much of this technical meaning, as we should expect, has been lost, and the word means simply the impression, true or false, which one is able to make upon others. Such

5. "New Meanings in Current English," in *Philologica: The Malone Anniversary Studies*, edited by Thomas A. Kirby and Henry Bosley Woolf (Baltimore, 1949), pp. 321–25.

6. The word is listed in the *OED* in the sense 'one who takes part in a performance,' with a single citation (1821). *Exhibitionism*, in the psychopathic sense, is entered only in the *Supplement* of 1933, the first citation being from 1908; but by the 1920s the figurative and general use had begun to occur.

an image is almost invariably *projected*, and would seem to be vastly more important than what a person or an institution really is. An interview with some very eminent members of the American Psychiatric Association around the time of the political conventions in 1960, syndicated by the Women's News Service,[7] disclosed that women, particularly those with weak husbands, wanted a "father image" as president. Dwight David Eisenhower, it was thought by the psychiatrists being interviewed, had projected just such an image,[8] whereas Mr. Nixon was "not quite old enough for a father image and not quite young enough to appeal to women as a boy," that is, presumably, as a son image. One pundit feared that Mr. Nixon's appearance on television, when with the aid of his family and the little dog Checkers he defended himself against slush-fund charges, had affected him adversely, but added, in what must be considered a little gem of voguish diction, "However, I am not discounting the fact that the Nixon image can be repackaged before the next election." Mr. Kennedy's chances were not rated high by the psychiatric mahatmas. In what was probably the most inept prophecy of the year 1960, they agreed that, although there was no doubt of his appeal to women as "the image of their little boy," they "will not vote for him because they do not want a boy in the White House." Nowhere in the article, it should be noted, was there any reference to a husband image. But this omission may be attributable to the fact that the assembled magi were by and large speaking for the American homemaker (she used to be a *housewife*), for whom a mere husband cannot be expected to project much of an image—or, to put it in another way, almost equally voguish, husbandwise she is left cold. An eminent lady doctor put the cap on the interview when she remarked that "the man who will be the next president will have to be presented to women in the image of a salesman."

More recently, according to Ben A. Franklin in an article copyrighted by the *New York Times*, government historians have agreed that in the earliest days of his presidency, Lyndon B. Johnson "projected a very strong image."[9] We should all feel a great sense of security, inasmuch as it is

---

7. *Jacksonville Florida Times-Union*, 9 February 1960, p. 10.

8. This fantasy was very widespread. Cf. Ralph McGill, "The Image of the President," in his column *Conscience of the South*, *Gainesville* (Fla.) *Sun*, 24 February 1964, p. 4: "They [poll takers] could explain that General Eisenhower was the father image for which all of us instinctively and psychologically seek . . . the universal father who knows best." President Johnson, however, has also built up an image, "not that of a comfortable and comforting father," but that "of a competent man who knows how to get things done." We shall see more of the Johnsonian projection later.

9. *Gainesville* (Fla.) *Sun*, 4 December 1963, p. 4.

only the image, the appearance, which seems to be really important. In "The Image of a Simple Man," *Time* reports an official White House "adviser" as declaring "I believe—and I'm sure he believes—that the best image for him now is that of a serious, able, competent man who understands the office of the presidency."[10]

The physical and biological sciences have supplied comparatively few vogue words. Nevertheless, the awesomeness of their mysteries, as well as the tremendous prestige which they enjoy in the lay mind, is indicated by the use of *lab(oratory)* in nonscientific contexts (for instance, *composition lab*, *writing lab*). The use of *potential* as a noun may come from physics; it is now very fashionable and may in time supplant *potentiality* altogether.[11] Medical terminology is widely used—and doubtless misused—but it is primarily in the employment of *allergy* for 'distaste,' as in *an allergy to learning*, *clinic* as in *reading clinic* and *high school football coaching clinic*, and *intern* for 'novice schoolteacher' that similar extensions and laxations may be observed. It is likely that *condition* as a euphemism for practically any sort of ailment originated with doctors: "You have a liver condition" is far less alarming to the victim than "You have cirrhosis of the liver."[12]

Charisma seems to have dribbled into vogue usage from theology; in very high-toned circles it is used as a synonym for *glamour*. It is impossible to account for the resuscitation of this rather rarefied word. The adjectival form *charismatic* was occasionally used by the tonier columnists in reference to the late President Kennedy. *Mystique*, with similarly metaphysical overtones, is even commoner in voguish use;[13] the craze for it is echoed in the title of a very popular book, *The Feminine Mystique*, by Betty Friedan. There has been a similar upsurge in the more or less figurative use of *viable*, and *methodology* has practically ousted the once fashionable *technique*, being frequently used to mean simply 'method of scholarly pro-

10. 27 March 1964, p. 14.

11. Thus Charles Reid, music critic, in the London *Spectator* (6 March 1964, p. 316): "For all the sudden throat trouble that marred her big coloratura number and made her duck a high note or two, Elizabeth Harwood is obviously a Zerbinetta of rare potential."

12. But *condition* as verb (*air-conditioned*, *flight-conditioned*, and the like) in the sense 'adapt' seems to have grown out of similar uses by psychologists and sociologists. To *recondition* means 'to repair' ("Let Us Recondition Your Shoes") and was probably born of the desire, laudable enough in a democracy, to dignify what might otherwise be thought of as humble work. A reconditioned car, as everyone is aware, is a second-hand one.

13. Thus Murray Krieger, "The Poet and His Work," *College English*, 25 (1964), 406: "Seeing the intimate relationships between the materials of the poem and the surrounding world which provides them, Spitzer refuses to engage in the mystique that cuts them off as 'not-words.'" Cf. the use by Henry C. Wolfe in the *Saturday Review* of 21 March 1964, p. 46; "Only his [Franz Josef's] sense of duty and his dynastic mystique sustained him."

cedure.' *Climate*, which many of us have been so naive as to associate primarily with the weather, has come to have a much more metaphysical meaning, as in "The preface of the document [issued by the Florida Legislative Investigations Committee and labeled 'obscene and pornographic' by Dade County State's Attorney Richard Gerstein] said the report could be of value to all citizens, 'for every parent and every individual concerned with the moral climate of the state should be aware of the rise in homosexual activity noted here.' "[14] *Time* has reported that, according to Senator Jacob Javits, "It is up to Latin American governments . . . to do more to improve the climate for business."[15] Finally, at the trial of Jack Ruby for the murder of the alleged assassin of President Kennedy, Judge Joe Brown "rejected a defense demand that all prospective jurors as well as spectators be searched for concealed weapons, on the ground that there is a 'climate' in Dallas of fear and animosity."[16]

Though a few rare and cantankerous souls may object to such words and their uses as have been cited thus far, it cannot be denied that many of them have connotations and associations which make them at least interesting. The same cannot be claimed for a group of almost completely colorless words which are nonetheless very stylish: *media* (as in *advertising media*, *news media*), for instance, and the interchangeable *level* and *bracket* (as in *teen-age level*, *income bracket*). *Area* is also very fashionable: what used to be a field of study is now an *area of research* and, as everybody knows, the once humble kitchen has become the *food preparation area* and the dining room the *dining area* in all the swanker advertising media and, doubtless, in split-level Suburbia as well. The dedicated (another very voguish word) men and women who write the nation's advertising copy and those who read their "messages" over television and radio are arbiters of amazing potency.

The vogue words which we have hitherto been concerned with have been on the whole learned words, some of them flashily so, a few downright exotic. There is, however, an opposite tendency at work in the Land of the Free: a self-consciously coy use of native words in place of words which, though of learned origin, are perfectly familiar to most people: *analysis*, for instance, has been largely supplanted by *breakdown*, as *to analyze* has been supplanted by *to break down*.[17] Other examples of this

14. *Jacksonville Florida Times-Union*, 19 March 1964, p. 22.
15. 20 March 1964, p. 29.
16. UPI item from Dallas in the University of Florida *Alligator*, 18 February 1964, p. 1.
17. A "quaint result" of the craze for this word is cited by Sir Ernest Gowers in *Plain Words: Their ABC* (New York, 1954), p. 128: "Statistics have been issued of the population of the United States, broken down by age and sex."

particular tendency are *to spell out* 'to explain,' *to fill in* 'to furnish background information,' and *rundown* 'summary.' Furthermore, in really high-powered circles an appointment is never arranged; it is *set up*. A problem is not investigated thoroughly or completely, but *in depth* or *in its totality*. One's attitudes and points of view concerning it are put in the form of a *position paper*, whatever that form is. *Breakthroughs* are much in evidence, practically all of them "major" or "revolutionary,"[18] and they may be achieved through the efforts of a *task force*, that is, two or more persons working on a single project, usually of industrial research, though the term has by now invaded the groves of Academe, ever on the alert for fertilization by industry.

Commenting on a plan for Protestant unity proposed a few years ago by the Reverend Doctor Eugene Carson Blake, chief administrative officer of the United Presbyterian Church, the Right Reverend James A. Pike, Bishop of California [d. 1969], said that it was "a great prophetic breakthrough." That Bishop Pike knows his way around in vogue talk is indicated by his ghostly pronouncement "I know of no event in American church history of greater overall significance,"[19] for to the man who has mastered this type of verbal communication *overall* is always to be preferred to *total*, *comprehensive*, *general*, or even *average*. Programs, plans, objectives, philosophies, pictures, views, and the like are practically always overall, just as surely as fundamentals are always basic. I note in passing that the sermon topic of the pastor of the First Methodist Church of Jacksonville, Florida, on 6 December 1959, was "The Big Break Through" and devoutly hope that God broke through somewhere in the course of the homily.[20]

Fashion alone would seem to be responsible for the widespread vogue of such self-consciously homely yet essentially newfangled expressions as *screen* 'examine with a view to classifying,' *pinpoint* 'determine exactly,' *undercut* 'take unfair advantage,' *fact-finding* 'investigative,' *cutback* 'reduction,' *kickback* 'enforced return of part of wages or commission,' *spot check* 'random verification,' *bottleneck* 'hindrance,' and *slant* 'represent with bias.' Changes in American sleeping habits may well render the literal

---

18. I have cited a number of examples of these in " 'Task Force' Makes 'Breakthrough,' " *American Speech*, 35 (1960), 155–56 [Selection 6 of this volume], including one in polyethylene wrapping proudly announced by the Scandia Packaging Machinery Company. *Breakthrough*, like *position paper* and *task force*, seems originally to have been a military term, though apparently a fairly recent one, since it is not listed in either the *OED* or the *OED Supplement* of 1933.

19. *Jacksonville Florida Times-Union*, 5 December 1960, p. 1.

20. *Jacksonville Florida Times-Union*, 5 December 1960, p. 8.

meaning of *featherbedding*, a voguish homespun metaphor meaning 'lim-
itation of work to make more jobs,' as archaic as that of *chamber pot* and
nightcap (except in the alcoholic sense). *Knowing* and *knowledgeable* are
practically synonymous as vogue words, but somehow they lack the true
homespun quality; there is about them a big-city slickness in contrast to
the rural wholesomeness of *know-how*, with its pleasantly American connotations of horse-trading, whittling, wooden nutmegs, and tinkering. Truly
homespun (and very fashionable nowadays) is the laying of *guidelines*
instead of the setting up of criteria or the making of plans.

Thought and *thinking* have held their own for some time as voguishly
homespun synonyms of *opinion*, and seem well on the way to displacing
pseudo-learned *reaction* in the same sense. "Will you give me your thinking
about [or *in regard to* or *in relation to*] this?" has come to be indicative
of a sophistication even greater than that implied by "What is your reaction
to this?" *Thought* in the answer would go far toward maintaining the same
high tone, thus: "My thought is that it is not too outstanding,"[21] though
one's diction would by no means be lacking in tone if one merely replied
"I don't subscribe to it," "I won't buy it," or "I don't go along with it."

One of the most voguish of phrases nowadays is *way of life*, which
may replace *philosophy* in its popular sense 'body of practical opinions,'
regimen ("vegetarianism as a way of life"), or simply *life*, as in the statement
some years back of a poltergeist-ridden housewife, then very much in the
news, to Mr. Ed Murrow on his television program *Person to Person*:
"We are just leading a normal, quiet way of life." Preceded by *American*
or *democratic*, the phrase has inspiring connotations of patriotism, high
living standards, technological progress, freedom, equalitarianism, and high
ideals. *As of now* is preferred by stylish speakers to *now* or *at present*,
though *presently* in the same sense has by no means gone out of fashion.[22]
Of one's choice is also widely heard, as in "Go to the church of your
choice this Sunday," as if it really didn't matter, one being just as equal
as another. It may be recollected at this point that the platform of the
Democratic Party in 1960, as read over television by Mr. Chester Bowles,
affirmed the right of "every qualified boy to go to the college of his choice."
It is perhaps just as well that this was never taken literally, for it is unlikely
that Harvard, to name a possible choice of many, would hold all the qualified

21. *Too* as a simple intensive, replacing *very*, is quite widespread, as in "He didn't
know too much about it."

22. *Presently* in the sense 'now' was widely current in older English. According to the
OED, the growth of the blunted sense insisted upon by certain present-day prescriptivists
"was so imperceptible, that early examples, esp. before *c* 1650, are doubtful."

boys who might choose it. But it all sounds fine, modern, and democratic, like the ubiquitous *regardless of race, creed, or color*.

Of voguish affixes *-ize* stood well to the front until a few years ago. A brand of condensed milk, for instance, was *instantized*; a certain hair-dressing *moisturized* the scalp; fountain pens of a certain brand were *genderized*, since it was obviously degrading to the national character for men and women to use the same style of writing implement; and T-2 tankers were *jumboized* by increasing their length. Though these may be for the most part ephemeral creations, they nevertheless indicate the vogue of the suffix. Other examples are *personalize, hospitalize, editorialize, accessorize, formalize*, and *glamorize*, with *finalize*[23] the most successful of all, doubtless here to stay.

But it would seem, on the basis of my recent researches, that the adverbial suffix *-wise* has pushed far ahead of the verbal suffix *-ize*. Previously occurring only in a few words like *lengthwise* and *crosswise*, this suffix has proliferated, as they say, like mad. There is no point in illustrating its proliferations, amusing as some of them may be.

Adjectives in *-type* are an equally interesting development: there are, for instance, *modern-type* refrigerators, *prescription-type* formulas (for headache remedies), and *city manager–type* governments. A single documented example should suffice—a reference to "Cesare Siepi, the glamour-type leading basso of the Metropolitan."[24]

Now that the New Testament has been made readily available to us in understandable present-day English, it is high time that certain important older literary and political monuments be put into a form of our language "understanded of the people," to use the old-fashioned, naive morphology of the Book of Common Prayer. I have attempted to do this with our most important American national document—a position paper spelling out a somewhat antiquated-type American mystique—which must be almost unintelligible to the modern reader conditioned to the lucid prose of writers of advertising copy, press releases, book reviews, and the like. How inept, from our more enlightened point of view, were the founders of this great democracy, which in their simplicity they chose to call a republic, when they wrote such stuff as this: "We hold these truths to be self-evident, that all men are created equal, that they are endowed by their Creator with certain unalienable rights, that among these are Life, Liberty, and the pursuit

---

23. The tempest in teapot over this word is one of the most amusing phenomena of our times. Its inclusion in *Webster's Third* has apparently given many critics the notion that they are required to use the word.

24. *Jacksonville Florida Times-Union*, 8 January 1961, p. 75.

of Happiness. . . . That whenever any Form of Government becomes de-
structive of these ends, it is the Right of the People to alter or to abolish
it, and to institute new Government" — and so on. I conclude with a sample
of my translation of this cumbersome and archaic language into the racy
and voguish diction of our own day, in the hope that others may follow
suit with similar important documents:

> Our thinking as of now is to the effect that prioritywise these facts
> are basic and fundamental and definitely in no need of spelling out
> in depth: that one man should not be placed in a lower bracket than
> any other man, regardless of race, creed, or color, due to the fact
> that God the Father Image has implemented all men with certain
> human-type rights, among these being a democratic way of life and
> the right to indulge in the group recreational pleasures of their choice
> so long as approval of these pleasures has been finalized by respon-
> sible-type top-level coordinators; that if, after making a careful
> breakdown, it becomes possible to pinpoint the fact that any admin-
> istrative setup in any area whatsoever, high-level or low-level, is
> dedicated to a philosophy that will activate a climate of opinion
> conducive to a cutback in these aims and objectives, then it is the
> right of all freedom-oriented personnel to condition themselves rev-
> olutionwise for a major breakthrough. . . .

8

The English of VIPs

IF they accomplished little else, the Army-McCarthy hearings provided us with sustained specimens of the language of a group of men who must be conceded to be Very Important Persons—in Attorney Joseph N. Welch's phrase, "pretty big stuff." It follows that a record of the speech of such colossi, most of it the most formal variety of which they were capable, is in effect a record of current American English on what is perhaps its most sublime level.

Unfortunately an official transcript of the hearings, which would run into many volumes, is beyond the financial reach of most scholars. It is therefore devoutly to be wished that such a transcript will be preserved in every university library, so that linguistic scientists of, say, the early years of the twenty-second century may make use of these monumental texts as primary sources in their reconstruction of the morphological and syntactical features of the English language as it was spoken A.D. 1954 in the United States of America by men of awe-inspiring distinction and prestige. But only the more than eighty miles of tape recording would enable the Ph.D. of the post-atomic age—if there is to be any such—to study the various types of pronunciation, regional and social, represented in the speech of the august participants in the drama. Modern spelling being so highly conventionalized, the reportorial transcript would be of no aid in a study of the phonology of the American English of our own day. A reporter, for instance, hearing Senator McCarthy's pronunciation of *grievous* to rhyme with *previous*, would merely transcribe the word in what is thought of as its "correct" spelling—that is, as I have recorded it, rather than as *grievious*.

Failing at first to realize fully the immense linguistic significance of what I was hearing over the radio, I did not begin to take notes until June 3, when the urge to do so became irresistible. The time required for making phonetic transcriptions and for writing phrases and occasionally whole sentences in longhand prevented my getting down in every instance the complete context in which a cited pronunciation or grammatical construction occurred, but the locutions themselves are, I believe, accurately recorded. In addition to the usages of the senators and the Secretary of the Army, I have included a few specimens drawn from Counsel Ray Jenkins's majestic hillbilly speech, for Mr. Jenkins, though he has not attained to the ineffable mysteries of senatorship, is certainly possessed of a dignity and an ability befitting so exalted a station in life. The same is doubtless true of Counsel Welch, who demonstrated, especially in the early days of the hearing, that he is a great stylist; but his Iowa-cum-Boston speech presents comparatively little of linguistic interest, perhaps because it conforms for the most part to what is popularly regarded as "correct" English. Mr. Roy Cohn and Mr. Francis Carr are, it is true, merely the satellites of greatness, but both are educated men who, from the point of view of, let us say, a university professor, have risen to positions of considerable eminence on the American scene. I have therefore not hesitated to draw a few examples from their speech.

Although only four of the participating senators (McCarthy, Mundt, Potter, and Jackson) actually hold college or university degrees, unless for reasons of modesty or political expediency Senators Symington ("student Yale, 1919–23") and Dirksen ("student U. of Minn., 1913–17") have omitted this academic distinction from their biographical sketches in the current *Who's Who in America*, all are, in the usually accepted sense, literate and highly articulate men, quite capable for the most part of quoting Shakespeare, the Bible, and Edgar A. Guest at the drop of a point of order. Of the two senators who lay claim only to a public school education, one, Senator McClellan, rose to a position of prominence as a lawyer after being admitted to the bar of his native Arkansas at the age of seventeen. Listening to his booming hill-type speech, no one could doubt that he is a man of dignity and superior ability. The other, Senator Dworshak, who had little to say in the course of the hearings but said that little well, has been, among other things, a newspaper editor.

When Senator McCarthy said "grievious" (at least three times, in expressing the moral indignation which comes so readily to him), he was using a fairly widespread variant pronunciation of *grievous*, but an unconventional one in the sense that it is not recorded in the dictionaries and, like some of the others to be cited, is included in lists of words "commonly mispronounced" prepared by persons who know how words "ought" to be pronounced and offered for sale to other persons who worry about their speech and are convinced that only its "incorrectness" has prevented them from climbing to the top of the tree. The same is true of Senator McClellan's loss of an entire syllable in *deteriorate*, which he consistently pronounced as "deteriate." On one occasion the word occurred in the Senator's cross-examination of Mr. Roy Cohn in such a way that Mr. Cohn had to repeat it in his response. With a slight hesitation natural to a courteous man faced with such a linguistic situation, Mr. Cohn used his own five-syllabled pronunciation of the word. The Senator from Arkansas, not in the least fazed, went right back to his own natural pronunciation and proceeded to use it twice in the colloquy which followed. The quadrisyllabic pronunciation, which is probably more usual than lexicographers are willing to admit, was also that employed by Mr. Jenkins's junior, Mr. Pruitt.

The *i*-sound which Senator McCarthy inserted where it does not historically belong was omitted where it does historically belong by Senator McClellan in "prev'ous," "mim'ographed," "appropr'ate" (the adjective), "per'od," and "immed'ately," and in Senator Potter's *current* (a monosyllable, rhyming with *burnt*) "esp'onage." Other unconventional pronunciations—and it must be remembered that I use the word only in the sense "not recorded in dictionaries"—were *Communist* as a homophone of *commonest* (McClellan, Potter); *dereliction* rhyming with *fair election* (Jackson); *particularly* with *warily* (Dirksen); *obstacle* with *Bob's pickle* (McClellan); *recognize* with *beckon eyes* (Potter); *substantiate* with *Bub, can't you wait* (McClellan); *jugular* with *smuggler* (McCarthy, with McClellan repeating the word and using the same pronunciation); *accurate* with *slacker it* (Mundt, McClellan); and some which, like the "fu'ther" of Mr. Jenkins and the "he'p" of Senator McClellan ("Ah'm gonna he'p the Chair if Ah can, occasionally"), are primarily regional. Mr. Jenkins's "inordinantly" for *inordinately* was probably a malapropism rather than a matter of pronunciation, like Senator Mundt's *maledictions* for *malefactions* and Senator Potter's "cool, calm, and collective."

Those not acclimated to the intrusive *r* common in certain parts of America (for instance, in Eastern New England and the New York City area) and not infrequent in Standard British English seem to find its occurrence cause for amusement. For their benefit I record Senator Symington's "idear," "Korear," "isher" (for *issue*), "shadder" (for *shadow*), and "supeener" (for *subpoena*, pronounced by other participants as "supeeny" and "supeenya"). This unetymological *r* was also noticeable, not surprisingly considering their linguistico-geographical backgrounds, from Messrs. Cohn and Carr.

The dictionaries record two pronunciations of *inquiry*, one with stress on the second syllable, pronounced *choir*, and the other with the first syllable stressed, as "ínkwuhry." I did not observe that the first of these pronunciations, presumably the "preferred" one, occurred once in the course of the hearings; the second occurred only occasionally. The pronunciation favored by VIPs, it seems, places primary stress on the first syllable and something approaching secondary stress on the second, which is pronounced as *queer*. To me this sounded very impressive, especially when uttered in the butterscotch baritone of Senator Dirksen.

Senator McCarthy's *highth* would appear to many to be an "error," though it is actually a perfectly sound historical variant of *height*, occurring in Milton's "highth of this great argument." Senator Potter's fairly consistent pronunciation of present participles with the ending *-in* ("dropping the *g*," as it is popularly described), although deplored by all teachers and all writers on "correct" speech, is likewise ancient and honorable.

Untraditional, hypercorrect pronunciations born of a self-conscious desire to "speak well" were of fairly frequent occurrence. These are of course attributable to a faith in mere literacy which no doubt appears to those nurtured in an older civilization than ours to be somewhat naive; but, inasmuch as literacy has in our American way of life (to lapse momentarily into Senatorese) frequently superseded the cultivated traditions of the past, it is worth recording a few examples. Lieutenant Blount's traditional pronunciation of his name (as "blunt") was, for instance, blithely ignored by all those who had occasion to use it, though they must have heard him say it as well as I did. Knowledge of the spelling was sufficient, however, to cause all to pronounce it to rhyme with *count*. Throughout the hearings, Chairman Mundt pronounced the second syllable of *Monmouth* as *mouth*, doubtless under the impression that he was thereby speaking better than those who used the traditional "mónmuth." Linguistic overzealousness based upon the notion that using one's native language is an intellectual feat rather than a social accomplishment is probably responsible for such pronunciations as "o-casions" (McCarthy), "o-ficials" (Mundt), and "ee-ficiency" (McCarthy).

In the treatment of learned Latin (and Graeco-Latin) words, the entities to the dispute, as Chairman Mundt was fond of calling them, used pronunciations which remain unrecorded in dictionaries, though common enough in educated speech. *Semi* and *anti* were, for instance, pronounced with their final syllables as *eye* and *tie* (McCarthy, Cohn, Potter). Senator McCarthy's *modus operandi* showed traditional Anglicization until he got to the end of the phrase, which he pronounced to rhyme with *sandy*. (According to a tradition now practically extinct in American English, but still recorded in our dictionaries, *semi* and *anti* rhyme with *jemmy* and *panty*, *operandi* with *and die*.) The Greek name *Nike*, as applied to a new guided missile, was pronounced to rhyme with *Ike*; it is, however, perhaps going rather too far to expect that one with Senator McCarthy's tremendous responsibilities should be even on speaking terms with a pagan divinity.

But this is only to trip lightly over the surface of my phonological notes. It is necessary to pass rapidly on to other aspects of VIP speech—its morphology, its syntax, and finally some of its stylistic characteristics.

In the language of these decidedly effective citizens, verbs obviously do not agree in number with their subjects as consistently as prescriptive grammarians would wish them to: "The filing of the false, fraudulent charges are a complete contradiction of the character of Bob Stevens" (McCarthy); "You know what clearance each of your staff have" (Symington); "[to determine] what the order of the phone calls were" (Mr. St. Clair, Mr. Welch's junior); "as far as the infiltration of the armed services were concerned" (Cohn); "as far as coddling Communists are concerned" (Cohn); "if the charges was dismissed" (McClellan); "as far as Mr. Adams and Mr. Cohn is concerned" (McCarthy); "You was advised of [something in regard to Senator McClellan's coming back on the Committee], wasn't you?" (McClellan).

That the *everyone* (*someone*, *everybody*, etc.) . . . *they* (*their*, *them*) construction is normal and natural in modern English should be apparent to anyone with eyes and ears, despite the fact that prescriptive authorities— those who write handbooks telling us how we ought to speak our native tongue—will not allow that the locution is in good usage. It is likely that a statistical examination of writings in English since the seventeenth century would disclose the fact that *everyone* . . . *they* is of far more frequent occurrence, even in the works of the acknowledged masters of English literature, than *everyone* . . . *he* (*his*, *him*). With the assurance to my readers that the incidence of the construction in question was rather high during the hearings, I content myself with two examples: "Everybody has said three or four times exactly where they stand" (Mundt); "Nobody is going to say whether they're glad or sorry or anything else" (Welch).

Other transgressions of the senators, the Secretary, their aides, and their counsel against the dicta of linguistic Emily Posts follow. Some of these were, it should be pointed out, already in perfectly reputable use long before the Army-McCarthy hearings, though still widely supposed to be "errors":

Like as a conjunction: "like I am now" (Symington); "a spirit of compromise like I suggested" (Carr).

Historical nominative form of the personal pronoun in objective construction: "Now, Stu, let's you and I go to the woodshed" (McCarthy); "these calls between Secretary Stevens and I" (Dirksen).

Relative or interrogative *who* for *whom*: "I checked back with the people who I interviewed" (Cohn); (in monitored call to Stevens) "Who have you talked to?" (Dirksen); "and finally Senator McCarthy said, 'Who *did* you call?' " (Cohn).

Set for *sit*: "Actually, members of this Committee set in a semijudicial capacity" (Potter); "You've let them set there and testify day after day" (McClellan).

Different than for *different from*: "You give a different connotation than I would, and than I did" (Carr); "an altogether different meaning than it has for us" (Mundt).

Try and for *try to*: "We try and sort out all the mail from Wisconsin" (McCarthy).

Myself for *me*: "He was in contact with myself and Don" (Carr).

Kind (type) of a for *kind (type) of*: "this kind of a threat" (McCarthy); "that type of a threat" (McCarthy).

And which for *which*: "one other statement, and which is perhaps not a question" (Jenkins).

But what for *but that*: "no question but what . . ." (McCarthy).

Mad 'angry': (in monitored call to Dirksen) "Of course he didn't like it—got very mad about it" (Stevens).

Can for *may*: "Can I proceed without interruption?" (Symington).

Number of Latin neuter noun: Senator Potter, Senator McClellan, and Mr. Carr all very sensibly used the Anglicized plural *memorandums*. The following examples, all taken from the speech of Mr. Welch on June 15, are representative of the confusion which prevailed in regard to *memorandum, -a*: "these memorandum"; "the first memoranda [the context indicated that this was intended to be singular] which you dictated"; "about half of that memoranda"; "Schine is mentioned in the single paragraph of that memoranda." On one occasion Senator Potter used *memorandum* as a plural: "These are not all the memorandum you have prepared?"

Reason is because for *reason is that*: I failed to note a single occurrence of the "recommended" construction; even Senator Mundt, a teacher of speech before his translation to the dizzying heights which he now inhabits, used "the reason is because."

The style of a VIP can be close-packed and down-to-earth, as in Senator Mundt's "Send them a transcript of what transpired here today and ask them to transmit their reaction," or it can soar into the upper reaches of rhetoric, as in Senator McCarthy's metaphor about the Communists "holding a razor blade over the juggler [or was it *juggaler*?] vein of the nation," all the more effective for its delivery in his sweetly reasonable, long-suffering monotone. It may be inferred (a word frequently used during the hearings, incidentally, and usually in an older sense 'imply,' with Senator Symington playing safe by saying, "You have constantly inferred or implied") that on the more rarefied levels of American life events *transpire* rather than merely happen and that persons *cooperate together* rather than merely cooperate, *continue on* but sometimes have to *refer back*, and give a *rundown* of a situation instead of merely summarizing it. It is also apparent that in VIPese two words meaning the same thing are considered twice as effective as one of them used alone, just as a word of four syllables is considered twice as effective as a disyllabic synonym. Redundancy would seem in fact almost to be a desideratum: witness Senator Dirksen's "Did you [two] travel in the same seat together?" and Senator Mundt's "an effort to endeavor to solve [a problem]," "so that we won't have to be held here interminably and forever," and "Did you have a trepidation that something serious and dire was going to happen to the Army?"

With the senatorial imprimatur, we may conclude that *spearhead* and *pinpoint* are now verbs in the very best standing, despite the unreasoning prejudices of stylistically conservative persons, who may also find something distasteful (if only because of their novelty) about *hassle*, *and/or*, *target date*, and the clipped *recap* for *recapitulation*. Audible punctuation would seem to be gaining ground in the uppermost levels of the national life, as in Senator McCarthy's use of the word *period* to announce that, happily no doubt for many of his unregenerate listeners, he had arrived at the end of a sentence. This stylistic grace note also made itself evident in the speech of Mr. Cohn and Senator Dirksen. VIP metaphors were occasionally a bit confused, as in Senator Potter's "how to cure that problem" and Mr. Carr's "means of dangling a little pressure over us," but none of the other participants had the golden opportunities vouchsafed Senator Mundt, who seldom had to refer to himself in the first person. He was "The Chair"; hence we were told that "The Chair went to South Dakota to make some speeches" and "The Chair is not wearing his television shirt this morning." Even Senator Dirksen was unable to rise to such heights.

From the examples which I have cited, it is obvious that a good many grammatical and stylistic constructions proscribed implicitly or by implication in books on English usage and in dictionaries do in fact occur in the speech of our most high-powered citizens. If standard American English usage is indeed based upon the practice of men of such exalted position as the participants in the Army-McCarthy hearings must be admitted to be, then it seems high time that some of the "rules" be revised. It is, however, a fairly safe prediction that nothing of the sort will actually be done.

[Addendum: The Watergate hearings of 1973 were probably as rich a mine for students of usage as the Army-McCarthy hearings of 1954. Having done what I considered my stint in the language of VIPs, I did not bother to listen to the 1973 broadcasts, suspecting that by that date they would leave me cold. I devoutly hope that some younger observer of similar interests listened and took notes. T.P.]

9

The Auditory Mass Media and U

IN the era of auditory mass media in which we are privileged to live, an American may willy-nilly hear more talk in the course of a waking day than it would have been possible for him to hear in a similar space of time in any previous period of history. Even the day's news is read aloud to him, and frequently explained to him as well. Students of usage, most of whom are, fortunately for their sanity, able to attend mainly to the manner of speech while almost totally disregarding its matter, have thus an unprecedented opportunity of observing stylistic varieties occurring within the context of standard English, which from a democratic point of view can mean only "educated" English.

Our national ideal of equality, so highly esteemed that we are willing to surrender many individual liberties to ensure even its semblance, commits us to the proposition that standard speech is attainable by any man who makes an effort to acquire it. We must continue to assume that conscientiously following a set of reasonably easy precepts involving the avoidance of double negatives, split infinitives, dangling participles, and the like will enable any man to speak as well as any other man, and that such characteristics as those which in less enlightened times were embodied in what was referred to as a "good background" are or should be more or less negligible. Such an assumption implies among other things that a cultured tradition in the apparently outworn sense of the term is of linguistic significance only so far as the style of speech of those who used to be vaguely regarded as "privileged" might be easily imparted to those now fashionably regarded as "culturally deprived."

The subtleties and nuances of the style to which I refer—qualities which those who employ it are for the most part quite unaware of—are of course not teachable; not even, in fact, capable of any thoroughgoing analysis. It would be difficult indeed to say precisely what qualities differentiate the speech styles of, say, Ellsworth Bunker, Senator Hugh Scott, Henry Cabot Lodge, the late Adlai Ewing Stevenson (but not his son Adlai III), William Frank Buckley, Jr., and William Averell Harriman from those of, say, Richard Milhous Nixon, the Kennedy brothers, Lyndon Baines Johnson, Melvin R. Laird, Nelson Aldrich Rockefeller, and Chester Robert ("Chet") Huntley. The two groups of speakers cited cover a fairly wide political, geographical, and cultural range, and all speak, or have spoken, what is definable as standard American English, despite widespread prejudice against the regional characteristics of Johnson's speech.

To designate these two varieties of standard American English, I shall henceforth, for want of any terms which might be less offensive to democratic sensibilities, use abbreviations applied to British English by A. S. C. Ross in his well-known "Linguistic Class-Indicators in Present-Day English":[1] *U* (upper class) and *Non-U*. The terms were given wide currency by the Hon. Nancy Mitford's use of them in her article "The English Aristocracy," first published in *Encounter* and later in her anthology *Noblesse Oblige* (London, 1956). Miss Mitford gives full credit to Ross for having provided the terms and the specimens that she exhibits. *Noblesse Oblige* begins with Ross's "U and Non-U: An Essay in Sociological Linguistics," a condensed and simplified version of his earlier article.

Like Ross, I use the terms "factually and not in reprobation" and, as previously stated, I take them as designating varieties of standard American English. I do not regard U speech as particularly worthy of emulation by those who do not have it by tradition or as necessarily any more "beautiful" than any other type of speech. Like their British counterparts, American U speakers are, in Ross's words, "not necessarily better educated, cleaner, or richer" than Non-U speakers. They have by and large come from what are thought of, if only locally, as "old families"; and they are conscious of the fact without being particularly proud or ashamed of it. As a rule they give little thought to matters of linguistic usage, and it would probably not occur to most of them to consult a dictionary to find out the pronunciation of any word that they used themselves, since from their point of view the way to say it would obviously be the way they said it.

Although some will regard Ross's term *U* as snobbish, it is certainly as accurate as anything else that I have been able to come up with—*elite* has connotations of caste equally offensive to egalitarians as *U*—and it has the advantage of being widely known as a designation for a type or

1. *Neuphilologische Mitteilungen*, 55 (1954), 20–56.

style of speech which almost inevitably must exist in all societies, including those that pride themselves upon their classlessness. It is, incidentally, unlikely that any adult takes this notion of classlessness very seriously, including the political spellbinders who pay lip service to it. Ross points out that even in present-day Russian the distinction between the two plurals of *ofitser* 'officer' —*ofitsery* and *ofitsera*—"is certainly one of class." As for Germany, although the "good Potsdam society of the late twenties," which frowned upon "küss' die Hand" (on being introduced to a lady), may be gone forever, Germans with all their talk about "democracy" are still very conscious of linguistic class-indicators. I was told by a tobacconist in Göttingen, upon my inquiring about the matter, that she had the impression that it was "eleganter" to ask for "ein Pakete (Zigaretten)" than for "ein Päckchen." Whether or not her impression has any validity I do not know, but the concept of German U was there. Germans of high status have informed me that *auf Wiederschauen* (for *auf Wiedersehen*) and *Mahlzeit!* (as a mealtime greeting or valedictory) were avoided by gentlefolk, though it seems likely that these may be merely regionalisms.

It has already been implied that, unlike the more or less standardized speech of those who speak professionally over mass media—the commentators ("news analysts"), the "anchor men," the interviewers, the announcers, and those who deliver the messages (sales talks)—and unlike its British equivalent, American U speech is by no means unmarked by regional characteristics. The speech of Franklin Delano Roosevelt bore the characteristics of his region as well as of his class, but the former were somewhat different from those of Albert Cabell Ritchie, Governor of Maryland throughout the 1920s until 1935. Yet both men were unquestionably U speakers; the usage of both was that of those whom they grew up with, without much regard for the schoolroom prescriptions— which does not mean that they made "grammatical errors"—and for the supposed necessity for euphemism of which Non-U is always keenly conscious.

Differences between U and Non-U word choice are fairly well known, despite the almost complete lack of any scholarly study of these differences as they are manifested in American English.[2] One salient characteristic of U has just been alluded to—the preference for plain and forthright terms

2. They are treated somewhat superficially by Vance Packard in *The Status Seekers* (New York, 1959), who cites (p. 41) contrasting examples of upper-class (U) and middle-class (Non-U) word choices from E. Digby Baltzell's *Philadelphia Gentlemen* (Glencoe, Ill., 1958), and by Clifton Fadiman in "On the Utility of U-Talk," which appeared in *Holiday* magazine and in his *Any Number Can Play* (Cleveland, Ohio, 1957) and is reprinted in *The World of Words*, edited by Barnet Kottler and Martin Light (Boston, 1967), pp. 179–87.

instead of euphemistic ones, particularly when the latter are voguish terms smacking of advertising or social uplift, or appear to be employed by Non-U speakers as mealy-mouthed attempts to gloss over facts of life which they may regard as shocking, such as death, excretion, and sex. The male U speaker (for the female of the U species would probably not refer to the activity at all) would of course use some such learned term as *fornication* or *coitus* rather than the more "folksy" word for the same thing, but practically always with a vague sense that he was being foolishly and unnecessarily evasive and a bit pompous.

Where sex is not involved, however, the U term very often coincides with the term used by speakers of nonstandard (that is, sub-Non-U) English, who say *crazy*, *old man* (or *woman*), and, in formal circumstances at least, *toilet paper*, not so much as a matter of taste as because they are unfamiliar with such namby-pambyisms as *mentally ill*, *senior citizen*, and *bathroom tissue*.[3] But U speakers are generally quite tolerant of Non-U terms and may even find them faintly amusing; they respect the right of anyone to say *finalize*, *budgetwise*, *in depth*, and *breakthrough*, but they would not use these terms themselves, perfectly standard though they are. Perhaps it would be more accurate to say that they would not use them in talking to other U speakers, for it is an ironic fact that many such modish terms are the concoctions of men in popular journalism and advertising who are, as Fadiman points out in the article cited, U by birth and education, meaning that they come from "old" families and have gone to Ivy League schools.

U pronunciation, unhappily for those who may yearn for it but do not have it by tradition, is shot through with subtleties of one sort or another rather than being consistent or reasonable as the old textbook rules dictated. For instance, loss of the first [r] in *February* might occur in U pronunciation, but never a similar loss in *secretary* and *library*. There is nothing Non-U about the loss of [n] in the second syllable of *government*, but the assimilatory [m] for [n] at the beginning of the second syllable of *hypnotize* is decidedly Non-U. What is popularly called "dropping the *g*" in words ending in *-ing* is unquestionably U, though by now somewhat old-fashioned; this conservative practice is still widespread in nonstandard speech, but not in Non-U, where it has been "taught out." Such apparent inconsistencies, such infringements of regulations highly regarded by Non-U

3. Ross points out that *toilet paper* is Non-U in British English, the U term being *lavatory paper* (in 1954). Both *toilet* and *lavatory* are of course euphemisms, but they supplanted plainer terms so long ago as to require other euphemisms for the squeamish: *rest room*, *comfort station*, *little boys'* (or *girls'*) *room*, and the like. The "plainer terms" referred to are not themselves very plain; one would have to go very far back to find really plain ones in general use. There is need for a sound historical study of cloacinal semantics.

speakers, occurring as they do within a type of speech which is usually marked by a blithe self-assuredness, are both annoying and baffling to those who, like the aforesaid Non-U speakers, have learned by the book.

The pronunciations to be treated in the discussion which follows have been taken down from the mouths of persons who are much in the news, most of them professional commentators from the auditory mass media, but some from speakers who appear on the media as interviewees, panelists, and the like because of their importance in American life. If not invariably professional public speakers, all are by any conceivable definition prominent Americans, and most have political potency on a national or metropolitan scale. There are no citations from speakers who, deservedly or not, have been publicly pilloried for their malapropisms, fractured syntax, markedly regional speech, and the like. Thus Chicago's Mayor Richard Daley, who except for an occasional [d] for [ð] has spoken what I consider to be standard English on the few occasions when I have heard him, is not represented. My present concern is with a variety of speech which no one acquainted with the cultural and social vagaries of the "American way" could possibly impugn as nonstandard.

As for the pronunciations of network newscasters, commentators, "anchor men," and those of almost equal prestige who exhort us to buy their particular brand of deodorant, laxative, headache remedy, detergent, or shampoo cream, many may be regarded by a handful of U speakers as affected, naive, or simply in a vague sort of way Non-U. Nevertheless, all pronunciations cited represent what must be accepted by any truly democratic criterion as standard; all represent "educated" usage—the usage of expensively groomed, high-salaried, mellifluous speakers, whose voices exude a self-confidence which cannot but be tremendously impressive to their considerable following of admirers. If the usage of such high-powered speakers be not adjudged standard English, I know not what should be.

Usually, it is to be suspected, the auditory media do not originate but merely reflect Non-U usage and, because of the eminence in the popular mind of those who speak professionally over these media, lend it authority and prestige. Thus, when Eric Sevareid, a widely respected pundit, solemnly pronounces *particularly* and *regularly* with penultimate secondary stress, he is certainly not using idiolectal pronunciations but rather ones that have been fairly widespread in Non-U speech for some time, though as yet unrecorded in the dictionaries.[4] But the prestige of Mr. Sevareid is

---

4. The words in question may also in Non-U speech have an extra syllable, as if written *particularily* and *regularily*, perhaps by analogy with *ordinarily*, *primarily*, and other adverbs in *-arily*.

awesome; and it is likely that, even without supporting usage by other TV "personalities," his usage would suffice to give final sanction to the pronunciations cited. U speakers may consider them either affected or naive, or both, but U speakers are doubtless best regarded as a moribund species; it is certain that no U speaker is anywhere near as impressive as Eric Sevareid. Similarly, when an even more frequently audible and visible reporter-commentator-analyst—an LL.D. *honoris causa*, no less—charged by his network with "covering" Sir Winston Churchill's funeral some years ago inserted a svarabhakti vowel between the *n* and the *s* of *Westminster*, he was merely giving authority to a Non-U pronunciation of the word symbolized by the spelling *Westminister* which appeared on the TV screen in the same program. Although labeled "substandard" by *Webster's Third*, the pronunciation cited is used by many quite respectable and some quite prominent Americans in addition to the commentator cited, in view of which fact I should hesitate to call it even nonstandard. Non-U it certainly is.

Some of the pronunciations to be cited as Non-U seldom occur in non-standard or substandard speech for the obvious reason that the words themselves seldom occur in such speech; the pronunciations indicated are thus pretty much confined to standard Non-U. Others, such as the common pronunciations of *premises* and *processes* as if these were third-declension Latin plurals in [-iz],[5] like *crises*, *analyses*, and *indices*, may have seeped down into nonstandard usage but certainly originated in rather rarefied intellectual circles, where they are heard from speakers of unquestionably high status. They are by no means unknown in the groves of Academe, which are not inhabited exclusively by U speakers nowadays, if indeed they ever were. U speakers, whether or not they are aware that *premises* and *processes* are not Latin loanwords, are in their stodgy traditional way likely to consider the Latinized pronunciation somewhat showy or, what is usually equally repugnant to the U linguistic psyche, newfangled.[6]

The increasing frequency in all positions of [ž]—earlier confined to medial position in loanwords taken into English from Old French, like *vision*, *pleasure*, and *azure*—is a phenomenon of recent times strikingly reflected in, and perhaps originating from, the auditory mass media. In all types of

---

5. They are in fact not even taken from Latin. *Sequence*, which often has Non-U plural in [-iz], is genuinely Latin, from *sequentia*; its Latin plural is of course *sequentiae*. For a few other spurious Latin third-declension plurals, see John Algeo, "More False Latin," *American Speech*, 41 (1966), 72–74.

6. The traditional English pronunciation of the Latin plural ending written *es* is of course [iz]; but *mores*, a genuine third-declension Latin plural, usually has pseudo-classical [es] or [ez], pronunciations doubtless promulgated by the sociologists, for whom the word is a technical term. It is of fairly recent adoption into English.

educated speech, U and Non-U alike, it occurs initially and finally only in a few quite recent loanwords from French, like *genre* and *beige*, in which it is taken directly from Modern French. Nonstandard speech lacks initial [ž], since French words beginning with the sound are no part of the word stock of the unschooled; in final position, in a few words like *rouge* and *garage* having currency in such speech, [ǰ] replaces standard [ž]. Non-U speakers, including those on the media, have extended this originally non-English consonant to a number of words in which there is no historical reason for it. It is, for instance, fairly usual in Italian *adagio* and may be heard in *Borgia*, (*Di*) *Maggio*, and (*Vesti la*) *Giubba*, although the Italian value symbolized by *gi* is of course [ǰ]; it is apparently also assumed to be the sound symbolized by *j* in *rajah* and *Taj* (*Mahal*) and by *sh* in *cashmere* and in other words recognized as non-English, no matter what their precise provenience. The pronunciations cited are almost certainly of American origin; some are recorded in American dictionaries, none in British dictionaries. The *g* of *menagerie*, genuinely French, has apparently been pronounced [ǰ]—the only pronunciation recorded in the *OED* and other British dictionaries—since its adoption into English in the early eighteenth century. Non-U has, however, Gallicized the consonant as [ž]. Less easily accounted for is the recent occurrence of [ž] in the Latin loanwords *coercion*, *fission*, and *subterfuge*.

Although of genuine French provenience, *liege* has been a part of the English word stock since the thirteenth century, about as long as *marriage* has been. Its final consonant is nevertheless sometimes pronounced as if it had been recently adopted. Even Prince Charles, on the occasion of his investiture as Prince of Wales, swore to be his mother's [liž] man, so that the pronunciation in question is obviously on its way to becoming the King's English—or so it is devoutly to be wished. The word is of course of rare occurrence in current English; it is thus not surprising, in view of its French "look," that it should have acquired a Modern French final consonant that has not as yet, it should be noted, occurred in the more familiar *siege*.

In U, particularly older-generation U, the Latin plural ending *i* is usually [aɪ], as in *fungi*, *cacti*, *stimuli*, and *alumni*,[7] but otherwise final *i* in Latin loanwords is [ɪ], as in the prefixes *anti* and *semi*. Non-U, however, pronounces the plural ending [i] but usually has [aɪ] in the prefixes when they are easily recognizable as such, as in *anti-intellectual*, *antisocial*, *antiaircraft*, *semiofficial*, and *semimonthly* (in contrast to *antiseptic* and *semicolon*, in which prefix and root are completely welded). Equally perverse from the

---

7. Note that the Non-U pronunciation of *alumni* is thus identical with the older (and doubtless still U) pronunciation of *alumnae*, with traditional English-Latin [i] for -*ae;* and that Non-U *alumnae* (with [aɪ]) likewise becomes identical with U *alumni*.

point of view of the U speaker is Non-U's un-English [i] for [aɪ] in the first syllables of *biography* and *biotic*; in *antibiotic* Non-U reverses the traditional English vowels of the second and third syllables.

Overcareful speech, frequently based upon spelling, is characteristic of the professional mass-media speaker, whose standards of linguistic propriety demand something less devil-may-care than schwa in the first syllables of such words as *collaborate*, *occur(rence)*, *opinion*, *obedient*, *official*, and *offensive*; typically, he uses [o] in these and similar words, so that their traditionally unstressed initial syllables receive a very slight degree of stress lacking in less painstaking, if more traditional, U speech. Similarly, he prefers [i] to traditional [ɪ] (or schwa) in *essential*, *effect(ive)*, *efficient*, *effeminate*, and the like.

The concern with giving every syllable what is regarded as its just dues is likewise evident in the mass-media treatment of the final syllables of the names of the days of the week and of *holiday*, which become [de]. Analysis of these previously amalgamated compounds is, it should be mentioned, now usual among younger-generation speakers, who pronounce the words in question with the same stressing as in *birthday*. John S. Kenyon's labeling of the use of the unreduced vowel in these words as "semiliterate formal" will not do for today's speech.[8]

Spelling is certainly responsible for the supposedly hifalutin (but decidedly Non-U) pronunciation of final *-or* with unreduced vowel, thus carefully distinguishing words with this ending from words in *-er*. There is not always complete consistency: I have recorded *senators and legislators* in the formal speech of a Non-U politician with [-ərz] in the first word and [-ɔrz] in the third. The unreduced vowel may nonetheless occur in *senator* or indeed in practically any word ending in *or*, whether or not an agentive suffix, for instance, *ambassador*, *competitor*, *juror*, *Bangor*, and *creator* (with reference to God, the full vowel giving the word a certain mouth-filling dignity felt to be appropriate to such elevated reference).

Unreduced final vowels also occur in the type of speech under consideration in *window*, *widow*, *narrow*, *thorough*, *borough*, and the like. The judgment of Kenyon and Knott in 1944 (unrevised in subsequent printings of the *Pronouncing Dictionary of American English*) that the ending *-ow* (or *-ough*) is "seldom pronounced" with a full vowel "except with artificial care" is no longer strictly accurate; the final [o] is now usual not only in the auditory mass media but also on all levels of younger-generation speech. Older-generation U speakers continue to pronounce [-ə].

8. "Cultural Levels and Functional Varieties of English," *College English*, 10 (1948), 32.

Whether to their credit or not, network professionals have by and large given up certain pronunciations which have been the subject of puristic objurgation in the press, for example, that for *nuclear* as if written **nucular*,[9] favored by Dwight David Eisenhower, Melvin R. Laird, Secretary of Defense in the Nixon cabinet, and Robert Miller, manager of the Nevada Test Site, among many others; that for *column* riming with *volume*, which used to be heard much more frequently than it is nowadays; and that for *escalate* as if written **esculate*, still preferred by many of high rank in our armed services. These and other pronunciations to be indicated which may by now be eschewed by the professionals nevertheless occur again and again from speakers of unquestioned status—government officials, physicists, social scientists, medical gurus, business leaders, and the like—who in our society are eminently newsworthy. (U speakers by and large have only a local prominence and thus are seldom in the national news.)

But subtler Non-U designators have hung on in network usage, such as *congratulate* as if written **congradulate*; *dissect* riming with *bisect*; *mineralogy* and *genealogy* with antepenultimate [ɑ], by analogy with many words in *-ology*; *schedule* as if written **schedual*; *potential* and *substantial* as if written **-tual* (and *substantiate* as if **-tuate*); *grievous* riming with *previous*; *insidious* and *invidious* as if written **-duous*; *stupendous* and *tremendous* as if written **-dious*; *portentous* as if written **-tious*; *deteriorate* as if written **deteriate* or **deterorate*; *priority* as if written **priorority*; and *beneficiary* as if written **beneficiarary*.[10]

Non-U practically always has strongest stress on the initial syllables of *millionaire* (frequently with loss of [l]), *cigarette*, *magazine*, *dictator*, and *spectator*, though initial stress in the last two words is now so widespread that it can hardly be considered a Non-U designator in any American speaker under sixty. Perversely enough, from the point of view of the U speaker, Non-U reverses the traditional initial stress of *berserk*, *Barnett*, *Bernard*, *Purcell*, *Gerard*, and *Maurice*, perhaps to give these words what is felt to be a tony Gallic flavor. The first name of the actor Maurice Evans, now that he has become an American, is [mə'ris] rather than ['mɔrɪs], though when the same name is spelled *Morris* the traditional pronunciation is always used.

Such pronunciations as have been here cited, taken from what I conceive

9. Respellings and riming words, rather than phonetic transcriptions, will be used henceforth whenever possible; they have the virtue of suggesting analogies—in this instance with *circular*, *jocular*, *particular*, and the like.

10. The pronunciation cited for *beneficiary* was that used by our thirty-sixth President in a broadcast telephone conversation with the Gemini astronauts Cooper and Conrad on 29 August 1965. He did not originate it.

to be standard speech as heard over the auditory mass media, will probably strike most older-generation speakers who are perceptive about such matters as Non-U designators. In any event, they are all innovations, which from the usually conservative U point of view amounts to much the same thing.

But, despite the conservatism of U, it is certain that much of the Non-U of one generation becomes the U of the next. When, in the latter part of the eighteenth century, conservative speakers like Dr. Johnson deplored the retraction of [æ] to [ɑ] in what Kenyon calls the *ask*-words, they could not have been aware that such vulgar pronunciations (vulgar to their ears, at least) would ultimately prevail in Standard British English, though the older vowel survives in the speech of most Americans.

Likewise, in the early years of the present century, pronunciation of the *t* in *often* was a Non-U designator; but pronouncing the *t* is now widespread in U speech, both American and British. Pronunciation as the spelling seems to indicate has occurred in formal broadcast speeches of two English kings, Edward VIII and George VI. Whether or not the present sovereign lady and her family pronounce the *t* I have not had the opportunity to observe, but I should be surprised if they did not.

It is thus likely that many of the pronunciations here cited (but not reprehended) as Non-U will occur in the U speech of the next generation. Such is the course of linguistic history. My own grandfather, born in 1857, thought my pronunciation of *a* before *lm* (the only one current today, except for *salmon*, in which U has [æ]) utterly reprehensible; an almshouse was to him an "amshouse," he read the "sams" in church, and, had he been an evangelical, would doubtless have been soothed by the "bam" of Gilead. His usage, it should be said, was somewhat retarded even for his generation.

There were no auditory mass media on which to blame newfangled pronunciations in Grandfather's day; they must then have been attributed to the natural perversity of what was regarded, always with disapproval, as the rising generation. In the more enlightened days in which we live, however, there can be little doubt that these mass media have hastened the dissemination of pronunciations which those of us who have the misfortune of being older-generation are quick to stigmatize as Non-U, albeit more in sorrow than in anger—untraditional pronunciations mostly stemming from a highly regarded if rather easily acquired literacy.

Without the media, on which we are all to some degree "hooked," it is doubtful that we should be particularly aware of such changes as have been discussed. With the media, we may witness the emergence, if not indeed the fruition, of a cultural and social level of speech that, though it may lack such outworn and undemocratic qualities as elegance and sophistication, must be regarded, as it has been here regarded, as a variety of standard English which is both widely admired and widely emulated. It is difficult to conceive of a more appropriate means of communication for the brave new world envisaged by our more advanced thinkers—a classless world in which tradition and elegance will, it is hoped, play no part.

Semantica et Etymologia

10

Innocuous Linguistic Indecorum:
A Semantic Byway

THERE can be no doubt, as the *OED* points out, that Browning's use of the plural form of a word ordinarily taboo in polite literature, as always in polite society, in *Pippa Passes*, 4.2.96 ("Then, owls and bats, / Cowls and twats"),[1] is a reflection of the lines in *Vanity of Vanities* (1660): "They talk't of his having a Cardinalls Hat, / They'd send him as soon an Old Nuns Twat." The word in question, riming in present English with *squat* rather than as Browning's lines would indicate, was commonly used for *pudendum muliebre* in the bawdy talk of schoolboys in my childhood, and may still be so used for all I know.[2] Browning's usage does more

1. If Browning's use of *twat* is, as Eric Partridge calls it, "the literary world's worst 'brick' " (*A Dictionary of Slang and Unconventional English*, New York, 1937, p. 919), George Meredith's use of *verteth* (i.e. 'farteth') in his parody of "Summer Is Icumen In" in *The Ordeal of Richard Feverel*, chapter 25, and his later use of the participial form *verting* in the same chapter, must surely run Browning a close second. See in this connection E. E. Ericson, "Bullock Sterteth , Bucke Verteth ," *MLN*, 53 (1938), 112–13, and the remonstrance of T. C. Hoepfner in *Explicator*, 3 (December 1944), 18, as well as the contributions of Huntington Brown and J. S. Kenyon, *Explicator*, 3 (February 1945), 34, and 3 (March 1945), 40, both of whom support Ericson and the *OED*. Mr. Hoepfner re-entered the lists, *Explicator*, 3 (June 1945), 59, still unconvinced.

In this connection, the "brick" dropped by Captain Marryat in chapter 20 of *Peter Simple* is worthy of mention: "O'Brien declared that he was a liar, and a cowardly *foutre*." For further comment on *foutre*, see infra, note 13. It is highly doubtful that the Puritan dandy, Nathaniel Parker Willis, had this passage in mind when he wrote, in a letter to the *New York Mirror* (18 April 1835): "Captain Marryat's gross trash sells immensely about Wapping and Portsmouth," a statement which was to precipitate the famous bloodless duel of Willis and Marryat.

2. In some sections, I am informed, the word now denotes the buttocks of either sex, a somewhat meliorative development comparable, indeed identical, to the moving rearward and loss of sexual discrimination in *fanny* (cf. Partridge, p. 265), now a "cute" euphemism in the social intercourse of respectability. Vice versa, *tail* and *arse* (i.e., *ass*) seem to have shifted frontwards, though they frequently include the entire female sacro-pubic region—in

117

credit to his breadth of reading than to his comprehension of the vernacular of venery. G. B. Woods explains the word in a footnote to the Browning poem as "part of a nun's garb, corresponding to the cowl of a monk,"[3] which is almost certainly what Browning thought it meant.[4]

It is less easy to demonstrate how other verbal indecencies penetrate into the language of ordinary, informal speech, as *twat* may be said to have entered the language of polite literature in Browning's usage (though it has not, so far as I know, made any headway). Frequently, I suspect, the indecency is introduced as a daringly conscious *double entente* for the purpose of "getting a laugh" from the knowing, and is repeated and disseminated in all innocence by good, douce people.

The semantic shift of *puss*, once synonymous with *twat*, to 'mouth, face' may perhaps be so explained.[5] To decadent middle age the word still

---

a loose sense, of course. (Cf. the vulgar "piece of ———"and see C. E. Jones, "Chaucer's *Taillynge Ynough*," *MLN*, 52, 1937, 570).

3. *Poetry of the Victorian Period* (New York, 1930), p. 189.

4. The late Professor B. L. Gildersleeve, who took a consistently lofty moral stand on the subject of Browning, did not think the poet so innocent, accusing him of frequent salacity (*American Journal of Philology*, 31, 1910, 488–89; 32, 1911, 484). But worst of all is that "notorious word which smirches the skirt of Pippa Passes" (32, 1911, 241).

5. A. E. Hutson, "Gaelic Loan-Words in American," *American Speech*, 22 (1947), 21, points out that *puss*, meaning 'face,' is derived from Irish *pus*, meaning 'mouth.' Although this Gaelic etymology may account for the introduction of the word in its innocent sense, there can be no doubt of its double associations for many as it is now used. The embarrassed titters and the uninhibited guffaws with which its use is likely to be greeted cannot be accounted for by any theory that it is thought of as a "quaint" Irish word.

I have long been tantalized by the possibility that *puss* in its pudendal sense may have developed from *purse* with loss of preconsonantal *r* (no doubt quite early, because of the dental consonant which follows: see A. A. Hill, "Early Loss of [r] before Dentals," *PMLA*, 55, 1940, 308–59): cf. *cuss*, *bust*, *fust* 'first,' *nuss* 'nurse.' The labial consonant of course accounts for the Modern English absence of unrounding of early [ʊ]—an unrounding which on the contrary is usually to be heard in *pussy* 'fat,' from *pursy*, which is quite another word. Long-established sexuo-zoölogical analogy (Eng. *cony*, *malkin*, *merkin*, Fr. *chat*, *angora*, *lapin*, Lat. *porcus*, Gk. χοῖρος, with its diminutives χοιρίον and χοιρίδιον. [In the Latin and Greek terms is there a suggestion of Oriental depilation?]), would have provided semantic support for the phonological development. For *purse* with yonic significance see Donne's "Love's Progress" (*The Poems of John Donne*, ed. H. J. C. Grierson, Oxford, 1912, 1:119, line 92); Beaumont and Fletcher's *Little French Lawyer:* "And put a good speed penny in my purse, / That has been empty these twenty years" (*Beaumont and Fletcher*, ed. A. R. Waller, Cambridge, 1906, 3:451); the broadside song "The Turnep Ground" (ca. 1720), printed in J. S. Farmer's *Merry Songs and Ballads* (London, 1897), 1:224: "When gently down I Layd her, She Op't a Purse as black as Coal, To hold my Coin"; "A Pleasant New Ballad" ("Being a pleasant discourse between a country lass and a young tailor"), reprinted as from the *Roxburghe Ballads* in *Poetica Erotica*, ed. T. R. Smith (New York, 1927), pp. 305–7, which uses similar metonymy in *fringed bag*, as does Durfey in his use of *sack* in the same sense. See also Farmer and Henley's *Slang and Its Analogues, Past and Present* (London, 1890–1904), s.v. *monosyllable*. The *OED* fails to give this meaning of *purse*, but lists equally appropriate uses of the word with the meaning 'scrotum.'

calls forth its earlier connotations, as is evidenced by the sniggers and the howls of ribald laughter which issue from the loudspeaker whenever the word is used, as it all too frequently is, by *soi-disant* comedians on the radio. Nevertheless, this word with its anatomically altered meaning may be said to have passed into ordinary slang, particularly in the phrase "a sock in the puss," which, though somewhat crude, is felt to be in no way indecent. *Cony*[6] 'rabbit' by a similar metonymic process, perhaps supported by the suggestion of *cunnus* and its English equivalent (*Quaere:* Was the author and illustrator of a book called *Country Matters*, published in 1937, aware of the outrageous paronomastic implications of the phrase as it is used in *Hamlet*, 3.2.123?), came to acquire, by 1591 at the latest, the same indecent signification as did *puss*(*y*) somewhat later. Readers of Elizabethan drama will be perfectly familiar with the frequent playing upon the double meaning of this word (similar to the many jokes involving the double meaning of *firk* in early Modern English), which survives with its historical pronunciation in the schoolboy expression *cunny-thumbed* 'having the fist closed with the thumb turned inward under the fingers,' used in the game of marbles.[7]

The word *ballock* (OE *bealluc* 'testicle'), with its variant *bollock*, is archaic, in metropolitan usage at least, save in the phrase *ballocks up*, variously spelled, in which it is employed frequently, not to say usually, with no sense of its original significance and hence with no idea of impropriety.[8] Much more common is *ball up*, with identical present meaning

---

6. The historical pronunciation is indicated by the spelling *cunny*. According to the *OED*, "It is possible . . . that the desire to avoid certain vulgar associations with the word in the *cunny* form, may have contributed to the preference for a different pronunciation in reading the Scriptures. Walker knew only the *cunny* pronunciation; Smart (1836) says 'it is familiarly pronounced *cunny*,' but *cŏny* is 'proper for solemn reading.'"

7. Not in the *DAE*, though the term was perfectly familiar to me as a boy. The *English Dialect Dictionary* records both *cunny-fingered* and *cunny-thumbed*.

8. Barnacle Bill the Sailor, a sort of nautical Paul Bunyan, was Ballocky Bill in the original ballad commemorating his adventures, usually amorous and on a scale in keeping with his original name. The popular song heard a few years back was presumably a bowdlerized version of this ballad, with toning-down of subject matter similar to the toning-down of the hero's name, which would have been a bit too bald to fool anybody. No such feeling, however, attaches to *ballocks up*. A young woman of unimpeachable modesty shocked her elderly uncle when, employing the phrase as learned from his own lips, she remarked to him that circumstances had occurred to "ballocks up" certain of her plans. In Arthur Kober's "Dilemma in the Bronx" (*New Yorker*, 7 September 1946), Mac (*né* Max), who is of the essence of refinement and much given to euphemism—witness his delicacy in referring to his "kidney condition"—writes to Billie (*née* Bella) Gross of his regret that World War II had come along to "bollix" everything up (p. 32). Conscious that the word is not quite standard English, he primly puts it within quotation marks. The word, with the spelling *bolix*, is to be found in the presumably chaste pages of a periodical known as *The Family Circle* (5 April 1946),

('disarrange, put out of order, confuse, disconcert, thwart,' etc.), which the *OED* (1933 Supplement) labels "U.S." and defines as 'clog' or 'become clogged,' presumably with balls (of snow, clay, etc.), adding that the expression is also used figuratively. This may be so, but it seems to me highly likely that *ball up* and *ballocks* (*bollocks*) *up* are merely formal variants. The British *balls-up*, labeled "low" by Partridge, is unquestionably the same.[9] Otherwise, the similarity in form and the identity in meaning taken together must be accounted a truly remarkable coincidence. In any case, there can be no doubt of the original indelicacy of *ballocks up*, which, with the obsolescence of *ballock*, has passed into fairly general familiar use.[10]

A similar contempt for the appurtenances of sex—a contempt more apparent than real, and manifesting itself largely in linguistic behavior—is indicated by the now uninhibited use of *nuts* as an exclamation of disgust or disparagement and in the phrase "Nuts to you (it)." As H. L. Mencken points out, when the word in this application came into general use, "its etymology must have been apparent to everyone old enough to vote, yet it seems to have met with no opposition from guardians of the national morals."[11] For a while the word was euphemized to *nerts*, which fooled nobody; but this flimsily disguised form is now quite old-fashioned. *Balls*, used in exactly the same way, has not fared so well socially: it is distinctly "low" on either side of the Atlantic. Whereas the American coed, or even her maiden aunt, may unblushingly hiss, "Nuts to you!"[12] taboo continues to operate against its British equivalent, "Balls to you!" Incidentally, it is just possible that the familiar *boloney* (*baloney*, *balony*), popularized

---

according to an inquiry as to its meaning in "Miscellany," *American Speech*, 22 (1947), 158, where it is "surmised to be of recent origin."

9. The use of the plural form of the noun is unquestionably responsible for the lowly transatlantic status of the phrase. *Ball*, like *breast*, is likely to become indelicate with pluralization.

10. The word *ballock* is not listed in any of its forms in Berrey and Van den Bark's *American Thesaurus of Slang* (New York, 1945), Harold Wentworth's *American Dialect Dictionary* (New York, 1944), or Farmer and Henley's *Slang and Its Analogues*. All "commercial" dictionaries save *Webster's New International* omit it, perhaps because it is felt to be obsolete, perhaps *pudoris causa*. Wright's *English Dialect Dictionary* lists the compounds *balack-handed*, *bollocky-'anded* 'left-handed' hence 'clumsy,' and the derivative *ballocky* (*bollocky*) 'left-handed.' *Ballocks up* is recorded in none of the dictionaries consulted.

11. *The American Language* (4th ed., New York, 1936), p. 300.

12. Despite its widespread distribution and apparent respectability, the word may not be heard in the cinema. In 1941, Will Hays, then head of the Motion Picture Producers and Distributors of America, Inc., included it among a list of words to be omitted from all pictures. It may, however, be used in the sense of 'crazy.' Presumably Mr. Hays's successor has not rescinded this order, for, in a long career of movie-going, I do not recollect a single occasion when my ears were sullied with the word in the sense under discussion.

by the late Alfred E. Smith, is also an example of unconscious obscenity, if, as Partridge believes, the word had originally nothing to do with Bologna sausages, but is derived from Gipsy *peloné* 'testicles.' Be that as it may, "That's all boloney" is exactly the equivalent in meaning of British "That's all balls" (printable in England since 1931, but held to be obscene in 1929).

The familiar expressions "not to give a fig for something (somebody),", "not worth a fig," and "a fig for it!"[13]—all freely used in polite society and in polite literature as well—had originally, it is to be suspected, an obscene signification, *fig* being in the beginning used not merely as a symbol of valuelessness, but as a symbol of obscenity, as in similar expressions never heard in mixed company and implying the same indifference to or contempt for something or somebody held to be of no worth—again the denigration of sex, which may be considered almost a minor linguistic phenomenon. According to the *OED*, *fig* is used as "a type of anything small, valueless, or contemptible" from ca. 1400. Although the word does not occur in English with manifestly sexual connotation until 1579, according to the same authority (i.e., as the equivalent of its use in French *faire la figue*, meaning to make the indecently insulting gesture of thrusting the thumb between two of the closed fingers, with biting the thumb, as in the opening scene of *Romeo and Juliet*, a less obviously indelicate variation),[14] I think that it is not straining the imagination too much to suspect that the sexual significance of the word, as well as the accompanying gesture, were known in England long before that date. In all the earlier uses of *fig* cited by the *OED*, in which the word is presumably used as "a type of anything small, valueless, or contemptible," the alternative indecent meaning might well be present.

The vowel of the first syllable of *shitepoke* has perhaps tended to becloud its scatological origin. At any rate, it is certain that the ladies of our

13. Cf. Pistol's "A footre [i.e., *foutre*] for the world and worldlings base!" and "A footre for thine office!" (2 *Henry IV*, 5.3.103 and 121). The *OED* chastely refrains from defining the word, listed under *foutre*, *fouter*, from OF *foutre* (Lat. *futuĕre*), also the source of Sir Richard Burton's verb *futter*. Except in Burton's coinage, the infinitive is used substantively in English, both as a symbol of worthlessness, as in Shakespeare's use, and as a contemptuous appellation, as in Marryat's doubtless innocent use, cited supra, note 1.

It is just possible that the exclamatory (*Oh*) *foot!* 'pshaw!' is a survival of some such phrase as "a foutre for it!" The *OED* labels obsolete this use of *foot* as an oath or exclamation, which it derives from "Christ's foot!" by way of "'s foot!" but I have frequently heard it as a sort of girl's-boarding-school profanity, though not very recently. In any case, it was by no means obsolete fifteen or twenty years ago.

14. Cf. Italian *fico* and Spanish *figo*, used also in early Modern English, both occurring in Shakespeare along with English *fig* in this meaning (*Henry V*, 3.6.60, 3.6.62, 4.1.60; 2 *Henry IV*, 5.3.121; *Merry Wives*, 1.3.31).

grandmothers' generation had no idea of the significance of the word when they used it jocularly and endearingly to their children and grandchildren as the equivalent of "little rascal." *Bugger* (['bʌgər] and, more frequently in American English ['bugər]), one of the most unprintable words in British English,[15] was, and doubtless still is, used by unsuspecting souls who would be appalled if they knew its origin and its present meaning in standard British English (though dialectally it is, as in American English, simply the equivalent of 'chap, fellow': cf. French *bougre*, with precisely the same status).

Feist (also *fice*, *fist* [faɪst], *phyce*, *fise*, *fiste*, *faust*) has long been a perfectly proper designation for a small, worthless cur in American English, whence the adjective *feisty*, sometimes applied to a restless, troublesome, fussy child.[16] The noun, originally meaning '*flatus ventris*' (as opposed to '*crepitus ventris*'), actually denoted a frequent failing of dogs not usually referred to *coram populo*. But its original meaning has become quite obsolete, as also in the related *fizz*, *fizzle*, and *foist*. A similar gastric metaphor is evident in *peter out* (Fr. *péter*), the equivalent of *fizzle out*. It is to be wondered how many who quote Hamlet's "Hoist with his own petar(d)" are aware of the coarse joke in the etymolgy of *petard*, or, for that matter, whether Shakespeare was himself aware of it. *Pétard* as a military or pyrotechnical term would seem to have no indecent connotations in Modern French. *Pétarade* with its literal meaning is of course low in that language, but, for all I can discover, apparently perfectly proper as a military term for 'useless cannonade'; similarly, *pet-de-nonne* 'apple fritter' and *pet-en-l'air*[17] 'short morning gown'; yet French verbal delicacy prefers *impasse* to *cul-de-sac*, *vespasienne* to *pissoir*.

But there is really no need of multiplying examples. Enough has been written to demonstrate a minor aspect of linguistic behavior which has not, so far as I know, been pointed out before—the unwitting indecency of respectability. It will be noted that euphemism is not involved, as it is in such expressions as *horse-feathers*, *bull* (or *b.s.*),[18] *s.o.b.*, *S.O.L.* (explained as 'short of luck'), or the many *-fu* words of army slang;[19] the

15. Actionable in British English until 1934, according to Partridge.

16. For other applications, see Phyllis J. Nixon, "A Glossary of Virginia Words," *Publication of the American Dialect Society*, no. 5 (May 1946), p. 21.

17. For an amusingly fanciful etymology of this expression, see the chapter "The Pet en l'Air" in the continuation of Sterne's *Sentimental Journey* by John Hall-Stephenson ("Eugenius") (New York, 1795), pp. 281–82.

18. See H. L. Mencken, *The American Language: Supplement One* (New York, 1945), p. 657.

19. *Snafu* was explained to "Mom" as "Situation normal—all *fouled* up," but G. I. Joe knew perfectly well what the italicized word really stood for. Euphemism is here involved,

full, unmutilated form is uncompromisingly and unhesitatingly employed, frequently by a class of speakers who are, when they are actually conscious of verbal indelicacy, highly intolerant of it, people who are indignant at any literature which employs words connected with sex or excretion with which they happen to be familiar. They are, as has been said, good, sweet people for the most part, who are sometimes more offended at verbal indecency when they recognize it as such than at downright immoral conduct, like the old gentleman who objected to Joyce's *Ulysses*, not because of what the people in the story did, but because of certain words they used. There is, as we have seen, a largish class of verbal indelicacies, including some of those discussed in this paper, which have undergone a toning-down or a complete loss of their original content; these are freely and undisguisedly used in all innocence by speakers who are, when aware of the slightest hint of verbal impropriety, careful to avoid it at all costs. The cream of the jest is that those who would wear fig leaves on their lips should be unintentionally guilty of even a limited use of words and phrases as shocking a few generations ago as would be much of the fireside and dinner-table talk at the great houses of Elizabethan England or, for that matter, of Colonial Virginia, were we privileged miraculously to hear it.

---

in both the word itself and the bowdlerized phrase. See J. A. Fleece, "Words in -Fu," *American Speech*, 21 (1946), 70–72.

11

Bollicky Naked

IN a letter to his friend Mrs. Shakespear, W. B. Yeats tells an amusing story of a certain stage manager at the Abbey Theatre who, knocking at the dressing-room door of a charming and "seemingly very shy" visiting actress, was bidden by the lady to enter. According to the manager's report, "I went in and there she was, saving your presence, bollicky naked," which I take to mean that she would have been naked to the ballocks had she been provided with such inappropriate impedimenta. Like many simple men—though it is difficult to understand how a stage manager, even an Irish one, should have remained so unsophisticated—he was offended rather than regaled at what he saw, and had to be dissuaded from bringing the matter before the Board: "I don't mind seeing a comedian in her knickers but nothing like this was ever seen in the Abbey before. . . . They do that kind of thing in England but not here." I am indebted to Professor F. D. Cooley for the reference to this interesting usage, which appears in Joseph Hone's *W. B. Yeats, 1865–1939* (New York, 1943), p. 480. In the light of earlier euphemizing of *ballock* to *bullock* cited by A. W. R. in *American Speech*, 24 (1949), 153, the temptation to label the Abbey stage manager's locution an "Irish bullock" becomes well-nigh irresistible.

[The *OED* Supplement of 1972 has *ballock-naked*. The single citation is from another eminent Irishman, James Joyce. Though I shall probably never have occasion to use it, I prefer the more rollicky *bollicky* of Yeats. T.P.]

12

Ophelia's "Nothing"

ERIC Partridge, in his *Shakespeare's Bawdy* (London, 1947), has failed to perceive the beautifully apt climax of the "country matters" dialogue in *Hamlet*, 3.2.119–29. Ophelia's reply to Hamlet's outrageously paronomastic "Do you think I meant country matters?" (adequately explained by Partridge, p. 95, though editors have pretty consistently shied away from pointing out the indelicacy) is, "I think nothing, my lord."

> *Ham.* That's a fair thought to lie between maids' legs.
> *Oph.* What is, my lord?
> *Ham.* Nothing.

Hamlet (or Dick Burbage) might well at this point have made the "nothing" symbol by joining thumb and forefinger, although the gesture is not at all necessary to "get over" the joke: the word itself in this context would, I think, have been sufficient to titillate the quicker wits in the audience.[1] In any event, Ophelia's "You are merry, my lord" indicates that she got the point well enough, though it is doubtful that many modern readers do—even including so perceptive an observer of "country matters" in literature and language as Partridge.

For Hamlet's *nothing*, a reflection of Ophelia's earlier use of the word, is unquestionably yonic symbolism, a shape-metaphor intended to call to mind the naught, or O, which is elsewhere in Shakespearean, if not in modern, "bawdy" a symbol of *pudendum muliebre*. So understood, the passage takes on a beautiful clarity. "Fair thought" is, of course, a quibble—

1. For *thing* with similarly "broad" meaning, cf. Partridge, s.v.

"happy idea" and "pretty trifle" (*OED*, *thought*, definition 6), as Professor Dover Wilson has recognized;[2] "That [*nothing* meaning 'pudendum']'s a fair thought [a pretty trifle] to lie between maids' legs," in addition to the more readily apparent meaning.

Partridge has recognized that there is a wealth of yonic symbolism in Shakespeare. If the Elizabethan meaning of *nothing* and *naught* (*nought*)[3] be recognized and added to those "country" references which he glosses, this anatomical localization of sexuality becomes considerably more impressive. There is certainly pudendal suggestiveness in Flute's "A paramour is, God bless us, a thing of naught" (*Midsummer Night's Dream*, 4.2.13–14), which Partridge thinks means no more than 'worthless' and 'obscene'; but the pun is actually triple-barreled, if *naught* be understood as a sexual reference, as I am convinced it would have been at the Globe. *Naughty* has similar triple paronomasia in Elbow's "This house, if it be not a bawd's house . . . is a naughty house" (*Measure for Measure*, 2.1.77–78). It seems likely also that Cressida's "You smile and mock me, as if I meant naughtily" (*Troilus and Cressida*, 4.2.38) is more indelicate than it first appears. In any case, I think it safe to assume that Shakespeare was perfectly well aware of the "loose" meaning of *nothing* and *naught(y)* in the bawdy talk of his day, and that the use of these words in the passages cited, and perhaps in others, could not have failed to provoke guffaws from the groundlings and civil leers from the gentles.

2. *Hamlet* (Cambridge, 1934), p. 199. Dover Wilson also got the point of *nothing*, as his reference to *O* with identical meaning in *Romeo and Juliet*, 3.3.90, and *Cymbeline*, 2.5.17, would indicate. To these he might appositely have added a reference to the more obvious synonym *naught* (or *nought*), which I shall later cite.

3. Cf. the erotic symbolism of *circle* (*Romeo and Juliet*, 2.1.24) and *ring* (*Merchant of Venice*, 5.1.307, reminiscent of Hans Carvel's ring). Partridge thinks the sexual circle "physiologically inaccurate" (s.v. *circle*, p. 87), but it is no more so than the conventionalized lozenges which carnal-minded moppets used to (and may still) scrawl on walls and fences as a representation of what, following the chaste example of the ending of Sterne's *Sentimental Journey*, I shall indicate here merely as ———.

Onomastica

13

Dan Chaucer

THE poet Spenser, in what is probably the most widely known of all Chaucer allusions, refers to his distinguished predecessor as "Dan Chaucer, well of English vndefyled" (*Faërie Queene*, 4.2.32). "Dan Chaucer," in its prefixing of title to surname, is the equivalent of "Sir Ralegh" (instead of "Sir Walter");[1] in fact, *dominus*, whence *dan* is ultimately derived,[2] was sometimes rendered by *sir* and used, "with the surname of the person, to designate a Bachelor of Arts in some Universities" (*OED*, s.v. *sir*).[3] Unless Spenser had this university practice specifically in mind,[4] and was

1. R. W. Chapman refers to "Sir Richmond" (for "Sir William [Richmond]") as a continental error (*Names, Designations and Appellations*, SPE Tract 47, Oxford, 1936, p. 252). He might with perfect justice have written "continental and American." Dr. Oliver St. John Gogarty reports a conversation between an American millionaire and Sir Horace Plunkett in which the American addresses Sir Horace as "Sir Plunkett" (*As I Was Going Down Sackville Street*, New York, 1937, p. 118). There must be many such examples of American ineptitude in the use of English titles.

2. Despite the belief of a sadly muddled gentleman who wrote to *Notes and Queries* (30 May 1863, pp. 427–28) to inquire as to the origin of *dan*, remarking that "to modern ears it has an air of grotesque familiarity, derived perhaps from 'Old Dan Tucker' and other Yankee associations." His selection of "Daniel" as a nom de guerre would seem to furnish a key to his confusion.

3. Says Robert Nares (*Glossary*, ed. 1859, s.v. *sir*), "*Dominus*, the academical title of a bachelor of arts, was usually rendered by *sir* in English, at the Universities; so that a bachelor, who in the books stood *Dominus* Brown, was in conversation called *Sir* Brown," adding that "this was in use in some colleges even in my memory." (He died in 1829, in his seventy-sixth year.) He points out, however, that, except for this archaic university custom, "*sir* is prefixed to the Christian name," explaining that "sirnames [*sic*] were little used, when the practice began."

4. This seems most unlikely, inasmuch as only the English *sir* and the Latin *dominus* were so used, not the derivative *dan* of the latter; nor is the at present familiar Oxford and Cambridge *don* used as a title of rank prefixed to a name.

thinking of Chaucer as a learned "clerk," perhaps even as a university man, it is difficult to see why he did not here write "Dan Geoffrey," since the meter would in no way have been affected, unless he wanted to make doubly sure that the reader would make the proper identification; indeed, later in the poem he does use what would seem to be the more orthodox form, i.e., "Dan Geffrey" (7.7.9). In both cases, however, identification is equally certain because of references to works of Chaucer. It seems most likely that Spenser was using the title *dan*, already old-fashioned, to connote antiquity, dignity, learning, and respectful affection for his avowed literary idol, and that the usage which we should expect to find (by analogy with earlier nonacademic[5] and with present-day *sir*, as well as with earlier *dan*) was not fixed in his day.[6] There can be absolutely no question, however, that prefixing *dan* to the surname was at any period exceedingly rare.[7]

It is worthy of note that Chaucer himself uses the title *dan*, or *daun*, like *sir*, in the more usual fashion, i.e., with given names, e.g., Albon, Burnel, Gerveys, John, Piers, Russell, Thomas; though, when he prefixes it, sometimes facetiously, I suspect, but quite in accord with tradition, to classical and biblical names, he of course uses either the single name by which the character was generally known or the only name borne by the character, e.g., Antenor, Arcite, Claudian, Constantyn, Cupido, Eneas, Eolus, Ethiocles, Jupiter, Lucan, Pharao, Phebus, Plato, Polymytes, Pseustis, Ptholome, Rupheo, Salomon, Scipio.

J. M. Manly, in his edition of the *Canterbury Tales* (New York, 1928), says of Chaucer's *dan*, or *daun*: "It is, apparently, not used with family names, but only with given names. Tennyson therefore in 'The Dream of Fair Women' should have said 'Dan Geoffrey,' not 'Dan Chaucer'" (p. 546). Of course, Tennyson's "Dan Chaucer" is only a reflection of Spenser's more famous usage, as are probably all references to "Dan Chaucer" subsequent to Spenser—and there are many, the misnomer (as it almost certainly is) having acquired an affectionate, reverent, and sometimes even a jocular connotation.[8]

Spenser was not, however, the first to refer to the older poet as "Dan

5. Used "rarely" before the surname, according to the *OED*, which labels such use obsolete.

6. Except for "Dan Chaucer" and "Dan Geffrey," Spenser applies the title only to figures from classical story and myth: Aeolus, Cupid, Faunus, Jove, Orpheus, Perseus, Phoebus. With none of these is there any question of choice between two names.

7. The cognate *don* and *dom* in Spanish and Portuguese always precede the Christian name.

8. Washington Irving, "To Lancelot Langstaff, Esq." in *Salmagundi*, February 1807 (*Works*, 1880–83 ed., 16:68) refers to "Dan Spenser" as well as to "Dan Chaucer," both of whom, "though covered with dust, are yet true sterling gold."

Chaucer." Caroline F. E. Spurgeon cites two earlier uses,[9] both in manuscripts written around the middle of the fifteenth century, which may
possibly have been known to Spenser. The readings of both manuscripts
are the same except for the spelling of one word, and the sentence, because
of its stereotyped nature, was probably of frequent occurrence, with change
of title according to the poem, as a head line or an end line in texts of
Chaucer's poems: "Explicit Pyte dan Chaucer lauture."[10] Except for these
two references to "Dan Chaucer," the only other widely known example
of *dan* prefixed to a surname antecedent to Spenser's usage is "Dan Lidgate"
in "William Baldwin to the Reader," prefaced to the *Mirror for Magis-
trates*.[11]

There can be little doubt, then, not only that all subsequent "Dan
Chaucers" are simply reflections of Spenser's usage, as has been stated
above, but also that all subsequent uses of *dan* with surname stem from
his famous "blunder" (if it may be so called). In the eighteenth century,
dan, though quite obsolete, was apparently well known, thanks to Spenser,
and was bestowed by the poets upon their fellows in facetious and somewhat
affected manner. Thus, Prior refers to "Dan Pope" ("Alma," 2.120), and
Pope in turn refers to "our friend, Dan Prior" (*Imitations of Horace*, Bk.
2, Sat. 6, line 153). The final stanza of the *"Bouts Rimés* on Signora
Domitilla," attributed to Swift and usually included among his poems,
also contains a reference to "Dan Pope."

In any event, it seems certain that Spenser's use of the title, unorthodox
though it may be, has established for "Dan Chaucer" a position of affectionate
regard in the hierarchy of "dans" second only to that held by "Dan Cupid."
Surely Dan Chaucer (for the writer is quite willing to do his bit in perpetuating
so worthy a solecism) would have desired no more exalted station.

9. *Five Hundred Years of Chaucer Criticism and Allusion* (Cambridge, 1925), 1:45 and
50.
10. The second instance cited by Miss Spurgeon has "Lauceire" for "lauture," but both
forms obviously stand for *l'autour*.
11. Ed. L. B. Campbell (Cambridge, 1938), p. 69.

14

British Titles of Nobility and Honor
in American English

EXCEPT for the no doubt apocryphal "You said a mouthful, Queen" variously attributed to Mrs. Mayor Hylan (to use a somewhat old-fashioned but useful Americanism) and to Mayor "Jimmy" Walker,[1] the royal style has presented little difficulty to Americans—certainly none in the third person. It is true that during and immediately after the First World War the Kaiser was frequently referred to editorially as William (or Wilhelm) Hohenzollern (sometimes preceded by *Mr.*), the implication being, apparently, that for all his ancestors, his uniforms, and his fiercely upturned mustachios, he was really no better than, even if superficially somewhat different from, Mr. John Smith, American. But this was intentional perversity on the part of writers who knew perfectly well that dynastic names like Hohenzollern, Windsor, and Hapsburg are not the equivalent of surnames. Although it is unlikely that a majority of our citizens are aware of these facts, Americans are nevertheless given to referring to the British monarch as Queen Elizabeth, not as Elizabeth Windsor or Elizabeth Mountbatten (the styles are equally incongruous, inasmuch as Mountbatten is merely a partial translation of Battenberg, a dynastic name like Windsor). This is dictated largely by a tradition which is easy to follow, but also to some extent by an awesome respect for royalty as such.

For there can be no serious doubt that, as Eleanor Roosevelt has written

1. Mrs. Hylan's remark is by some unkind persons said to have been made to Elizabeth, Queen of the Belgians, by others to Queen Marie of Rumania. On chronological grounds the former version is the more likely. But Grover Whalen, who certainly ought to know, denies that she ever made the remark and believes that attribution of it to her broke the poor lady's heart ("For City and For Coty," *New Yorker*, 14 July 1951, p. 36). *Life* attributes it to Mayor Walker, speaking to Queen Marie (21 April 1952, p. 32).

in *This I Remember*, "Even in this country, where people have shed their blood to be independent of a king, there is still an awe of and an interest in royalty and the panoply which surrounds it."[2] The awe and the interest of which this great democrat writes are reflected, if somewhat distortedly, in the multiplicity of queens—with an occasional king—who adorn modern American life: apple blossom queens, bobsled queens, citrus queens, not to mention radio's "Queen for a Day." One can hardly throw a stone on the campus of an American coeducational institution without running the fearsome risk of hitting royalty of some sort: there are homecoming queens, engineering queens, poinciana queens, and even F.F.A. (Future Farmers of America) queens, to mention only a few. An Englishwoman, visiting one of our state universities in the midst of a contest to choose a queen of something or other and noting the prominently displayed placards announcing rival candidacies, was moved to ask, "Whatever did you people fight the Revolution for?" It is probably not without sociological significance that the late Huey P. Long's battle cry was not "Every Man a President" but "Every Man a King."

Quite aside from his emotional response to royalty, it is equally obvious that, for all his perfervid professions of equalitarianism, the American dearly loves a lord; nor does he turn up his nose at a baronet or even a knight, though it is sometimes doubtful whether he knows the difference between them. It is thus not surprising that Colonel Robert R. McCormick's suggestion of a decade or so ago that all British titles be dropped by American newspapers was never taken very seriously in this country. Whether in the first place the proposal was simply a matter of convenience—the complexities of British usage being too much for the copyreaders of the *Chicago Tribune*— or whether the Colonel was inspired by the same sort of Anglophobia as the late Mayor "Big Bill" Thompson, who threatened to punch King George V in the "snoot" if he ever decided to spend his vacation in Chicago, I cannot tell.

Despite a certain grass-roots disapproval of all titles of nobility and honor, which the cynical observer of the national folkways may suspect to be somewhat fraudulent, we are yet impressed by such titles, mouth them lovingly, and sometimes even go so far as to bestow them gratuitously, as when the learned author of an article on Shakespeare elevates to the peerage both Arthur Broke (or Brooke), author of *The Tragicall Historye of Romeus and Juliet*, and Sir Thomas North, translator of Plutarch, as

2. She was telling of the elaborate preparations for the visit of the King and Queen of England to this country (Installment 14, as reprinted in the *Jacksonville Florida Times-Union*, 22 January 1950, p. 4).

Lord Brooke and Lord North respectively.[3] The nonexistent peerage implied by the designation Lord Bacon for Francis Bacon is a classical example, probably not confined to American usage. In fact, this particular blunder may be said to have become practically traditional.[4]

As for knighthoods (or it may be baronetcies), they would also seem to be conferred quite recklessly *honoris causa* in this country. W. G. Marshall, an Englishman who visited the United States in the 1880s, was thrice knighted by American newspapers, according to his own testimony. He was not particularly pleased: "It is beyond a joke . . . when the newspapers take you up and proclaim your name with a . . . spurious title attached to it, thereby causing you to become a laughing-stock to your friends."[5] *Webster's Biographical Dictionary* (Springfield, Mass., 1943) and *Words: The New Dictionary* (New York, 1943) concur in giving the accolade to the former British prime minister by listing him as Sir Clement Richard Attlee. *Macmillan's Modern Dictionary* (rev. ed., New York, 1944) is equally gracious to Mr. Eden, who appears as Sir Anthony. [Attlee was knighted in 1956 and created an earl upon resigning the leadership of the Labour party. Eden was knighted in 1954 and raised to the peerage (as Earl of Avon) in 1961. The American reference works thus anticipated Her Majesty by a decade or more.] An editorial in the *Florida Times-Union* (Jacksonville) of 1 April 1951 refers to "that great thinker, Sir Edmund Burke, the British statesman," though so far as I can discover Burke was never so dubbed by his sovereign.

With all our somewhat naive susceptibility to its elegance, the British noble and honorific style is far too complex for most of us. Even the redoubtable H. L. Mencken throws in his hand with the statement that "the intricacies of British titles are so vast that I can't go into them here."[6] Nor is there any point in my going into them either except as they become relevant to the matter under discussion. The curious will find a brief but fairly adequate treatment in R. W. Chapman's *Names, Designations and*

3. W. S. Knickerbocker, ed., *Twentieth Century English* (New York, 1946), pp. 448, 449.

4. Two examples will suffice: William Shirer, reviewing Mary Borden's *You, the Jury* in the *New York Herald Tribune* Book Review for 14 September 1952 (p. 5), and the Funk and Wagnalls *New College Standard Dictionary* (New York, 1947), s.v. *Bacon*. It is true, of course, that Bacon was a peer; but the style "Lord Bacon" is one which, for a very good reason, he never assumed. From 1618 to 1621 he was Lord (i.e., Baron) Verulam, and thereafter Lord (i.e., Viscount) St. Albans. To refer to him by either of these "correct" titles, however, would be to invite confusion.

5. Cited by H. L. Mencken, *The American Language: Supplement One* (New York, 1945), p. 534.

6. *The American Language* (4th ed., New York, 1936), p. 279.

Appellations (Oxford, 1936), in the section "Titles of Honour" (pp. 248–52). Recommended to those wishing a more detailed treatment are *Titles and Forms of Address* (8th ed., London, 1951) and Valentine Heywood, *British Titles* (London, 1951).

Inasmuch as Heywood's book is subtitled "The Use and Misuse of the Titles of Peers and Commoners with Some Historical Notes" and *Titles and Forms of Address* is described as a "Guide to Their Correct Use," it is obvious that the matter presents some difficulties to the British as well as to us. Indeed, it is possible to turn up a number of instances of British blundering. In *Oscar Wilde: His Life and Confessions*, Frank Harris, who spent the greater part of his life among Englishmen, though he was Irish by birth and American by naturalization, at least twice refers to Lord Alfred Douglas, a younger son of the eighth Marquess of Queensberry, as Lord Douglas,[7] though he usually employs the more conventional style. And long before the *Encyclopaedia Britannica* acquired the stigma of Americanization it had referred to Lord George Gordon as Lord Gordon (11th ed., 12:253). That these are far from being isolated instances is indicated by H. W. Fowler's caveat, "The permissible shortening [of *Lord Arthur Smith*] is not *Lord Smith*, but *Lord Arthur*" (*Modern English Usage*, s.v. *lord*). Nevertheless, it is probably safe to say that the distinction between the peerage title and the courtesy title of younger sons of dukes and marquesses, with Christian name intervening between *Lord* and surname (usually different from the father's peerage title, which in the case of all dukedoms and all but two marquessates is territorial), is by and large well understood and scrupulously observed by educated Britons.[8]

Leaving the duke and duchess out of the picture—their style is difficult[9] to get wrong in the third person—the peers are, in descending order, the marquess,[10] whose wife is the marchioness; the earl, whose wife is the

---

7. New York, 1930, pp. 412, 418, in footnotes which Harris supplied for portions of *De Profundis*.

8. The reference to "Lord Alfred Tennyson" by a character in Dylan Thomas's *Portrait of the Artist as a Young Dog* (Norfolk, Conn., 1940, p. 181) is certainly intended to represent provincial usage, not that of Thomas, who languished in the purlieus of the B.B.C. long enough to know better.

9. Difficult because the Christian names of nonroyal dukes and duchesses seldom come before the public eye, but not impossible, as in an article entitled, with unconscious irony, "Newspapers Err in Use of Foreign Titles." Its author, Carlos J. Videla, cites "Duke John and Duchess Mary of Galaxia" as a correct alternative of "the Duke and Duchess of Galaxia" (*Editor and Publisher*, vol. 71, no. 41, section 1, 8 October 1938, p. 35).

10. Also written *marquis*, which is according to Fowler "the prevailing spelling in literary use." Both Heywood and the anonymous compiler of *Titles and Forms of Address* use the form *marquess* in all their examples; the latter states that "peers of this rank use whichever form they prefer, and their choice should be ascertained and observed in addressing them

countess; the viscount, whose wife is the viscountess; and the baron, whose wife is the baroness. All these are referred to in ordinary, everyday British usage as *Lord* and their wives as *Lady*, regardless of the exact rank.[11] These titles are always immediately followed by the peerage name, sometimes the same as the surname (e.g., Byron, Tennyson, Curzon), sometimes not (e.g., Lord Halifax, whose surname is Wood; Lord Salisbury, whose surname is Cecil; Lord Derby, whose surname is Stanley). A Christian name does not intervene: thus, when the poet Tennyson was elevated to the peerage by his grateful sovereign as the first Baron Tennyson, he became Lord Tennyson, not Lord Alfred Tennyson, and thenceforth signed himself simply "Tennyson." To those not previously on Christian-name terms with him, he was "Lord Tennyson" (third person), "My Lord" (second person), and very formally "The Lord Tennyson," from which last-named style it would follow that he was a baron.[12]

In addition to being the everyday title of marquesses, earls, and viscounts, and practically the only title of barons, *Lord*, as we have seen, is also used as a courtesy title for younger sons of dukes and marquesses, e.g., Lord Peter Wimsey, Lord Hugh Cecil.[13] Younger sons of earls and all sons of viscounts and barons are designated in writing as "The Honourable," the adjective being prefixed to the Christian name, just as with *Lord* when it is a courtesy title.[14] All daughters of dukes, marquesses, and

---

[in writing]" (p. 54). Regardless of the spelling, the British invariably use the Anglicized pronunciation ['mɑkwɪs] in reference to a British peer, though the French title might be pronounced in the French fashion, with [-'ki] in the final syllable.

11. When Viscount Halifax was elevated to an earldom, he became formally the Earl of Halifax, but informally his style did not change; he was still for ordinary wear (to use Fowler's phrase) Lord Halifax. There is, however, a growing tendency in journalistic usage to employ the more exact prefixes, except for *baron*, which is probably thought of as too continental in flavor for an English noble. *Baroness* is hardly ever used, though Baroness Burdett-Coutts, who was a peeress in her own right, was so styled. According to Heywood, "the elder daughter of the late Marquess Curzon of Kedleston, who succeeded to her father's barony by special remainder, is referred to as Baroness Ravensdale," because "Lady Ravensdale" would indicate that she was the wife of a Lord Ravensdale.

12. More exalted rank would be formally designated by "The Viscount Tennyson," "The Earl Tennyson," or "The Marquess Tennyson." *Of* usually intervenes in the formal titles of peers above viscounts if the titles are territorial: thus, "The Marquess of Lothian," but "The Marquess Townshend"; "The Earl of Beaconsfield," but "The Earl Russell." (There are a few exceptions to this rule.) *Of* is always used in ducal styles. It is, of course, never used after the blanket title *Lord*, which, as we have seen, is formal only in the case of the baron. This *of* is not to be confused with the *of* which sometimes is a part of the name of the title, as in "The Earl Lloyd-George of Dwyfor," "The Viscount Cecil of Chelwood."

13. Their wives would be Lady Peter Wimsey, Lady Hugh Cecil, to distinguish them from the wives of peers.

14. "The Honourable" as a title is never spoken, but is punctiliously written on envelopes. As Heywood says: "It is a style of reference only. It is absolutely ignored in conversation

earls use the courtesy title *Lady* prefixed to their Christian names, e.g.,
Lady Mary Pierrepont, daughter of the first Duke of Kingston (better known
to literary historians by her husband's compound surname Wortley Mon-
tagu), Lady Eleanor Smith, daughter of the first Earl of Birkenhead.
Permissible shortenings are Lady Mary, Lady Eleanor — never Lady Pierre-
pont, Lady Smith. Daughters of viscounts and barons are designated
"The Honourable" exactly like their brothers, e.g., The Honourable Dorothy
Brett, The Honourable Nancy Mitford.

It is perhaps unnecessary to add that the only British peers are the actual
holders of peerages. Heirs to dukedoms, marquessates, and earldoms use
their father's second peerage title by courtesy only; thus, the eldest son
of the Duke of Marlborough is known and referred to formally as the
Marquess of Blandford (informally Lord Blandford) and the eldest son of
the Marquess of Salisbury is similarly Viscount Cranborne (or Lord Cranborne); but, like their younger brothers, they are commoners in the eyes
of the law. In other words, Blandford is a marquess by courtesy only; he
is not entitled to a seat in the House of Lords as is the Marquess of Salisbury.
Nor is Viscount Cranborne a peer like Viscount Montgomery. But there
is hardly any way of telling by the designation alone. The wives of the
bearers of these courtesy titles are designated precisely as if their husbands
were peers.

Enough has been said to give some notion of the pitfalls attendant upon
the use of a set of appellations based upon a long and complicated tradition
with which Americans have had no first-hand acquaintance. The difficulties
are easy to underestimate if one has little or no familiarity with that tradition,
as my specimens will indicate. Particularly troublesome is the distinction
between *Lord* for a peer, without the Christian name, and the same title

---

and should never be printed on visiting cards" (*British Titles*, p. 118). The wife of an
"honourable" is designated "The Honourable Mrs." followed by the husband's name. It
should be noted that, although neither *Mr.* nor *Miss* is used after *Honourable*, it is both
correct and necessary to use *Mrs.* after it.

For the American use of *Hon.*, usually written and frequently spoken without a preceding
the, for practically any freeman with shoes, see Mencken's wondrous "Bulletin on 'Hon.,'"
American Speech, 21 (1946), 81–85; his *The American Language* (4th ed.), pp. 275–78;
and his *Supplement One*, pp. 535–46. For the first time in a singularly undistinguished
career as a citizen, I was myself recently so addressed by an aspirant to Congress who was
soliciting my support at the polls. My initial feeling was exaltation—this might indeed have
been one of those "Honors, Rights, and Privileges" to which my diploma declares me entitled,
but whose heady pleasure I had not hitherto savored. Sober reflection convinced me, however,
that such discrimination would have been undemocratic in the extreme, and further inquiries
revealed the disheartening fact that the gentleman, who unhappily will not represent me on
Capitol Hill, had conferred an identical honorific upon every single one of his potential
constituents. I nevertheless treasure the envelope and from time to time regard it wistfully.

for younger sons of those peers stipulated above, with the Christian name. Thus the distinguished occupant of the "Editor's Easy Chair" of *Harper's Magazine* in 1886 unwittingly conferred a peerage upon the father of Winston Churchill when he referred to Lord Randolph Churchill, a younger son of the seventh Duke of Marlborough, as Lord Churchill and to his wife as Lady Churchill (instead of Lady Randolph Churchill).[15] Only recently a learned writer has similarly elevated Lord David Cecil, a younger son of the fourth Marquess of Salisbury, as Lord Cecil.[16] The *Congressional Record* was considerably less gracious to Lord Keynes (i.e., the first Baron Keynes), treating him as a mere younger son by designating him Lord John Maynard Keynes.[17] Newly created peers or men who, like Bertrand Russell, succeed to peerages after they have acquired a reputation in this country are exceptions to Chapman's statement that "the Christian names of peers do not much come into public" (p. 249). A common American practice is simply to prefix Lord to the Christian name, if known, so that Russell becomes Lord Bertrand Russell, as in G. Legman's *Love and Death* (New York, 1949), p. 23.

The American tendency to retain the Christian name is intensified if the peerage name is the same as the surname. Thus, when Russell succeeded his elder brother in 1931, it was difficult to think of him as (informally) Lord Russell and (formally) The Earl Russell. The fact that the title is a surname rather than a territorial designation is here a complicating factor. Had he become the Earl of (say) Trelleck, a complete change of style would have been involved, with the possibility of less confusion, though it is still probable that he would have occasionally been called Lord Bertrand Trelleck in this country. Those acquainted with him as a writer would of course continue, quite justifiably, to refer to him as Bertrand Russell, just as Lord Passfield never ceased to be known as Sidney Webb.

Since the former Lord Louis Mountbatten became a peer in his own right—he was created Viscount Mountbatten in 1946 and Earl Mountbatten the following year—no younger son of a peer has been much in the news. Because of Mountbatten's eminence as Lord Louis Mountbatten, he will doubtless be referred to by that style for many years to come—a contributory factor being the frequent American assumption that, just as "Mr. John Smith" is an expansion of "Mr. Smith," so is "Lord Louis Mountbatten"

15. 72:317. The first reference to Lord Randolph uses the conventional British form, but thereafter he becomes Lord Churchill for short.

16. Margaret M. Bryant, "Current English Forum," *College English*, 11 (1950), 345.

17. Cited by Mencken, "Bulletin on 'Hon.,' " p. 85.

an expansion of "Lord Mountbatten" (his present everyday designation). Conversely, he was frequently "Lord Mountbatten" in American usage before 1946, this style having been felt to be a proper shortening of "Lord Louis Mountbatten."

But despite the present dearth of newsworthy younger sons, many who are peers are, if their Christian names are known, designated by American custom precisely as if they were younger sons. My collectanea include in addition to those already mentioned, Lord Lionel Hastings Ismay,[18] Lord Arthur William Tedder,[19] Lord Josiah Stamp,[20] and a good many others. [*Who's Who in America*, volume 37 (1972–73), has "Lord Kenneth McKenzie Clark," "Lord Hugh Mackintosh Caradon," and "Lord Harold Anthony Caccia," among others.]

On the distaff side comparable misunderstanding prevails. Lady Cavendish[21] for Lady Charles Cavendish (the former Adele Astaire, who married a younger son of the ninth Duke of Devonshire) is the feminine counterpart of Lord Cecil for Lord David Cecil in its implication that its bearer is the wife of a peer. Conversely, the wife of Lord Rothermere is properly— that is, traditionally—Lady Rothermere, but *Time* has referred to her as Lady Ann Rothermere, as if she were the daughter of a duke, a marquess, or an earl (5 June 1950, p. 69). The former Mrs. Clark Gable appears in the news as Lady Sylvia Ashley somewhat less often than as the former Lady Ashley.[22] The latter designation is correct enough though hardly

18. A.P. dispatch in the *Florida Times-Union*, 13 March 1952, p. 1.

19. I.e., as "Tedder, Lord Arthur William" in *Who's Who in America*, vol. 27. This is obviously an editorial revision, like certain other forms to be cited from the same work; it is inconceivable that Lord Tedder could have indicated his style thus.

20. The *Baltimore Evening Sun*, 14 June 1938, reporting the graduation exercises at the Johns Hopkins University, at which Stamp was the speaker and the recipient of an honorary degree. Although the peerage title had only recently been bestowed—Stamp had had a distinguished career as Sir Josiah Stamp—the late President Isaiah Bowman of Johns Hopkins got it right.

21. As in Fred Astaire's biographical sketch in *Who's Who in America*, vol. 25. (Adele Astaire has remarried since the death of Lord Charles Cavendish, hence the omission of the misnomer—if it can be so called in American usage—from later volumes.) According to Deems Taylor, Marcelene Peterson, and Bryant Hale, *A Pictorial History of the Movies* (New York, 1943), Adele Astaire "deserted her career to marry into the British peerage" (p. 285); it is hardly necessary at this point to remind the reader that the son of a peer is not himself a member of the peerage. Jay Kaye, "The Gay Lord of Yogurt," *Pageant*, September 1951, refers to Adele Astaire as "Lady Cavendish, wife of the British nobleman" (p. 53), although according to Palmer's standard *Peerage Law in England* only peers and peeresses are noble.

22. A.P. dispatches in the *Gainesville* (Fla.) *Sun*, 27 May 1951, p. 1; 18 February 1952, p. 6; and 22 April 1952, p. 3. It is true that Louella O. ("Lolly") Parsons refers to her as "the former Lady Ashley," which is accurate enough ("Stars Who Have Cried on My Shoulder,"

necessary for any practical purpose other than to satisfy a democratic craving for noble titles, inasmuch as the lady has remarried several times since she ceased being the wife of Lord Ashley. The *Reader's Digest* of September 1950 refers to Lady Blessington, confidante of Lord Byron, as Lady Marguerite Blessington (p. 138), though she was the wife, not the daughter, of a peer; and Lady Astor, widow of the second Viscount, became Lady Nancy Astor in the A.P. dispatch reporting the death of Lord Astor (30 September 1952).[23] In this connection it is interesting to note that members of the "Ladies Auxiliary Patriarch Militant," a feminine branch of the Odd Fellows, prefix *Lady* indiscriminately to either the Christian name or the surname.[24] The president of the "department association of Florida" (as reported in the *Florida Times-Union* of 18 March 1952, p. 8) is Lady Birdie Cody. I am informed that within the order it is *de rigueur* to address her either as Lady Cody or as Lady Birdie. My own aesthetic preferences would leave me no choice in the matter: I should find the latter form altogether irresistible.

But these are all possible combinations, even though inapplicable to the persons they are intended to designate. Quite impossible, from the point of view of British tradition, are such forms as Earl Bertrand Russell,[25] Viscount Bernard L. Montgomery,[26] Countess Elizabeth Mary Russell,[27]

Modern Screen, December 1951, p. 94). I have found no references to her as, say, Mrs. Douglas Fairbanks, Sr., or Mrs. Clark Gable, without a statement to the effect that she was once Lady (or Lady Sylvia) Ashley: such is the prestige of the noble style in this great democracy.

23. The same style appears on the letterhead of the International Mark Twain Society, of which Lady Astor is an Honorary Vice President.

24. So far as I can discover, there are no fraternal organizations the members of which are called *Lord*. The Masons, however, have a Council of Anointed Kings, each member of which is presumably addressed as *King*, though I have no way of ascertaining this; in the Council there are also princes, along with such plebeian functionaries as a grand captain of the guard, a grand conductor of council, a principal conductor of work, and a grand sentinal [*sic*, according to the *Florida Times-Union* of 16 May 1951, p. 17]. In solemn conclave, the Knights Templars, an order of Masons, call each other "Sir Knight."

25. F. C. S. Schiller, "How is Exactness Possible?" reprinted from his *Our Human Truths* in Irving J. Lee's *The Language of Wisdom and Folly* (New York, 1949), p. 147. The excerpt, it should be said, has nothing to do with exactness in the use of titles of nobility. The same impossible style—impossible unless *Bertrand Russell* were assumed to be a compound peerage title like *Milford Haven*—was used in the U.P. dispatch from Stockholm concerning the awarding of the Nobel Prize to Lord Russell (*Florida Times-Union*, 11 November 1950, p. 1).

26. *New York Times* News Service, in the *Florida Times-Union*, 13 April 1952, p. 1. He is listed in vol. 26 (1950–51) and the current volume (27) of *Who's Who in America* as Field Marshal Viscount Montgomery of Adamier [*sic*, for *Alamein*].

27. *Webster's Biographical Dictionary*, s.v. *Elizabeth*.

and Viscount Louis Francis Albert Victor Nicholas Mountbatten,[28] all culled from American sources. The ultimate in absurdity is probably "Marquess Henry and Marchioness Henry of Coney Island," cited by Carlos J. Videla in his "Newspapers Err in Use of Foreign Titles"[29] as proper alternatives of "the Marquess and Marchioness of Coney Island." Mr. Videla, who was and may still be Latin-American Editor of the North America Newspaper Alliance, is presumably regarded in journalistic circles as something of an authority on the use of foreign titles.

The baronet and the knight are not peers, though, as Mencken observes, "it is almost an everyday occurrence for some people to speak of a knight or a baronet as a peer" (*Supplement One*, p. 558). He cites a New York newspaper headline "Lord Sassoon, Briton, Dies," referring to the late Sir Philip Sassoon. To this may be added "Young Briton in Baronetcy is Perplexed" from the *Florida Times-Union* of 8 April 1951: this article concerns the succession of Lord Ravensworth, who is correctly identified therein as the eighth baron of his line. Kenneth Horan Rogers's review of Angela Thirkell's *Happy Return* in the *Saturday Review* of 27 September 1952, pp. 16–17, refers to Sir Cecil Waring, a character in the book, as Lord Waring, and is quite properly taken to task by a peerage-minded reader from New Orleans, Beryl Donnath, in the issue of the same journal for 1 November 1952 ("Letters to the Editor," p. 23). Says Miss Donnath, with some measure of indignation, "If the review has blessed [Sir Cecil] with a barony due to his wife being called 'Lady,' this is because Lady Cora is the daughter of a duke and therefore entitled to the appendage regardless of her married name," at the same time taking the hapless reviewer to task for speaking of Lord Lufton, a baron, as Lord Ludovic.

Both baronet and knight prefix *Sir* to their Christian names, e.g., Sir Walter Scott, Sir Ralph Richardson, the traditionally permissible shortening being Sir Walter, Sir Ralph. But blunders of the "Sir Scott" type occur fairly frequently, as when the president of a large provincial university formally introduced Sir Josiah (later Lord) Stamp as "Sir Stamp." This is not an isolated boner from the more rarefied reaches of academe: the form "Sir Frobisher" (for Sir Martin Frobisher) occurs in an American reference work to be found in many libraries.[30] The University of Chicago *Maroon*, the campus newspaper, heralded the arrival in this country of

28, *Who's Who in America*, vol. 27 (1952–53). He was created Earl Mountbatten as long ago as 1947, as has been pointed out, but has apparently neglected to apprise the editors of *Who's Who in America* of this new honor.

29. As in n. 9 above.

30. Harry R. Warfel, *American Novelists of Today* (New York, 1951), p. 293.

Sir William and Lady Craigie with the headline "Chicago Welcomes Sir Craigie and Lady Sadie" (cited by Mencken, *Supplement One*, p. 558), but it is most likely that this was the conscious waggery of an undergraduate wit. In *Head of a Traveler* (New York, 1949), by Nicholas Blake (C. Day-Lewis), a rustic refers to Sir Adrian Boult as "Sir Boult" (p. 27). This is, of course, an intentional error on the part of the author, but it indicates that what Chapman calls "a Continental [he might well have added "and American"] error" (p. 252) is altogether possible in England, if only on the lips of the uneducated.

Wives of baronets and knights have no official title other than *Lady*; thus, Lady Scott, Lady Richardson. If there were a Lord Scott, his unfortunate spouse could not be distinguished in ordinary address from the wife of Sir Walter. Very formally, however, the peer's wife would be "The Lady Scott," the baronet's (or knight's) wife merely "Lady Scott." "Lady Walter Scott" would indicate that its bearer was the wife of a younger son styled "Lord Walter Scott"; "Lady Mary Scott" as the designation of a married woman would be proper to the daughter of a duke, a marquess, an earl, or a peeress in her own right who had married a commoner named Scott.[31] The "Lady Sadie" [Craigie] of the *Maroon* headline is therefore preposterous.[32] No such laudable attempt at humor is responsible, however, for "Lady Alice," of an A.P. dispatch of 5 October 1952, referring to the American-born wife of Sir Roger Makins, British ambassador to this country.

Of *Dame*, the title of Dames Grand Cross and Dames Commanders of the Most Excellent Order of the British Empire, Mencken writes, "American reporters, when they have to mention a *dame*, commonly call her *Lady Smith*" (*Supplement One*, p. 560). This usage I have not encountered. It is likely, however, that Americans would be unaware that *Dame*, like *Sir*, is traditionally prefixed to the Christian name. Probably one "Dame" most widely known in this country was the late Dame May Whitty, who was frequently, if not customarily, referred to as "Dame Whitty" rather than correctly as "Dame May."

It is strange that, with all our love of titles of nobility and honor, we should have made so little effort to learn how to use them in the traditional, i.e., "correct" fashion. Mastery of some of the complexities here dealt with is doubtless too much to expect, but certainly the writer for the

31. But this merely skims the surface; see also Chapman, pp. 244–45, where there are such fascinating items as the fact that "Sir Samuel Hoare's wife is Lady Maude Hoare [rather than Lady Hoare] because before her marriage she was Lady Maude Lygon, daughter of Earl Beauchamp."

32. Purely incidental is the fact that the lady's name is Jessie, not Sadie.

Gainesville (Florida) *Sun* of 24 March 1950 might with a minimum of research have done better than to say of the city's new Director of Utilities, "If you should put a monocle in his right eye he might pass for an English duke or marquis, or even a lord for he dresses quietly but neatly." The writer is apparently under the impression that a lord is somehow higher than a duke or a marquis. (Is it also to be inferred that wearing the monocle in the *left* eye would enable the Director to pass for an earl or a viscount, or perhaps even for a baronet provided he dressed quietly but neatly?) Even this is less surprising than Cleveland Amory's statement in *Life* (21 January 1952, p. 92) that the third husband of Arthur Bradley Campbell's mother was the eleventh Marchioness of Huntley—surely one of the rarest matrimonial arrangements of all times. It is nevertheless obvious that, like the tender-hearted Pirates of Penzance, with all our faults we love our house of peers, nor are we unimpressed by baronets, knights, and dames, even though we frequently designate them by a method all our own.

15

Onomastic Individualism in Oklahoma

THE Southwest—Oklahoma in particular, though some of my specimens
come from Texas and other neighboring states—is a land where nomenclature is fanciful, colorful, and sometimes highly imaginative. While such
given names as I shall discuss are not confined to this section, they abound
here in such numbers and on such an indisputably high social level that
they may, I think, be regarded as characteristic of the section. Their patterns
should furnish an interesting sidelight on a certain somewhat restricted
type of linguistic behavior.

I am aware that "made-up" names, which comprise my largest category
(I have collected literally hundreds of specimens in the comparatively short
time that I have been a resident of Oklahoma, and every reading of a
local newspaper brings to light new ones), are to be found in all sections
of the country. H. L. Mencken cites Le Esta, Emavida, and Uretha, among
others, from my own (and his own) native Maryland.[1] It is the frequency
of such given names in the Southwest and their highly reputable social
standing which principally concern me here. The bearers of the names
later to be cited are for the most part personable, highly sophisticated (even
"glamorous") in appearance, scions of families of wealth and position.
Many of the feminine names are borne by young women of my own
acquaintance, students in the University of Oklahoma, who might have
stepped from the pages of *Vogue*, *Harper's Bazaar*, or at the least *Ma-
demoiselle*. "Fancy" names in other sections with which I am acquainted
are usually, though not always (see for example those taken from the New
York Social Register by Mencken), indicative of a lack of sophistication,

1. *The American Language* (4th ed., 1936), p. 522.

144

education, social standing; they are bestowed usually among the under-privileged (to use the fashionable euphemism for 'poor and lowly'), and are due either to a misguided aesthetic sense or to a desire to be somehow distinctive. In the Southwest these facts, as far as their sociological and economic implications are concerned, certainly do not hold true; for instance, among those pledged to national sororities during "rush week" of 1946 are Aletha, Cloa, Conna, Florine, Garalene, Glennes, Ilva, Joella, La Nelle, La Voime, Ludille, Marijo, Minnette, Nil, Olla, Sharna, Uana, and Wil-burta.

I have been confronted with such a wealth of material that systematic search was quite unnecessary. Perhaps my greatest single source has been class admission cards signed by the bearers of the names themselves — those of my own students and the students of some of my colleagues. I have also made some use of commencement programs, yearbooks, the student newspaper (checking where a misprint seemed likely, as it fre-quently did seem), and, in a few instances, the *Norman Transcript* and the Oklahoma City papers. Records in the University Registry Office have also been consulted, but a thoroughgoing examination of these would have resulted in such a mass of material that housing it would have been impos-sible. I have also relied to a very small extent upon information from trustworthy friends. As far as I know, no Negro names are represented. I have also tried to eliminate all Indian names, which would furnish material for a separate study.

Conspicuous by their almost total absence in Oklahoma are such "swank" names as Anthony, Christopher, Geoffrey, Peter, Michael, Stephen, Brenda (although the daughter of a former President of the University of Oklahoma is so named), Cynthia, Moira, Deirdre, and Sylvia. The names Wayne and Duane are very popular for boys,[2] and may well have the same sort of "tone" in Oklahoma as Peter and Michael in the East. Nicknames are likewise very popular; they are presumably bestowed at the baptismal font, since they are signed on the most official of records. Among girls, only slightly less frequent than "fancy" names are "double-barreled" names such as Mary Lou, Betty Jo, and the like. These latter are no doubt attributable to Southern influence, and are felt to be somehow "cute" in a land where juvenility is highly regarded; the nicknames are perhaps due to a desire for easy-going informality—a sort of bonhomie that might conceivably

2. I have no idea why. Perhaps researches into Oklahoma history would divulge the reason. The University of Oklahoma Honor Roll has five Waynes, one Duane out of a total of 409 names (Program, War Memorial Service, 5 May 1946).

pay political dividends in later life.[3] The incongruity of the nickname preceded by hieratic or academic title may well startle the newcomer. The faculty of the University of Oklahoma includes, according to its official catalogue, three Professors Jack, two Professors Joe, a Professor Abe, a Professor Sam, a Professor Gus, and a Professor Margie. The Reverend Bill Alexander, six feet and more of Titian-tressed, eye-dazzling, Hollywood-tailored male pulchritude, is perhaps the most widely publicized man of God in Oklahoma. On the occasion when I was privileged to hear him preach, he was introduced by the Reverend Ray. I have also come upon a Reverend Sam, a Reverend Tommie, and a Reverend Doctor Phil.

"Fancy" names are presumably born of the desire to designate what to parents' eyes is a uniquely beautiful creature—an infant, usually a female infant—by a uniquely beautiful name. Obviously Jane and Mary and Elizabeth are inadequate for a bundle straight from heaven and divinely darling; and so, to fill what is thought to be a real need, NaeAtha, Thellys, and Ladelle are created. The list below, which is highly selective, includes pure root creations and variations of more familiar names. Some have feminine suffixes, or what are felt to be feminine suffixes, in *-dean*, *-elda*, *-elle*, *-etta*, *-ice*, *-ena*, *-ine*, *-eta*, and the like. The prefix *La* is also common, occurring, for instance, in La Verne (also written Laverne), which, though usually feminine, is also occasionally borne by men, and, amazingly, in La Carl and La Don. Some of the names listed show a high degree of ingenuity; others, like Corene, which might have been suggested by Cora plus *ene* (or perhaps by Corinne), are considerably less imaginative. Names to my knowledge borne by men are designated (m.). [See p. 147.]

Perhaps the oddly spelled name is the next best thing to the "fancy" made-up name. What must be the mortification of soul suffered by the Southwestern moppet, incipiently conscious of a tradition of onomastic individualism, upon learning that others bear his or her name! Fortunately, something can be done about this unhappy situation: Earl may make his name *look* more unusual by writing it Irl, or even Yrl, and Lilian may just as easily become Lylyn. Until Miss Bette Davis came along, Bettye was a popular schoolgirl spelling all over the country; now Bette is very widespread and, by analogy, Besse, Nelle, Bobbe, and the like. *Y* for *i*

3. Among candidates for public office in the Oklahoma elections held 5 November 1946 were the following, as taken from the official ballot: Mickey (governor), Mike (congress), Mac (attorney general), Joe (president, state board of agriculture), Jim (commissioner of labor), Buck (commissioner of charities and corrections), Ben (supreme court), Andy (clerk, supreme court), Jo (clerk, supreme court), Sam (assistant mine inspector), two Joes (assistant mine inspectors), Jim (state senate), Dick (county sheriff), Cliff (court clerk), Bernie (state examiner), Toby (district judge).

Adine
Adnell (m.)
Aletrice
Aprienne
Auwilda
Avece
Bevelene
Bronnell
Brunetta
Bytha
Cartha
Chlorine
Cirrelda
Clarill
Cleron (m.)
Coeta
D'Ann (also
	De Ann)
Dathel
Deatha
De Frank (m.)
De Owen (m.)
Dejuana
Delvoris (m.)
Denna Fo
Deroy (m.)
Donavea
Dormilee
Dorweta
Doryle
Eardean
Edale
Estyl
Euris (m.)
Ezella
Flay (m.)
Freedis
Gala

Gathel
Glathu
Ivaleen (sister
	of Kartaleen)
Ivo Amazon (m.)
Janellia
Jedolyn
Jeeta
Jenneth (m.)
Jerean
Jiola
Jodice
Juhree
Jur (m.)
J'Val
La Joy
La Reau
Lavata
La Voice
Lavora
Lazelle
L'Deane
Le Delle
Ling (m.)
Louiezon
Lueverine
Maravon
Mardiece
Medrith
Melva
Mertice
Moita
Moneer (m.)
Mozetta
Maidae
Nathena
Naul (m.)
Nelda

Neleeta
Nodelle
Noveline
Odeal
Odema
Ovetta
Ozella
Phygenia
Predirta
Quilla
Quintelle
Raysal (m.)
Rinda
Rojean
Rulema
Sanjean
Trecil
Twyla
Tyty
Va Anne (also
	Vayann)
Vainna
Valenia
Venrean
VeRee
Veroqua
Virjama
Voline (m.)
Vyrdane
Wadia
Wendaleen
Windell
Wylodean
Yerdith
Zava Roe
Zazzelle
Zefferine
Zerene

or *e* (Jacquelyne, Marye, Helyn) and *k* for *c* (Karol, Kassie) have been
schoolgirl orthographical devices for as long as I can remember. Such
devices are neither new nor distinctively Southwestern except in the high
frequency of their occurrence. Most of the examples which I have collected
are obviously born of the desire to give tone and to confer individuality
in a land where individualism must in these dull days of the common man
perforce confine itself to externals; this desire for nomenclatural distinction
is equally evident in those forms which are simplifications of the conventional spellings (Orval, Ilean) as in those which are elaborations thereof.
Further examples follow: Amanuel, ArLette, Arrendell (m.) (Arundel?),
Bessae, Betty-le, Burndean, Deaune [dwen] (also Duwain, DuWayne,
Dwayne), Dorrace, Dwite, Everette Myrl (m.), Evonne (also Eyvonne),
Gae, Geraldean (also Jeroldine, Jerrelldine), Hurschel Vern (m.), Jayne,
Joean, Lahrue, LeeRoy, Lieonnie Janeal, Loyce, Malcomb, Michieal, Jarita
Pyrl, Safronia, Syble (also Syebelle), Tomme (m.), Virgle, Wanita, Wyl-
lys.

Double names are frequently written solid, and blends, such as Clyola
(from Clyde and Iola, parents), are fairly frequent. The following are a
few of the more colorful of the compounds and blends which I have come
upon: Arahmae, Carolee, Carrifae, Cinnebell, Clairavan (m.), Daisybee,
Dillagene, Doloresanne, Dorthyle (Dorothy Lee?), Ellulyn, Emalu, Em-
majean, Halgene (f.), Henrianna, Inafay, Jimell (m.) (Jim L.?), Joidel,
Junann, Lucynthia, Marada (Mary Ada?), Marialice, Marjeleene, Neljean,
Robbylee, Robray (m.), Winigene (also Winnogene).

Many a girl in these parts bears a name formed somehow (though usually
by the addition of a feminine suffix) from the given name of her father
or a clipped form thereof. This method of naming a female infant may
be indicative of initial disappointment over the sex of the child when a
son has been anticipated or simply of the father's desire that the daughter
be "daddy's girl." The following are some examples of this type of feminine
patronymic, if it may be so called: Bobbette, Charlsie, Davene, Dennisteen,
Donita (d. of J. Don), Earldean, Earlene (also *-ine*), Elmerine, Johniece,
Johnita (d. of Johnny), Leoneita, Lloydene, Orvillyne, Philelle (d. of Rev.
Dr. Phil), Raydene, Rossine, Royleen, Royleta, Tollie (d. of Tol).

The fondness of Southwestern adults for nicknames, clipped forms, and
diminutives has already been referred to. The names listed below have
been taken from official signatures and may be assumed to be baptismal
names; the coupling of hypocoristic with formal, as in Billie Edward and
Teddy Daniel, adds strength to this assumption. To the stranger there is
an element of incongruity, to say the least, when a cowboy-booted six-

footer answers to a name like Bobby Gene or Billy Bob; this incongruity apparently does not occur to the native. The list which follows is, like all preceding lists, highly selective: Arch(ie), Benny, Bett (f.), Billy Joe, Caddie, Cy, Dan Finley, Frankie (m.), Guss [*sic*], Hez, Hi, Ike, Jeddie, Jodie Edgar, Louie Sam, Newt, Ollie, Otey, Sim, Steve Arch, Willie.

The bisexual name, such as Marion and Carol (and Evelyn and Vivian in England), is frequently a source of annoyance and embarrassment to the letter writer, who, if he does not know his ambiguously named correspondent personally, has only a fifty-fifty chance of using the appropriate title of address. In Oklahoma (and no doubt in the Southwest generally) many names are thus interchangeable; Royce may be feminine,[4] June may be masculine. A class admission card frequently fails to disclose the sex of the signer, so that a feminine treble may answer to a surname prefixed by Billie Zach or Tommie Joe, and a booming bass to one prefixed by Doris or Cleo. Among those commissioned as ensigns in the USNR at the University of Oklahoma in 1946 were three stalwarts named Marion Beryl, Beryl Erwin, and Bobby Jean. Frequently a masculine name (usually a hypocoristic form), which is presumably the father's name, is borne as a second name by a girl, as in Betty Bill and Dorothy Jim. I have encountered the following puzzlers in the course of my researches: (masculine) Dixie, Jackie Jo, Jewell, Kay, Louraine, Rae, Sharon Lee; (feminine) Billie Joe, Bob, Danny, Deane, Devereux, Don, Jere, Jimmie, Neville, Newlin, Nigel, Oberon, Vincent.

Such appellations as Babe, Boy, and Sonny do not, it is true, occur so frequently in Oklahoma as in the Southern Highlands, but they are by no means rare in these parts. A Babe and a Boy of my acquaintance are now grandfathers; Sonny was a justice of the peace. Bink is no nickname, but apparently a baptismal name, since its owner formally signed "Bink A. ———." Cyclone was presumably so named because of meteorological conditions prevailing at his nativity. In one way or another, the following, all baptismal names (or their equivalent in churches rejecting infant baptism, which are both numerous and prestigious in the Southwest), seem to have something in common, though it is difficult to say just what: Armadillo (f.), Bat, Boss, Buck, Bud, Buena, Cherie, Cherry, Chuck, Colonel, Delyte, Doe, Dovey, Duke, Echo, Edelweiss, Fairy, Happy, Honey, John the Baptist, Junior, Laddie, Lady Percy (f., from name of favorite uncle), Major, Melody, Pink (m.), Pleasant (m.), Porgie (f.), Sir Maud (m.), Sunshine (f.). Certain combinations are worthy of record because of their

4. This particular name, if it is indeed a family name, may well be due to Southern influence. Cf. Faulkner's Temple Drake.

incongruity: Carlos Elmer, Carlos D'Arcy (McCullough), Olga Juanita, Martha Magdalene (Toot), Mary Marie. The temptation to use Okla and Homa as names (considered equally appropriate to either sex) has been frequently irresistible,[5] and many twins are so named. Similarly, local pride is responsible for Lahoma, the name of three girls of whom I know; there are doubtless many others throughout the state. The use of initials only, as in "R""G" (so written), may indicate a quite understandable, not to say laudable, distaste for the full names; this may also explain AB as the name of a young woman, pronounced [æb], I presume, rather than ['e'bi]. Literary influence is obvious in Kathleen Mavourneen, Ouida, and Trilby, all students in the University of Oklahoma, though chronological considerations make it seem likely that the names were suggested by grandparents.

Unusually frequent of occurrence in Oklahoma, it would seem from the number of examples which have come to my attention, is the combination of names to form a word, a phrase, or even a sentence. The reader may well be skeptical about some of these specimens, but he may be assured that I have discarded all which have been merely reported to me and which I was unable to check. Some of those named are or have been students in the University of Oklahoma. Although a few of these combinations are inadvertent, like Fairy Guy (f.), Modest Fowler (m.), and Virgin Muse (m.), most represent quite conscious jokes on the part of whimsical but misguided parents, like Ima Hogg, the name of the charming and gracious daughter of a former governor of Texas. It has been suggested to me that most of the bearers of jocular names come of families in which infant baptism is not practiced, inasmuch as (it is to be hoped) few clergymen would consent to make a travesty of the sacrament of baptism by bestowing such names in christening. This may well be an explanation of the frequency of such names in Oklahoma, a territory dominated by the Baptist Church and its offshoots, in which the minister need have no part in name-giving. I confess myself incredulous of names like those of the brother and sister Harry and Ophelia Legg, as well as of Pinky Bottom, all reported by trustworthy informants. The names which follow can be completely documented: A. Noble Ladd, Beverage Porter, Birch Rose, Bob Opp, Bob White, Bunker Hill, Charming Fox, Diamond Queen, Earla June Goode, Erie Lake, France Paris (member of Oklahoma State Highway Commission, 1945), Gunga Dean (from Agra, Oklahoma), Harness Upp, Harry Baer,[6]

5. There is to my knowledge an Okla Bobo—a combination of assonances which I believe deserving of the permanence of print. Whether Mr. Bobo has a twin named Homa I do not know. In the interests of euphonious nomenclature, I devoutly hope so.

6. Whether this was intentional I do not know. In a type of American pronunciation current in Oklahoma, *Harry* and *hairy* are homophones.

Hugh Hogg, Icy Day, Ima Foster (twin sister of Ura Foster? Both received the degree of M.Ed. in August, 1943), Ima Fox, Ima Goose, Jack Frost, Johnny Steele Casebeer, Liberty Bond, Mary Gold, Merry English, Pansy Leafe, Pearl Button, Rose Bush, Rose Early, Safety Reuel First, Winter Frost.[7]

Onomastic individualism has apparently become, for the Oklahoman at least, a succedaneum for a broader, more far-reaching individualism of the spirit. Such an independence of spirit was characteristic of his hardy ancestors, whom he tends to idealize; indeed, he goes so far as to think of himself as an individualist; but in truth his individualism has suffered emasculation, and must now manifest itself in such superficialities as cowboy boots, outlandish sects, and the type of given names which are the subject of this paper. Underneath, like so many of his fellow-countrymen all over the Republic, he really hates and fears freedom (except as a subject for political speeches), adores regimentation, and is a staunch adherent of the most extreme "kick-me-harder" school of political thought. He placidly allows his books to be taxed [as do we all today], his appetite for drink to be inhibited, and has in the past tolerated some of the crudest political chicanery, complete with hillbilly music, ever to be witnessed in the Land of the Free. But he preserves the sacred American right to bestow upon his children names which will individualize them wherever they may go.

7. A number of these names are from the collection of my colleague, Professor L. N. Morgan.

16

Bible Belt Onomastics; or, Some Curiosities
of Antipedobaptist Nomenclature

IN 1947 Mrs. Hoyette White, a former teacher and the mother of five fair daughters, graduated from Oklahoma City University. At the same time one of the aforesaid daughters, Norvetta, graduated from Oklahoma A. and M. University with a fine arts degree in piano and voice; a second daughter, Yerdith, graduated from Classen High School in Oklahoma City, where she distinguished herself as a clarinet player in the school band and as a member of the swimming team; a third, Arthetta, finished her work at Wilson grade school; and a fourth, Marlynne, did not graduate from anywhere, but got into the newspaper anyway. Mother Hoyette's fifth daughter, Wilbarine, had already graduated in 1943 from Oklahoma City University and married a man prosaically named John.

Even in Oklahoma such a clutch of euphoniously named females as Hoyette, Norvetta, Yerdith, Arthetta, Marlynne, and Wilbarine seems to have been noteworthy, if not the actual occasion for the newsworthiness of the White family, for the feature writer in the Oklahoma City *Daily Oklahoman* (19 May 1947, p. 1) asks, "Wondering where they got those names?" and goes on to give Mrs. White's explanation:

> When my mother saw I looked so much like my father, she made a girl's name out of the family name Hoyt and called me Hoyette. That started the names.
> When I named my own girls, I wanted names no one had ever had and names nobody would ever want. So I made them up.

On St. Valentine's Day, 1948, Mr. and Mrs. Finis Finch of Oklahoma City had been married almost sixty-eight years. It was evidently the opinion of the feature editor of the same newspaper cited above that this almost incredibly prolonged Darby-and-Joan existence qualified them as authorities on romantic love, and they were accordingly the subjects of an interview by one of the paper's feature writers. The entire family of the Finches at that time included five children, twenty-two grandchildren, thirty-seven great-grandchildren, and four great-great-grandchildren. It is not surprising that the Reverend Mrs. Finch, a preacher in the Holiness Church, had difficulty in remembering some of the children's names. She complained as follows: "They don't use old-fashioned names that are easy to remember. They name them things like Linda and Treva, Mickey Gail and Suevella and—" turning to her husband—"What is Eddie Sue's boy's name?" (14 February 1948, p. 1).

One more illustrative quotation, and then to my muttons. The speaker this time is the eminent Speaker Rayburn of Texas, as reported by Mr. Drew Pearson: "I was named Sam, not Samuel. We don't believe in putting on airs in our family" (*Jacksonville Florida Times-Union*, 16 April 1955, p. 11). [Speaker Rayburn's statement does not accord with the attested fact that his name was originally Samuel Taliaferro Rayburn. T.P.]

Here we may see three leading factors in American name-giving: the desire to be unique, to be fashionable, and to be folksily democratic. We shall encounter yet others as we proceed.

In a youth agreeably misspent *in partibus infidelium*, I was little conscious of the tendencies in name-giving with which I am here concerned. It is true that names which were thought strange or amusing did in those days occasionally come to one's attention, but they were almost invariably cited as curiosa and equated with naivete, inferior social standing, and ignorance. They were more or less sporadic even on the social level at which they were believed most likely to occur and were regarded as the creations of those who led drab and lowly lives—the onomastic *bijouterie* of the underprivileged.

It was not indeed until my translation, fairly late in life, first to the southwestern and later to the southeastern sector of the Bible Belt—in Mencken's classic definition, as utilized by M. M. Mathews in the *Dictionary of Americanisms*, "those parts of the country in which the literal accuracy of the Bible is credited and clergymen who preach it have public influence"—that I first became aware of such names in high places. To what extent the onomastic mores with which I am here concerned have become nationwide I do not really know. Thomas L. Crowell in *American Speech* (23, 1948, 265–72) contributes some very fruity specimens from Washington, a city which has a more or less transient population, and has

collected similar examples in New York City. Mencken also cites a good
many from outside the Bible Belt. It is likely that the isoglosses demarcating
the Fancy Names Belt have by now spread considerably beyond the limits
of the Bible Belt. Two World Wars have brought hosts of antipedobaptists
from the hills to the towns and cities, where their fecundity has shown
no signs of abating. Their places of worship have moved from deserted
stores to gaudy, neon-illuminated erections and, among the more sophisticated, to tabernacles of neo-Gothic and colonial meeting-house architec-
ture. But the moral, social, and ecclesiastical customs of the rural Bethels
linger on, as do also the naming habits of the remoter areas, despite increasing
prosperity, superficial sophistication, and considerable distinction in business, politics, and the professions on the part of many. In the towns of
the inland South and even to a large extent in the cities, the pastors of
these formerly more or less obscure religious bodies[1] have retained much
of the public influence which they and their predecessors had in the hill
country, but unlike the pedobaptist men of God whom they have displaced
in prestige, they exert no influence over the name-giving habits of those
committed to their charge. The naming of Christians is no part of their
ghostly office.

According to the 1958 *World Almanac*, the total Christian church membership in this country is 98,014,954 (excluding the Christian Scientists,
who release no figures). Of these, 26,011,499, or considerably more than
a fourth, do not practice infant baptism. These have their greatest strength
in the inland South. The effect of these circumstances peculiar to our American religious life in the matter of name-giving is obvious. Where name-
giving is no part of the sacrament of baptism, and where consequently a
clergyman with some sense of traditional onomastic decorum has no say,
individual taste and fancy may run riot—and usually do. It is highly unlikely
that any man of God, even though the canons of his church were not
explicit in the matter, would consent in the course of his sacerdotal duties
to confer upon hapless infants such names as Buzz Buzz, Coeta, Merdine,
Aslean, La Void, Arsie, Phalla, and Raz—all legal names borne by Bible
Belters of repute. And it is certain that Ima Hogg, the grande dame of

1. The Baptists were of course never obscure in American life. But there are now, according
to my friend and former student, the Reverend Dr. James Sims, himself a Baptist pastor,
at least 117 other antipedobaptist denominations among the 272 listed in the 1956 *World
Almanac*. (Of still others he was not sure.) The groups most prominent in the inland South,
in addition to the various Baptist bodies, are the Assemblies of God, the Churches of Christ,
the Disciples of Christ, Jehovah's Witnesses, the Churches of God, the Pentecostal Assemblies,
and the Church of the Nazarene.

Houston society, whose father was once governor of Texas, was so named without the connivance of any anointed priest.

One result of the increasing numbers and prestige of antipedobaptists has thus been, ironically enough, the decline of the Christian name in what is certainly the most self-consciously and vocally Christian of all lands, where God's name is minted into the very currency and He runs on all sides of every political campaign. It has also, incidentally, given rise to a new type of urban Christianity, quite unlike anything ever known in Europe and probably never known before even in this nation under God.

The proud bearers of the names which I shall shortly begin to cite are all, unless otherwise specified, Christian Caucasians of good standing in their communities — people of sufficient importance that their engagements, their marriages, their parturitions, and, alas, their deaths are recounted fairly fully on "society" pages and in full-length obituaries in the news-papers,[2] which are a veritable onomastic treasure-trove. Other important sources have been class lists, yearbooks, official lists of voters and of property owners, telephone directories, and commencement programs. These last have provided entertainment and instruction during many commencement addresses by atomic physicists, business executives, industrialists, gen-erals, and presidents of neighboring colleges and universities panting after yet another honorary doctorate to add to their string. Many of my hand-somest specimens were collected under such otherwise depressing circum-stances. It should be obvious that the names culled from these sources are not those of the underprivileged, the economically depressed, or whatever the current term for 'poor and lowly' happens to be. Nor are such names to be regarded as nicknames, since they appear in formal and dignified surroundings — those in the commencement programs being obviously the same as those which appear in Old English calligraphy on diplomas.

The formal and official use of diminutives by adults is quite common in the Belt. The most popular of these diminutives is Billy (with "clear" *l*), usually masculine, though considered perfectly appropriate for women also, with Bobby, Johnny, and Jimmy — also bisexual — running slightly behind. In a single year (1950), no fewer than eighteen Billys, including two Billy Joes, two Billy Genes, and one feminine Billye, received degrees from the University of Oklahoma. In addition, there were four Willies.[3]

2. Among my richest sources are the Oklahoma City *Daily Oklahoman*, the *Norman* (Oklahoma) *Transcript*, the *Jacksonville Florida Times-Union*, and the *Gainesville* (Florida) *Sun*.

3. The preferred spelling of the *W*-form seems to be *Willie* rather than *Willy*.

At the University of Florida in the same year, three Billys graduated from a single college, Business Administration.

So prestigious is Billy, in fact, that one of Florida's representatives in Congress, Hon. Donald Ray Matthews, has adopted the name, using the official style D. R. (Billy) Matthews. It is unlikely that many of his constituents are even aware that *Billy* is merely a nom de guerre. For similar reasons, doubtless, Rev. Billy Graham long ago abandoned the full form of his name, which happens really to be William. ("We don't put on airs in God's family.") Diminutive forms occur frequently in combination with clipped forms, as in the previously mentioned Billy Joe and Billy Gene, and with nonhypocoristic forms, as in Billy Donald, Larry Leroy, and Jerry Roscoe.

I have collected scores of printed instances of diminutives and apparent diminutives used as legal names by adults, some of them adults of advanced years, some recently gone to their Great Reward. Most of these are commonplace enough (like Dannie, Davie, and Maxie), most are bisexual, and some are diminutives by virtue of their endings, without being necessarily derivative. Only Zippie (Mrs. Billy), Sippie, Vandie, Watie, Beadie, Lamie, Collie, Cossie, Ossie, Carlie (Mrs. Bobby), Omie (f.), Fonzy, Lonzie, Lokie, Mammie, Toppy, Mealy, Bussie, Jadie Obie (m.), Nicy, Dicey, Ledgie, Raffie, Dilly, Coarsey, Sugie, Urksey, Skeety, and Ripsie seem to me particularly noteworthy, though I confess to a personal fondness for the comparatively conventional Early Bill and Jody Elijah.

Inasmuch as these diminutive forms occur in the most formal and dignified contexts, usually preceded by honorific, often with no front or middle initial, and sometimes with second name in full form, it is generally safe to assume that they are legal names. Occasionally, however, a newspaper item like "Mr. and Mrs. Bobby ——— are announcing the arrival of a son, Robert Craig" (*Sun*, 13 September 1951, p. 4) leads to a somewhat different conclusion. Perhaps we may infer that the right to use the seemingly less dignified and presumably more "democratic" diminutive form is the father's prerogative. We can hope that, reversing what used to be the normal procedure, young Robert Craig will wax in folksy virtues to such an extent that he too may in time merit the juvenile form of his name which apparently symbolizes complete acceptance by one's fellows. Then he will really "belong."

Nor does the Bible Belt perceive any incongruity in the prefixing of professional, ecclesiastical, or political honorifics to diminutives and apparent diminutives. Dr. Billy and Dr. Lonnie are respected physicians in northern Florida. Dr. J. Ollie,[4] a native of Georgia, is president of a well-heeled antipedobaptist university in southern Florida. Hon. Toby, formerly a judge, is now one of Oklahoma's representatives in Washington. Hon. Jimmie is State Auditor for Arkansas. Hon. Eddie became a member of the Oklahoma State Legislature in an election in which Hon. Billy Joe was defeated despite his onomastic advantage. Hon. Zollie is Texas's Secretary of State. Hon. Charley is a member of the Florida State Senate and a former governor of the state. Hon. Jodie was re-elected chairman of Florida's Jackson County Commission in 1956. The full name of the mayor of Pine Bluff, Arkansas, is Hon. Offie Lites. Rev. Dr. Billy Graham, the most glamorous of the antipedobaptist theologians, has already been alluded to. My collectanea include such lesser luminaries as Rev. Ikie, Rev. Willie Lee, Rev. Woody, Rev. Jimmy, Rev. Tommy, Rev. Johnny, and Rev. Sister Lessie, all entrusted with the cure of souls in northern Florida and southern Georgia, of which northern Florida is, because of its settlement history, a cultural as well as a linguistic extension.

Clipped forms, although lacking the connotations of eternal juvenility possessed by the diminutive forms, are perhaps even more redolent of bonhomie and camaraderie—qualities highly regarded in our democracy. Judging from the contexts in which they occur, these also must be regarded as legal names. The assumption is strengthened by the fact that they are sometimes used in combination with a more formal designation, as in John Bob, Leslie Ike, and Guss [sic] Herbert. I have already cited Congressman Rayburn's statement that in his family to name a child Samuel rather than Sam would have been regarded as putting on airs. Many of Hon. Sam's countrymen would seem to be at one with the Rayburn family. Oklahoma used to be represented in the U.S. Senate by Hon. Josh Lee, who in 1942 failed of re-election. He was opposed in the primary by two other Josh Lees, one a furniture dealer and the other a farmer. The state is now represented in the Senate by Hon. Mike Monroney,[5] and in the House by Hon. Ed and Hon. Tom, along with the aforementioned Hon. Toby. In the same legislative body Texas has, in addition to Hon. Sam Rayburn, Hon. Jim, Hon. Jack, and Hon. Joe. Representing Tennessee are Hon. Joe and Hon. Tom. Georgia, whose Secretary of State is Hon. Zack, is

4. The *J* stands for John. The preference for the style *J. Ollie* to *John O.* may indicate the superior standing of the diminutive, the feeling that John is lacking in distinction, or the prestige in America of an initial letter, preferably *J*, at the beginning of a name.

5. Originally Aylmer Stillwell Monroney and no antipedobaptist, he now uses the style A. S. Mike Monroney.

represented in Congress by Hon. Phil. Similarly with the hieratic title. There is no need to multiply examples; I shall content myself with citing the (doubtless inadvertently) alcoholically named Rev. Dr. Tom Collins (his full name), who is Moderator of the Jacksonville Baptist Association.

The extent to which this ordinary use of what were formerly considered nicknames has gone is indicated by the fact that 190, or more than 10 percent, of the 1,517 June graduates of the University of Oklahoma in 1950 bore names which were diminutives or clipped forms. This figure does not include hypocorisms unconnected etymologically with traditional names, coinages—the sort of "fancy" names to be discussed later—and names which were once regarded as nicknames but have long been commonly used as ordinary legal names, such as Ray, Betty, Harry, Frank, Don, and Bert.

Often a hypocoristic name becomes so closely identified with a person that it is customarily inserted in parentheses after his legal given names or initials. This retention of what in some instances must be bynames acquired in school is by no means confined to the Bible Belt, though it is probably of more frequent occurrence in antipedobaptist civilization than in the Sodoms and Gomorrahs of the Atlantic Coast. I must confess that I was brought up suddenly by the following item from the *Gainesville Sun* (1 October 1952, p. 5): "Friends of Mr. A. W. (Poopy) Roundtree, Sr., will be interested to know that he is recuperating following an operation in Lake City." Similar, if less colorful, specimens, all taken from printed sources, are Tootie, Tucky, Bus, Tiny (male principal of an elementary school), and Lefty. Hon. Juanita (Skeet)——, a former mayor of High Springs, Florida, is now languishing in durance vile at the State Penitentiary for moonshining activities. Hon. E. L. (Tic) Forester is a representative of Georgia in the U.S. Congress. Rev. Charles E. (Stoney) Jackson came into national prominence some time back as a participant in one of the TV quiz shows. Hon. J. Emory (Red) Cross represents his home county in the Florida State Legislature; his hair is not red.

The use of a parenthetical derivative nickname in one's formal style is of course not unusual among popular men, e.g., Hon. W. A. (Bill), the style of a Florida State Senator whose name is actually William. Sometimes, however, a popular man may use a nickname which is derivative from some name other than his own, for example, Hon. Harold L. (Tom) (former Chief Justice of the Florida Supreme Court), Rev. A. A. (Bob), who is pastor of the Ramona Boulevard Baptist Church, Jacksonville, and Rev. H. G. (Pat), who is pastor of a drive-in church, succeeding Rev. Jimmy. Judging by the frequency of their occurrence in such contexts, Pete and

Pat seem to be overwhelming favorites. That the style is not limited to the Bible Belt is indicated by its adoption by the Governor of California, Edmund G. (Pat) Brown.

I am convinced that such forms as Buddy, Bubba, Bud, Buck, Sonny, Bunnie, and Buster, which occur with an almost nauseating frequency, are legal names, not merely alternate names like those cited just previously, since they appear alone in formal connotations without quotation marks. They are frequently preceded by honorifics, as in an account of a reception following a large church wedding at which Mrs. Buddy was "floor hostess" — whatever that is — and Mrs. Buster greeted guests (*Times-Union*, 20 February 1949, p. 11). The ceremony might have been performed either by Rev. Buck or by Rev. Buddy, both of whom are in my files, but I regret to say that it was not. A third-generation Buddy is indicated in "A.O.M. 2-c. Buddy E. C. Kelly III, son of Mrs. Clara Kelly and the late Mr. Buddy E. C. Kelly, Jr."[6] A new trend may be indicated by the fact that a Mr. and Mrs. Buddy named their son Ronald Eugene and a Mr. and Mrs. Sonny named theirs Randy Allen (*Times-Union*, 18 August 1958, p. 22).

Because they share a certain indefinable folksy quality which is highly regarded in the inland South, I have grouped the following names, some of them derivative forms, together; all are borne by substantial citizens: Lum, Dub, Teet, Quince, Zack, Zeph, Zeb, Clem, Wash, and Sim. Had I never been privileged to live in the Bible Belt, I should have thought to this day that their only existence was in the literature of backhouse humor. *Ish*, though it had no previous associations for me, seems to me nevertheless to have the same homely, down-to-earth flavor. It is borne by Hon. Ish W. Brant, Superintendent of Public Instruction of Duval County, Florida (the county seat of which is Jacksonville), who has the additional distinction of being governor of the Florida District of Kiwanis International. When Hon. Ish was merely a candidate for the political office which he now holds with grace and distinction, his campaign slogan was "Ish Is Everybody's Wish." His opponents were Mr. Coke L. Barr and Mrs. Iva Sprinkle.

Many a Bible Belter who is a democrat by conviction boasts a title as given name. Etymologically Leroy, with principal stress on the first syllable in Bible Belt pronunciation, belongs here, but it is doubtful that parents who so name their male offspring are aware of its dynastic meaning. I have collected a Leroy King, and so has Crowell (*American Speech* 23:272), along with Roy King and Leroy Prince. From royalty and the peerage

---

6. This gem appeared in the *Gainesville Sun*. The cutting is in my possession, but I carelessly neglected to take down the date.

come Hon. Czar D. Langston, a high-ranking official of the State of Oklahoma, listed in the current *Who's Who in the South and Southwest*; King Pharaoh (d. *aet.* 65, *Times-Union*, 22 September 1951, p. 3), Queen Adina (d. *aet.* 81, *Times-Union*, 21 August 1951, p. 10), and Queen Victoria, whose surname is Cambridge (*Sun*, 2 July 1958, p. 8); three Princesses; Hon. Prince Preston, U.S. Congressman from Georgia, and Prince Albert, a Floridian whose only distinction known to me other than his name was his involvement in a minor automobile accident (*Sun*, 4 October 1953, p. 12); Regent Gaskin, who is a Master of Education; Rev. Dr. Duke McCall, who is President of the Southern Baptist Theological Seminary; Baron Darvis, a Bachelor of Arts in Education; three Ladies—Lady Grace, Lady Jane, and Lady Percy; and one baronet—or perhaps he is only a knight—Sir Maud. More democratically inclined were the parents of the gentlemen named President (*Sun*, 15 April 1956, p. 26), Electer (*Sun*, 6 May 1958, p. 1), and Chancellor (M.S. in Agriculture, University of Florida, 1951). The family doctor has perhaps been honored in the names of four Docs, one of them a Dr. Doc, whose dissertation subject was "Refinement of an Instrument to Determine Certain of the Working Patterns of School Principals" (Gainesville, Florida, 1956).

The armed services have been a prolific source of names. My collections include General Phillips and Lieutenant Tisdale, who were inducted into the army as privates at Knoxville, Tennessee (*Times-Union*, 11 March 1952, p. 5); Major General Williams, who at the age of 17 enlisted in Birmingham, Alabama, as a member of the Marine Corps, explaining to reporters that his parents decided to name him something "everybody else wasn't" (*Times-Union*, 11 January 1958, p. 17); and General Morgan, who died in Waycross, Georgia, in 1952, survived by a son named Colonel. But it is unnecessary to multiply examples of generals who have never heard the roar of cannon fire; I have many more. I consider General Salor [*sic*] (*Sun*, 24 September 1954, p. 8) and General Ulysses Grant (his full name) who graduated from the University of Florida in 1956 with a B.S. in Education, to be my prize specimens. I pray that General Grant does not encounter discrimination if he is now practicing his chosen profession in the Confederacy. Colonel and Major are also popular, but I have only a single Cap, a single Ensign, a single (aforementioned) Lieutenant, and, it is perhaps needless to say, no Sergeants, Corporals, or Privates. Bishop and Judge occur a number of times, but these are probably family names, particularly the first when borne by nonepiscopalians. Missie Frankie was a first-year student in the University of Florida in 1957–58, and may well now be a sophomore for all I know.

When one has the same surname as a great man or woman, the temptation to confer his or her given name (or names) upon one's offspring—and in the case of the aforementioned General Ulysses Grant, a title as well—is for many Bible Belters practically irresistible. (In the examples which follow I shall of course be required to give surnames.) Enrollment records at the University of Florida since 1900 disclose the fact that its student body has included, as is to be expected, a good many Robert E. Lees, along with a number of Andrew Jacksons and Benjamin Franklins. My researches in the newspapers and telephone directories have brought to light Lon Chaney, Gloria Swanson, Jefferson Davis, Woodrow Wilson, George K. Washington and his daughter Martha, William H. Taft, Dick Whittington, and Josh Billings. When Abe Lincoln of Oklahoma City made a contribution to that city's United Fund, the fact was considered newsworthy by the Associated Press (*Sun*, 4 December 1958, p. 7), but no Oklahoman would consider it anything out of the ordinary, for in that state alone Daniel Boone, Oliver Cromwell, Joe E. Brown, Mae West, Joan Crawford, Brigham Young, Al Jennings, Will Rogers, Huey Long, Jack Dempsey, William Cullen Bryant, and Robert Burns have all aspired to, and some have held, political office. As Secretary of the American Dialect Society, I was always delighted to receive a cheque for the subscription of the University of Texas signed by, of all people, Jesse James, Texas State Treasurer. Bryan Jennings, of Norman, Oklahoma; Lee Grant, formerly of the University of Florida; and De Leon Ponce, late of Jacksonville, Florida, present interesting anomalies.

The practice of naming children after celebrities is of course universal, only the choice of celebrity having any sociological interest. The classical influence is strong in the Bible Belt, e.g., Euclid, Orion, Marcus Tony, Plato, Corydon, Amazon (m.), Addicuss [*sic*], Hanabal [*sic*], Julius Cicero, Virgil Q., Ovid, Solon, and Leda. The French ending *-ous* in Latin names (and Hebrew names which have come to us via Latin) is found in Arelious, Olynthous, Romulous, Julious, Lucious, and the like. Omer and Ector, the French forms used in Middle English times and later replaced in educated usage by the classical forms with *h*, survive in the Southern hills and their settlement areas. Omar, as in the name of General Omar Bradley (b. in Missouri), is no Mahometan name, but merely a spelling of Omer and usually so pronounced. The Book of Books holds its own with Amanuel [*sic*], Jacob, the aforementioned King Pharaoh, John the Baptist, Dorcas, Nazarine [*sic*], Hezikiah [*sic*], Zadok, Hosea, Malachi, Juda, and Lazarous [*sic*]. An Onan who graduated from the University of Oklahoma in 1950 and another of the same name who died in Florida in 1954, aged 74 (*Times-*

Union, 23 January 1954, p. 7), were apparently not named from the ungallant gentleman in the thirty-eighth chapter of Genesis—at least it is to be hoped not; I think it more likely that the name in question is an independent creation of parental fancy.

Belles lettres, the drama, and music are represented in my files by Casanova (b. 1950), Amber, Marteen, two Romeos, Trilby, two Ouidas, Thais, Melba, Orlando, Tiny Tim, Oberon (f.), two Annie Lauries, Ivanhoe Elizabeth, St. Elmo, Kathleen Mavourneen, Tom Mix, Rob Roy, and, strange as its occurrence in a Deep-South Caucasian may seem, Othello. Tommy Tucker, Tom Sawyer, and Buster Brown are the full names of adults. Geographical names include Cuba (and Cubie, which may represent an old-fashioned pronunciation), which I should have supposed to be bisexual, though the two specimens which I have are males; Persia (f.), Savanah [*sic*] (f.), Utah (m.), Arizona (m.), Missoura [*sic*] (f.), and Venice (m.).[7] Botavia [*sic*] and Odessa are probably to be explained as fanciful creations rather than place names.

A number of bisexual names have already been cited. Lee, Pat, Jo(e), Robin, and Lynn are doubtless given to boys and girls indiscriminately all over the country nowadays, and can hardly be considered Bible Belt names. The following names, which are usually feminine or which one would expect to be feminine, are borne by males in the inland South: Paulyne, Pearlie, Delories, Fay, Adell, Ardelle, Ellie, Bonnie, June, Junell, Merrilett Jessie, Loice, Jewell, Bernice (also Burnice), Ivy, Buna Joe, Pink, Jonice, Dixie, Beryl, Nance, Bronzell, Alvine, Nolia, Cledith, Dee, Elizie, Gayle, Rae, Ovida, Jackie Jo, Sam Ella, Laurie, Carman, Verdell, Juadean, Lorraine, Sharon Lee, Amander, Berta, and Euzema, Jr. Conversely, the following apparently masculine names are borne by females: Terry (also -ie, -i), Gil, Stacy, Tracy, Bobbie, Laddie, Mick, Mickie, Ira, Bennie, Benjie, Mackie, Willie, Jimmie, Tommy, Kelley, Nigel, Vincent, Juan, Billie Joe, Danny, Deane, Don, Page, Toni, Maxie, Montez, Nathan, Sandy, Glen, Sammie, and Henri.[8] The popularity of LaVoid and LaVerne, both bisexual, I am totally at a loss to explain. It may be that some of these onomastic reversals of sex may be due to the desire to name a male child after his mother, or a female child after her father. A number of names borne by females are somehow formed from the given name of a male relative, usually the father, e.g., Julie Anne (dau. of Julian), Philelle,

---

7. Crowell, *American Speech*, 23:270, has many more specimens of geographical names used as given names.

8. This last is also cited by Crowell, p. 271, along with other bisexual names which I have not encountered.

Lloydene, Gina (dau. of Gene), Basilene (dau. of Alfred Basil), Charlsie, Dennisteen, Donita (dau. of J. Don), Elmerine, Johnita (dau. of Johnny), Orvillyne, Harolyn (dau. of Harold), and Methadene (dau. of Metha).

When, like Mrs. Hoyette White, quoted at the beginning of this paper, people set out to make up names, they tend to follow certain well-established principles. Pure root creations, some of which will be cited later, are somewhat less common than creations with conventional affixes. Blends and compounds occur fairly often, such as Sherliana, Jamesvee (f., perhaps from James V., father's name?), Beneva (Ben + Eva?), Neldagae, Bettijane, Joashley (m.), Texana, Charlouise, Vickianne, Loiciebelle, Kalynn, Annijane, Alimae, Jimtom (f., civil defense chairman for the Arlington Woman's Club of Jacksonville, *Times-Union*, 24 November 1957, p. 49), Marijac, Marynelle, Marytom, Suellen, JoNez (Joe + Inez?), and Joella. The highly ingenious ChaRu (*Sun*, 16 November 1952, p. 14) is probably a combination of Charles with Ruth or Ruby; in any case, the father's name is Charles. When bisexual Lugene (or Lougene) is a girl's name it is probably a blend of Lou and Gene, both of which are also bisexual. As a boy's name it may possibly be a riming form of Eugene, which is very popular in the South. The opposite tendency occurs in Joe Cephus, Emma Lena, Fitch Gerald, Cad Walder, Do Remus, Cull Pepper, Shir Lee, and Hezzie Kiye.

The riming principle just alluded to doubtless accounts for such curiosities as Jenneth, Jarold Flemuel, Arlysle (f.), Veryl (m., suggested by Beryl, common among Bible Belt males?), Vernice (bisexual), Rinda, Valcom, Dolive, Taura (f.), Burtis, Lurtis, Hertis, Burnest, Bernon, Harl, Bloria, Glennard, Verton, Floyce, Dorma, Derl, Verl, Flarain (m., suggested by bisexual Lorraine?), Lomer, Mevelin, and Delain. Occasionally there may be internal instead of initial change, as in Zenokia, which was almost certainly suggested by Zenobia.

I hasten to cite a few miscellaneous whimsicalities, all full names, which have appealed to me for one reason or another: Oleander Lafayette Fitzgerald III, Ed Ek, Shellie Swilley, Early Hawaiian McKinnon, Sandy Gandy, Earl Curl, Jr., Turkey Curd, Percy Nursey, Rev. Fay de Sha (m.), Lovie Slappey, Esperanza Le Socke, Pamela Gay Day, Staff-Sgt. Mehogany Brewer, Girlie Burns, Fawn Grey Trawick Dunkle, Peter Teeter, Alure Sweat (f., sister of Alfa, Alta, Sabry, and the late Cleveland Sweat, *Times-Union*, 12 February 1958, p. 22), Bloomer Bedenbaugh, Martha Magdalene Toot, Okla Bobo, and Melody Clinkenbeard. The last-cited given name may be bisexual, for a fellow townsman of Miss Clinkenbeard's is Hon. Melody Reynolds, an officer of the Veterans of Foreign Wars in Norman,

Oklahoma. The same bisexuality seems to be characteristic of Memory: Hon. Memory Martin is lieutenant governor of division 6, Florida Kiwanis district, as well as a former school teacher and principal; my files also disclose Memorie Frances Griner, whom I take to be female from the spelling of the second name. Hon. Cowboy Pink Williams, former Lieutenant Governor of Oklahoma, was defeated to succeed himself in 1958 despite a style which should have endeared him to all Southwesterners. It is possible that Cowboy Pink is merely a nom de guerre, but the hon. gentleman is so listed in the 1958 *World Almanac* and in the *Britannica* yearbook.

In the whimsies which follow I omit surnames: Dawn Robin, Kitty Bit, Lance Amorus, Lovely, Charme, Greek (f.), Pearl Garnet, Dimple, Dixie, Pixianne, Cherry, Orchid Favia (f.), Rose Bud, Satire, Fairy (a missionary of the Church of the Nazarene to Africa, *Times-Union*, 26 January 1952, p. 6), Acid, Buzz Buzz, Tyty, Hubert Herbert, Kae Rae, Mary Sunshine, Boysy, Madonna Ruth, Delyte, Doe, Dovey, Echo, Edelweiss, and Brunette (who turned out to be a blonde). The children of Mr. Stanford Bardwell, a realtor and a graduate of Louisiana State University, and his wife Loyola, are Stanford, Jr., Harvard, Princeton, Cornell, Auburn, and the twins Duke and T'lane. When the Bardwells go on holiday they travel in a specially equipped school bus called the "Collegiate Caravan" (*Times-Union*, 29 August 1954, p. 13).

The following combinations of given name and surname represent the conscious, if misguided, humor of parents with no priestly hand to guide or restrain them, though some are doubtless to be attributed simply to parental naivete: Pleasant Weathers, Honey Combs, French Crown, Golden Gamble, Royal Child, Goode Carr, Early Priest, Craven Angel, Robin Starling, Paris Miracle, Young Boozer, Etta Turnipseed, Summer Robbins, Shari Glass, Fannie Bottom, Love Snow (f.), Rocky Mountain, Alto Hooten, Early Wages, Drew Swords, English Piper, and Minor Peeples. Everyone has by now doubtless heard of Dill L. Pickle, of Rolling Fork, Mississippi, who grew up to be a pickle salesman for Paramount Foods, a Louisville concern. Less widely publicized are Never Fail of Oklahoma City, who did fail to graduate from Harding Junior High School in that city (*Sun*, 26 May 1950, p. 7), Dr. Safety First of Tulsa, Oklahoma, and Noe Moore, bailiff during a trial in Gainesville, Florida (*Sun*, 25 February 1959). I have elsewhere recorded Bunker Hill, Charming Fox, Ima Fox, Diamond Queen, France Paris, Jack Frost, Winter Frost, Merry English, Erie Lake, Pinky Bottom, Virgin Muse, and Fairy Guy, among a good many other such jocular and would-be-jocular names (*American Speech*, 23, 1947,

263 [selection 15 of this volume]). It seems to me unlikely that any of these names—and they are legal names, not nicknames—were conferred in the course of administering the sacrament of baptism.

The bulk of my collection comprises what for want of a better term we may call made-up names—many of them root creations, some with prefixes like *Le*, *La*, *De*, and *Du* (used without the slightest reference to gender, as in La Don [m.] and Le Vaughn [f.]) and suffixes like *elda*, *etta*, *eta*, *dean*, *ine*, *ena*, *elle*, and others which usually designate females, though I have some in *ell(e)* which are borne by males.

So that the full beauty of these manifestations of the linguistic fancy of a people unhampered by ecclesiastical or civil authority or by onomastic traditions may be savored, I have arranged a few from my collection in tetrameter couplets. When I began to do this, I expected very little, but what emerged has, it seems to me, a certain poetic quality, along with a certain power of allusiveness in its *Klang*-associations. *Metris causa*—i.e., because I needed a few monosyllables—I have had to include some names which more properly belong in other categories.

1

Yerdith, Virtus, Frow, LaDonna,
Nishie, Alderine, Zollie, Conna;
Garalene, Methalene, Ethelyne, Fal,
Bennilene, Gatsey, Ripsie, Ral.

2

Dolliree, Jetteree, Mauderie, Flem,
Nubit, Wogan, Omria, Kem;
Pheriba, Yuba, Twylah Jo,
Ovidetta, Zava Roe.

3

Leos, Cubie, Dicie, Metha,
Shi, Revonie, Sag, Uretha;
Arsie, Kissie, Bussie, Missie,
Yada, Telka, Clell, Elissie.

4

Ozena, Madula, Oleta, Zippie,
Ozella, Schiley, Florine, Rippie;
Amorus, Onan, Coeta, Pasco,
Reion, Merkin, Jeline, Vasco.

5

Incia, Phenis, Phalla, Icy,
Idlene, Birdene, Ala, Nicy.
Rectus, Dilly, Dally, Nil;
Mosco, Oco, Rumbo, Zill.

6

Stobo, Chlorine, Bamma, Floyce,
Willamane, Voncile, Thair, La Voice;
O'Leita, La Gita, Ludille, La Coy,
Arnetta, Loonis, Fanida, Hoy.

7

Shira, Reva, Terrayne, Aslean,
Etrelle, Mardelle, La Nan, Rudine.
Zazzelle, Glathu, Lavora, Troy,
Colonys, Wylodean, Cy, La Joy.

8

Alfa, Alto, Shyne, Arveta,
Pledger, Mortis, Cance, La Nita;
Anys, Cyrese, Bink, Eloyde,
Verdine, Merdine, Pink, La Void.

9

Raysal, Quintelle, Raz, Zerene,
Estyl, Bytha, Bevelene;
Boysy, Lugen, Lavator, Lake,
Eskaleen, Lueverine, Voline, Flake.

10

La Vada, La Voime, Donrue, La Nelle,
Kartaleen, Avalene, Zan, Jamelle;
Ronalene, Darlene, Denna Fo,
Japnel, Oynel, Wynell, Bo.

11

Vivett, La Carl, La Bruce, La Don,
La Vondus, Burtis, Joette, Lavon;
Zedro, Velpo, Bryna Lee,
Zefferine, Windell, Zim, La Mee.

Pseudodoxia Epidemica Linguistica

17

Linguistics and Pedagogy: The Need
for Conciliation

IT is obvious to the objective student of language that the English language
taught in the classroom is frequently not the same as that observed in the
writings of the masters of English prose and poetry and in the speech of
well-bred, cultivated people. This dichotomy disturbs me; for, as a professor
of English, I foresee that it is going to make the strange race of pedagogues,
to which unkind genes have doomed me, look pretty foolish one of these
days—even more foolish than our paltry compensation already makes us
look to successful men who build bridges and fill teeth—when a sufficiently
large number of our students detect the essential fraudulence of our position
as grammatical dictators. So esoteric have we made our cult that as yet
our pronouncements on English usage are regarded as coming straight from
a linguistic Mount Horeb; but a day of reckoning may come—my worst
nightmare may become a horrible reality: a generation of students may
yet rise against us and ask, "How do you *know* what good English is, if
it isn't the English written in the very books which you recommended to
us?" Well, on second thought, perhaps the possibility is remote, students
being what they are.

Nevertheless, too many of us schoolmarms—I use the term bisexually
and write as one of the family, free to criticize, albeit lovingly and humbly—
would seem to believe in an ideal English language, God-given instead
of shaped and molded by man, somewhere off in a sort of linguistic
stratosphere—a language which nobody actually speaks or writes but toward
whose ineffable standards all should aspire. Some of us, however, have
in our worst moments suspected that writers of handbooks of so-called
"standard English usage" really know no more about what the English

169

language ought to be than those who use it effectively and sometimes beautifully. In truth, I long ago arrived at such a conclusion: frankly, I do not believe that anyone knows what language *ought* to be. What most of the authors of handbooks do know is what they *want* English to be, which does not interest me in the least except as an indication of the love of some professors for absolute and final authority.

When Winston Churchill said "It's me" in a public speech, American schoolteachers were much alarmed. It is true that most "authorities" grudgingly "allow" this locution, hallowed by cultivated usage and found in the most reputable English writing and speech for centuries; but they take care to label it "colloquial," which to all too many of us means "wrong," a judgment which the grudging tone of the "authorities" does nothing to discourage. A letter-writer to *Time* from Brentwood, Tennessee, remarked: "Apparently we have arrived at a point where it is not necessary for . . . anyone . . . to learn the difference between the nominative and accusative cases. . . . Is this perhaps a Churchillian bit of undress in order to gain the approval of the masses?" I might comment that Churchill was almost certainly not departing from the usage of his by no means proletarian ancestors, the dukes of Marlborough. What is significant is that the writer from Brentwood, Tennessee, knew better what constituted "good" English than one of the most effective living users of our language. In truth, if the point of view of this gentleman from Tennessee, which is altogether too typical of teachers of English, were carried to its logical conclusion, we should be required to speak our language in its oldest and most complicated form. At the time when the dual number was going out of use in English because it was troublesome, complicated, and not at all worth preserving, people like our Tennessean no doubt shook their heads sadly and croaked that the English language was going to the dogs; for, in truth, from this point of view all languages, not English only, have always been going to the dogs. When the Old English nominative and accusative cases were leveled, English was going to the dogs; when natural gender superseded grammatical gender, English was going to the dogs; when the distinction between preterit singular and preterit plural was lost in all verbs except *be* (and the folk have lost it here in "you was," "we was," "they was," simply carrying on a tendency which was arrested by the spread of public education), English was going to the dogs. And when the languages derived from Latin lost case endings in the noun even more completely than did English, those languages had gone to the dogs. In fact, from the point of view of the classicist, Vulgar Latin had itself gone to the dogs. But I refuse to fret. I can get along very well without the fine distinctions which the classicist takes such pride in, for instance, those expressed by the subjunctive. The fact that the subjunctive is dead in British English and moribund, despite our misguided efforts to pump blood into it, in American English does not distress me in the least. I never liked to bother with the subjunctive anyway, except as a sort of mental exercise like working anagrams or crossword puzzles. And I see no point in teaching its niceties to freshmen, who will never use it outside the classroom except in a few stereotyped constructions, for the proper management of which their own *Sprachgefühl* will be a sufficient guide.

What these linguistic authoritarians really object to is linguistic change — or, rather, any departure from what they happen to approve on grounds of aesthetic taste or classical tradition or simply whim. Now objecting to linguistic change is like objecting to other facts of our existence: it doesn't get one very far along the road to understanding. Many find the physical facts of birth and death repugnant — in certain circles they are never referred to directly ("when Baby came," "when Father passed away," etc.); and, indeed, certain aspects of both, despite romantic sentimentalization designed to make them more bearable to the human consciousness, *are* shockingly inartistic, to say the least. But there just isn't anything we can do except sentimentalize; and sentimentalism isn't the same thing as facing the facts. It does little good to protest against the law of gravity, however inconvenient it may prove at times; as has been pointed out by an astute commentator on human folly, one doesn't repeal the law by stepping off a cliff, one merely demonstrates it.

Much of our teaching is based on the assumption that everyone ought to talk and write in exactly the same way — that there is a right way and that all departures from it are therefore wrong. For instance, the handbooks are unanimous in condemning colloquial "he don't," "it don't," "she don't." As a matter of fact, many cultivated speakers of southern American English, landed gentlemen and ladies who would grace even an Iowa drawing-room, do employ this contraction of "does not" instead of the more usual (in educated use) "doesn't." (Let it be borne in mind that, when used in the third person singular, "don't" is certainly no contraction of "do not," despite the too easy contention of the handbook-makers that it is.) I trust that no reader will so far misunderstand me as to suppose that I am recommending "he don't" for general American use (as if I could feel qualified to recommend to anyone how he ought to talk); I merely point out that any text that condemns this variant contraction as exclusively uncouth and illiterate is unaware of the facts of language, which I believe even freshmen are mature enough to be taught. There is absolutely no reason for an educated Iowan or Nebraskan to say "he don't"; only let him not suppose that the locution is invariably to be associated with indifference about washing behind the ears.

Not long ago it was my duty to find a longish paragraph—about 350 words—for analysis in a junior English achievement examination. Now in these sorry days of widespread, but only partial, literacy, paragraphs of such length are hard to come by. So I went to the Victorians, settling upon Cardinal Newman, whose usage in my innocence I thought would come up to our standards. I selected tentatively the famous description of a gentleman from *The Idea of a University*, which runs as follows:

> The true gentleman . . . carefully avoids whatever may cause a jar or a jolt in the minds of those with whom he is cast;—all clashing of opinion, or collision of feeling, all restraint, or suspicion, or gloom, or resentment; his great concern being to make every one at their ease and at home.

And at this point I had to throw Cardinal Newman out of my office window. He simply did not write well enough to satisfy undergraduate requirements in an American state university; poor gentleman, he was not aware, as are the authors of every little tuppenny-ha'penny handbook of English usage, that *every one* is always singular and should therefore always be referred to by a singular pronoun. Incidentally, in the section of the aforesaid examination dealing with usage, a colleague had contributed a sentence containing the same "error" to be corrected.

Now it so happens that this particular "error" has been made by the most prominent authors since at least the sixteenth century, not to speak of its decidedly frequent occurrence in cultured speech at the present day. How long, one wonders, does it take for a locution to establish itself as "good"? We could, of course, infer that Jane Austen, De Quincey, Arnold, Newman, and the rest would have written better, or at least more "correctly," had they "taken" English 1 or its equivalent in practically any American university; but it would be a pretty silly inference, I think. As a matter of fact, I believe that a statistical study—I have made none—would show that *they, their*, and *them* refer to *everyone, everybody, no one*, and *nobody* in the masterpieces of recent English literature somewhat more frequently than do *he, his*, and *him*. The painstaking observer of language habits can therefore only wonder whence is derived this favorite rule of the handbook-makers. Perhaps, like Swift's spider, they have spun it out of their own entrails, for it certainly is not based on the usage of the "best speakers and writers," who are, incidentally, not invariably teachers of English. He can only believe that the rule-makers have access to sources of information, above and beyond the corpus of English literature, from which he is debarred — a trunk line to some sort of linguistic Yahweh, maybe.

The honest teacher may well be troubled. He may reach a point where he can no longer condemn a locution simply because some rule-maker, frequently a linguistic illiterate, has blacklisted it. Even if he has no conscience and can therefore be perfectly cynical about the whole business, he still needs to fear for his scholarly reputation every time an observant student shows signs of interest in English literature. Fortunately, students are not as a rule observant of such matters, and they do not read Cardinal Newman any more. Perhaps they are spared "bad grammar" in the literary and elocutionary tinsel of Dr. Lloyd Douglas and Mr. Gabriel Heatter, both of whom have presumably "taken" freshman English. And so the schoolmarm maintains her little sway.

What is "good English"? The rule-makers say it is one thing, and the most prominent writers and speakers lead one to infer that it is something quite different, not at all bound down by thou-shalt-nots. Read the masters, and you will find that, according to the handbook-makers, they write very bad English indeed; for they are frequently unable to distinguish between *who* and *whom*, and they do not even know that *to be* can never take an object.

I pick up one of these handbooks of English usage, copyrighted 1943 (if it were 1949 it would make no difference, since each new text, with the exception of one or two not very widely used because teachers do not find them sufficiently "strict," seems simply to take over the rules and prohibitions of those that have gone before), and I find the following:

"The rules regarding case are arbitrary and are befogged by shifting usages, but they are still on the statute books and the student must attempt to understand them." What statute books? Apparently, books which are closed to the linguist, who supposes in his innocence that the usage of the well-bred and the well-washed, however shifting, must be the criterion.

"Singular pronouns are required for the following singular antecedents: any, anybody, each, each one, either, every, everybody, everyone, nobody, person, sort, type." Required by whom? (Are *anyone* and *no one* exceptions to this rule, or were they merely omitted through inadvertence?)

In a list of principal parts, only *got* is listed as the past participle of *get*, despite the obvious fact — obvious, that is, to anyone with ears and eyes — that *gotten* is very much alive in the English spoken by the best speakers in our country and in that written by our best writers. It is by no means obsolescent, although the handbooks would have us either repudiate the evidence of our ears and eyes or assume that an overwhelming majority of nonacademic speakers and writers and quite a few academic ones (even in departments of English) are using old-fashioned English. Old-fashioned by what standard? As a matter of fact, in many cultured circles "have got" would seem somewhat questionable.

There is the usual warning, repeated from countless predecessors, to "distinguish between the adjectival 'due to' and the adverbial 'because of,' " with the statement that *"due to* should be directly attributable to a noun," a rule which has not had much validity in fact for a great many years.

After all this and much more with which anyone who has "had" freshman English must be perfectly familiar, it seems the height of broadmindedness for the authors to inform us that "a preposition may stand at the end of a clause or a sentence," as in "Whom did you ask for?" which, though certainly correct, still seems somewhat self-conscious: *who* in such a construction has very distinguished precedent, Steele, Lamb, Jane Austen, Conrad, Meredith, Yeats, and Kipling having used it in similar sentences in which only *whom* would meet the requirements set up by English 1.

It is to be feared that the time spent in instilling these rules—which, as I have tried to show, have little validity in fact but are, instead, based upon notions held by writers of handbooks—is utterly wasted. Students may learn to "correct" sentences involving the moribund subjunctive or the distinction between *shall* and *will*, a distinction seldom made in American English (and I am referring to "good," that is, to educated American English); but does any teacher fool himself into believing that these distinctions are carried out of the classroom? No, the moment the bell buzzes, *shall* and the subjunctive are completely abandoned.

I remember an elementary-school teacher with whom I was afflicted a long while past. This worthy man had learned from a book that people— presumably even people from that part of the Atlantic seaboard from which I derive—should pronounce the *h* in such words as *which, why, where, when, wheat, whisper*, etc. He drilled us carefully in this pronunciation, strange to us small descendants of London Englishmen who for generations had not pronounced the *h* in such words, and we docilely learned to pronounce the *h* in his class—and only there. To this day "the baby whales" and "the baby wails" sound exactly alike in my pronunciation, as they do in the pronunciation of many speakers in all parts of the country, cultured and uncultured alike. Speakers of the widespread types of American English which have characteristics of the English of the North of England pronounce the *h* just as naturally as I fail to do so. Who is to say which is "correct"? Incidentally, my son had exactly the same experience as mine at his school in Baltimore, where he had a teacher highly conscious of the supposed social importance of pronouncing the *h;* she had no doubt read about it in a book or had taken a course in "correct" speech, for she was herself a native of those parts and had probably learned laboriously to say [hw] because she thought it more elegant, though not to do so is literally the King's English, as well as Winston Churchill's and Anthony Eden's.

Many teachers, apparently not content merely to teach, believe that they have some sort of divine mission to "improve" the standards of American English. This is a laudable enough ambition. But what shall be our standards, assuming that people of any consequence would submit to such a process of standardization? Are we to accept the rules set up by academic arbiters, worthy people but many of them quite ignorant of the history of the language, most of them teeming with notions of what language *ought* to be, notions derived from heaven knows where? As for myself, I am not likely to; nor have I any desire to dictate how others shall speak and write. Frankly, I have no idea what is best to do for those who are more concerned with "improvement" than with sense, who think that the English language should be more elevated, more "proper," more subservient to eighteenth-century notions of logic than is the English language actually heard in Westminster Abbey, the House of Lords, or the meetings of practically any learned or professional society in our own country.

Any plea for a more realistic approach to English usage is likely to be met with some such question as "How would you like your child to go about using double negatives?"—a question which, incidentally, indicates complete misunderstanding of the point of view of the scientific grammarian. Its answer, I hasten to add, is: "I wouldn't, because the double negative is low; it has no social standing at the present time." For there is nothing "liberal" (in the current sense of that much-abused word) in what has been called the "liberal" point of view toward language. It is essentially aristocratic; the whole thing boils down to fashion, the usage of the well-bred rather than the fiat of the schoolmarm. A Texas millionaire speaks in one way; a Boston Brahmin in another; a Virginia landed gentleman in still another. All are speaking "correct" English, for reasons which, though essentially superficial, perhaps even meretricious from the point of view of sweet, earnest souls, should be obvious. There is no reason why all should speak alike, even if it were possible to make them do so. It is likewise with the doctrine of "correctness" in writing: fashion and good form justify many expressions at present condemned by the handbooks and by the linguistically untrained or unobservant teacher of English. And there is no higher authority, human nature being what it is—not what it perhaps should be—than fashion and good form. The scientific attitude will probably never be generally accepted because it is too difficult—much more difficult than learning a set of grammatical rules and then proceeding to make others learn them. Clarity, unity, straight thinking, organization, are all more important, I am sure, than the avoidance of *due to* as a preposition, the distinction between *shall* and *will*, and the uses of the subjunctive—and, incidentally, much harder to teach.

Because he has refused to proscribe what he knows from his own observation, supplemented by the painstaking research of more than a generation of scholars such as Otto Jespersen and Henry Cecil Wyld, to be perfectly reputable usage, it has been said that the scientific student of language has no standards. On the contrary, he has very high standards indeed—standards not based upon what someone thinks ought to be but derived from the practice of the best writers and speakers; standards which are frequently at variance with those set up by the prescriptive grammarians, the writers of handbooks, and the teachers, who, incidentally, would in all innocence maintain that they were simply following the "best usage," as if that could be done by refusing to admit the reality of linguistic change, by holding fast to a conception of language whose principal tenet would seem to be that practically any change which has occurred since circa 1700 (for the authoritarian grammarian is usually not conscious of what took place before that date) is to be regarded as deterioration and corruption. His standards are, I fear, frequently "undemocratic"; for, being a realist in this respect at least, he does not assume that schooling will make a gentleman or even that it can confer that air of well-bred ease which is by long tradition recognized as culture; rather, that the first business of education is the acquirement of knowledge and the learning how to deal with it. He is unwilling to assume, however flattering the assumption may be to him, that the potpourri of rules, regulations, and prescriptions cooked up by his guild of academic chefs has any relation to knowledge or, for that matter, that it has any real validity. He is, as the late H. W. Fowler has so neatly put it, "neither on the side of the angels (university professors, that is) nor on the side of the devil (who is the nearest vulgarian)" but takes his stand "with the ordinary (or lazy but civilized) human being." He makes no pretense of knowing better how the English language should be written or spoken than those who have written it and spoken it effectively, gracefully, powerfully; who have wielded it to great purpose with sincerity, clarity, lucidity. He is content to observe, putting his own aesthetic preferences aside, and to induce his rules—if, indeed, he is interested in rules as such at all—from the actual usage of these writers and speakers. He knows that he is merely hampering the process of communication so long as in the classroom he is expected to stress the singularness of *everyone* and the evil of the dangling participle, even when unambiguous, above sound learning, straightforward thinking, and effectiveness of expression— desiderata unlikely to be achieved by means of the current conception of an English language that never was on sea or land, a language which those responsible for the glories of English literature *ought* to have written but which, unfortunately for the best-laid plans of prescriptive teachers, they seldom bothered to write.

18

The Role of Historical Linguistics

IF we are to assess properly the tremendous advances of the nineteenth century in linguistic studies, it is necessary that we have some notion of what had gone immediately before. In the eighteenth century, and beginning somewhat earlier, writers on language were for the most part concerned with regularizing and "ascertaining." Their meaning of the latter word becomes clear to us if we stress its second rather than its third syllable. They believed in a "universal grammar" which postulated that all languages were governed by the same principles and that these principles were rooted in nature itself. These were notions which would have been completely dispelled by a study of exotic languages, but such study was far in the future. Inasmuch as nature seemed to them logical—that is, from their point of view, orderly, for as Pope put it, "Order is Heaven's first law" — they believed that grammar ought also to be. All of us would of course agree that language has orderly patterns, but they are not what the eighteenth-century writers on the subject were concerned with. By *orderly* they seem to have meant 'consistent' according to their more or less arbitrary definition, which was usually based on the preconceived notion of a relationship between language and nature.

Such notions went hand in glove with the general belief that language was of divine origin and hence in its beginnings perfect, but that it embarked upon a long process of deterioration as soon as man, ungoverned by reason and logic as he was likely to be, began to use it. The grammarians deemed it necessary to slow down this degeneration; they felt that it was their bounden duty to gain for themselves acceptance as authorities on what ought to be, and thus to keep language in line, lest it degenerate, presumably, into a few grunts and groans, or even into a single grunt. It apparently never occurred to anyone that the English language, to cite only one, had got along rather well in the course of eleven or so centuries, producing some decidedly superior literature along the way, without any regulation other than that of usage.

In any case, "governing principles" were formulated, and out of these grew a body of "rules" pretty much the same as those we encounter today in some of our freshman handbooks, as well as in practically all non-academic guides to "good English" offered for sale to the insecure; they are also the stock in trade of newspaper columns devoted to the subject of English usage. These rules grew for the most part out of arbitrary appeals to philosophical principles—logic, analogy, "reason"—made in order to settle matters on which usage was divided.

Those who attempted to write authoritatively about language—and we are here concerned specifically with those who wrote about the English language—had very few genuine qualifications for doing so, though it must be said that most of them were polished and urbane men with an acquaintance with Latin and its literature (and to a considerably smaller degree with Greek) which is nowadays regrettably rare. They were not, however, given to observing and recording, but rather to legislating. With their minds all made up about governing principles, they could blithely assume, as did Jonathan Swift, that most of the "best writers of our age" committed solecism after solecism. Except for their native tongue, they were little concerned with modern languages.

Probably the most successful of the eighteenth-century linguistic solons was Robert Lowth, a distinguished and scholarly clergyman who in 1762 published *A Short Introduction to English Grammar*, a work in which he wholeheartedly agreed with Dean Swift's earlier charges in his *Proposal for Correcting, Improving, and Ascertaining the English Tongue* (1712) that "our language is extremely imperfect" and that "it offends against every part of grammar," whatever that could have meant. Elegant people in eighteenth-century drawing rooms doubtless couldn't have cared less, and went on talking as they had always done. Nevertheless, Lowth's book was enormously successful; its preeminence remained unthreatened until Lindley Murray, a well-to-do American lawyer who had emigrated to Yorkshire, published in 1795 his *Grammar of the English Language*, a work along much the same lines as Lowth's. Murray's grammar, like Lowth's, went through many editions. Amusingly enough, it was originally prepared to teach young Quaker girls, to all intents and purposes cloistered in a Friends' school in York, how men of fashion spoke their native language. Though something of a magnifico in Yorkshire, Murray was himself a

Quaker. One cannot help wondering just how extensive or intimate his contacts with high life really were, for nonconformists were less gladly tolerated in English society then than now. In any event, his work became the standard textbook for half a century in both English and American schools.

In the early years of the nineteenth century certain brilliantly gifted men in the northern part of Europe—notably the Dane Rasmus Christian Rask, born in the very year of Bishop Lowth's death, and the Germans Jacob Grimm and Franz Bopp—began to investigate language without preconception or prejudice. Language itself was what they were interested in— the way people had talked in the past, as well as the way they themselves and their contemporaries talked. It is nevertheless quite true, as Kemp Malone has pointed out in his MHRA presidential address, "The Rise of Modern Philology" (1958), that the early Indo-Europeanists were interested in modern languages and literatures primarily for the light which they threw upon Indo-European antiquity—a period far more remote even than classical antiquity. According to Malone, "the faith was strong in those days that by such investigations we could . . . reach the very cradle of our culture."

Thus began the systematic study of medieval documents in Gothic, Icelandic, German, and English, by means of which we are able to reconstruct their common original, Germanic. Making use of correspondences of sound and structure in various languages, the pioneers of linguistic study were able to demonstrate what no informed person has since doubted, but which was earlier only dimly sensed if it was sensed at all: the relationship through common origin of Indian, Iranian, and practically all of the languages spoken in Europe (Finnish, Hungarian, and Turkish are the most important exceptions). This exciting hypothesis had been clearly, if of necessity somewhat incompletely, enunciated in 1786 by Sir William Jones, an English jurist stationed in Calcutta, who had studied Sanskrit because he had the good sense to realize the importance of knowing the language of the Hindu legal writings. In a paper read before the Bengal Asiatic Society, which he himself had founded, Jones made his famous statement regarding the "affinity" of Sanskrit to Greek and Latin, going on to say that there was good reason to suppose that a similar relationship existed regarding Germanic (or, as he called it, "Gothick") and Celtic.

Thus also began a truly disciplined, hence scientific, study of language. The early investigators, like those who followed them, permitted themselves no notions about how people *ought* to talk; they were in fact not in the least concerned with prescribing. Grimm was, as everybody knows, a folklorist; hence it is not surprising that in his *Deutsche Grammatik*, the second and more important edition of which appeared in 1822, he was not primarily concerned with what were thought of as the standard or literary forms of the Germanic languages. Faced with a fascinating body of evidence in older writings in the Germanic languages, the scholars of the early nineteenth century had little time for the kind of petit-bourgeois quasi-philosophical idealism about language which had previously seemed of such moment. The eighteenth-century grammarians can hardly be blamed, however, for not being modern linguists, inasmuch as their magisterial attitudes had been assumed in a period which, as far as language is concerned, we may regard as comparable to the pre-Copernican era in cosmology. It is less easy to exculpate Noah Webster, who, though considerably older than Rask, Grimm, and Bopp, was a vigorous sexagenarian at the time of the publication of Grimm's germinal work, with more than a score of bustling years ahead of him. Little concerned with what was going on in the German and Scandinavian Sodoms and Gomorrahs, he continued to accept the Biblical story of the Tower of Babel as a satisfactory explanation of the diversity of tongues and hence derived all languages from "Chaldee," or Biblical Aramaic.

Quite aside from the intrinsic importance of their researches—for Rask and Grimm showed abundantly clearly the relationship of the Germanic languages to other languages of what we now consider the Indo-European group, at the same time demonstrating the regularity of sound changes, and Bopp's further comparative studies added still other languages to the group—this first generation of historical and comparative linguists directed attention to the importance of the objective observation of language, in striking contrast to the vaporings of the eighteenth-century worthies, who really knew very little about language but had their minds all made up anyhow. The rigorous methods of Rask, Grimm, and Bopp put the historical and comparative study of language on its feet and set the tone for what was to follow.

This very earliest productive study of language as such provided in the course of the nineteenth century a more accurate description and appraisal of its phenomena than had ever before been available. Much of what we regard as of the first importance in current linguistic study was clearly perceived by the giants in those days, who were greatly concerned with linguistic structural patterns as these were discernible in the highly systematic way in which they observed sound shifts. Though they may not have enunciated every single one of them specifically, by precept and practice they laid down those general principles on which all subsequent linguistic study has been based. Furthermore, largely out of the accurate description of vernacular languages in early stages of development, which was so important a part of the historico-comparative discipline, came the urge to describe and analyze with equal accuracy later and even current stages.

A historical grammar of a language is in effect but a consecutive and concatenated set of descriptive grammars of that language. It is thus impossible to regard historical (diachronic) studies and descriptive (synchronic) studies as mutually exclusive. The latter have been, in a broad sense of the term, to a great extent the task of our own century.

Those who have done significant work in the study of modern English, which will be our principal concern from now on, have not always been native speakers of it; German, Dutch, and Scandinavian scholars have played a distinguished role. One of the most distinguished and influential pioneers in such studies was Henry Sweet, the unhappy prototype of George Bernard Shaw's Professor Henry Higgins in *Pygmalion*. Most of the work of Sweet, who did not in the least resemble either the late Leslie Howard or Rex Harrison, has held up amazingly well, considering the fact that he died as long ago as 1912. He may with a good deal of justice be regarded as the principal founder of modern phonetics, though he touched upon every phase of linguistic science, historical as well as descriptive; in his most widely known work, the two-volume *New English Grammar* (1900–1903), fewer than a hundred pages are devoted to phonology.

Another Englishman, Henry Cecil Wyld, is the author of *A History of Modern Colloquial English*, first published in 1920 with a third revised edition in 1936; this is still a work of great importance to the student. Wyld also wrote *A Short History of English*, first published in 1914, and was editor of the *Universal Dictionary of the English Language* (1932).

Though begun long before, the greater part of the *New English Dictionary on Historical Principles*, the most complete lexical record of a language in existence, first appeared in the twentieth century. Of great importance to the study of English has been the work of the Danish Anglicist Otto Jespersen, particularly his monumental seven-volume *Modern English Grammar on Historical Principles* (1909–49). Jespersen is best known for a semipopular book *Growth and Structure of the English Language*, first published in 1905. It has gone through many editions and is still readily available. It is not surprising that some of the notions expressed in this book, particularly in its opening chapter, are now outmoded. Jespersen's formative period, dominated ideologically by evolutionary doctrine, plus his daring, imagination, and philosophical turn of mind, led him into occasional fallacies; nevertheless, he is always stimulating to read, and no undergraduate has been led far astray by doing so.

In the same tradition as the *New English Dictionary*, nowadays increasingly called by its new title (1933) the *Oxford English Dictionary* (or the *OED*), is the *Dictionary of American English* (1938–44). In the study of American English, H. L. Mencken's *The American Language*, the first edition of which appeared in 1919, and George Philip Krapp's *The English Language in America* (1925) must be regarded as important pioneering works. The concern with spoken in contrast to literary forms which was engendered by the study of historical linguistics is reflected, as far as American English is concerned, in the publications of the American Dialect Society (*Dialect Notes*, 1890–1939; *Publication of the American Dialect Society*, 1944–), in the periodical *American Speech* (1925–), and in the Linguistic Atlas of the United States and Canada, work on which began in 1931. The Linguistic Society of America, founded in 1924, in its journal *Language* has published many articles dealing with Indo-European historical linguistics, some of which have been primarily concerned with the English language.

Such were some of the more important materials available for the scholarly study of the English language up to about the time of the publication of Leonard Bloomfield's *Language* in 1933. In this book Bloomfield, who had been thoroughly schooled in the historico-comparative discipline, laid a foundation for much of the work done subsequently in American linguistic studies, and in particular for that done by those who are by special designation structural linguists.

In advanced English studies, what with the comparatively recent emphasis on later periods, including the contemporary period, the older requirement of Gothic and Icelandic for all students working toward the doctorate has generally gone by the board. It is, however, obviously impossible to read our older literature unless one has a fair knowledge of forms of the language no longer current, or in some instances current only in dialectal usage. Hence the usual requirement of courses in Old English and Middle English still imposed upon all students by most graduate departments of English in addition to the more or less sweeping survey of the history of the English language required of, or at least strongly recommended to, advanced undergraduate English majors or beginning graduate students, some of whom enter graduate school knowing no more of Grimm's Law than of Gresham's.

To have to pass up *Beowulf* altogether save in translation and to understand *Sir Gawain and the Green Knight*, *Piers Plowman*, and even the seemingly more "modern" works of Chaucer only dimly is surely a woeful penalty for not knowing the earlier forms of the English language. Without the insights into change of meaning which even a modicum of training in historical linguistics inculcates, the student of literature is likely to miss — in fact, alas, frequently does miss — what so comparatively recent a writer as Shakespeare intended by even everyday words such as adverbial *still* in "We still have known thee for a holy man" (*Romeo and Juliet* 5.3.270) and "Pardon is still the nurse of second woe" (*Measure for Measure* 2.1.298), let alone such comparatively bookish loanwords as *admiration* in "This admiration, sir, is much o' the savour / Of other your new pranks" (*King Lear* 1.4.258) and *questionable* in "Thou com'st in such a questionable shape / That I will speak to thee" (*Hamlet* 1.4.43). Quite aside from the fact that such rimes as *defeat:great* and *love:move* will seem "bad" to him, ignorance of the pronunciation of this early modern period will cause him to miss a good many plays upon words of varying brilliance and bawdiness, which frequently throw light on the mores of Elizabethan life as well as on a by no means negligible aspect of the mind and art of our greatest writer.

The historically trained linguist is by virtue of his specialized learning bound to be tolerant of the supposed blunders of unsophisticated speakers, while realizing perfectly well that the sole criterion for determining the status of a given linguistic form at a given time is, as it has ever been, current usage. The fact that such a form as Chaucer's "is went" (as in *Troilus* 5.546 and elsewhere) once had high status is just as irrelevant as far as current usage is concerned as the eighteenth-century appeals to logic, reason, nature, or Latin grammar in defense of whatever construction the "authority" was attempting to legislate. (Then as now authorities did not always agree.) He is equally cognizant and perhaps, depending upon his individual temperament, somewhat less tolerant of the errors of the pseudo-learned born of pretense and presumption, even though these may have become standard.

To put it another way, he is unwilling, reprehensible as it may seem to his critics, to accept the easy assumption of the amateur arbiter that there is anything intrinsically erroneous, or un-English, about a good many grammatical forms eschewed for one reason or another by all educated speakers of current English, like the multiple negative construction in Chaucer's "For-why to tellen nas nat his entente / To nevere no man" (*Troilus* 1.738–39), or by most such speakers, like third-person *don't*. (The latter construction, though now somewhat old-fashioned, occurs frequently in the usage of fashionable speakers in the works of writers so recent as Shaw and W. S. Gilbert.) He is aware that such a form as *ax* 'inquire, request,' widely current among the "underprivileged" of the

American South, is not to be regarded as a bumbling mispronunciation of
ask, but as a variant form occurring in cultivated usage until well into the
sixteenth century, as in the Coverdale Bible's rendition of Matthew 7.7
as "Axe & it shalbe giuen you." Those who continue to use this variant
are not through ineptitude distorting the standard form; rather, they are
employing a perfectly sound traditional form which went underground, so
to speak, a good many years ago. In fact, as the historically trained linguist
knows very well, those usages of the folk which diverge from standard
speech—leaving out of the question the malapropisms which inevitably
occur when "bookish" language is attempted by unsophisticated people—
are almost invariably traditional in that they reflect the fashions in language
of an earlier period. Strangely enough, such information is sometimes
regarded as subversive by otherwise educated people, perhaps because of
a general inability to comprehend that a statement of a grammatical fact
does not constitute either an endorsement or a condemnation of that fact.
It is certain that this inability is a hangover from the prescientific magisterial
attitudes of writers about language.

In any case, when the historical linguist becomes involved, as he almost
inevitably does, in controversies over what is "good English" and what
is "bad," his disinterested, or at best highly conservative, attitude is
practically always misunderstood, not only by the general public but
frequently, if he happens to be a member of a department of English, by
those of his own literary colleagues who have forgotten, or more likely
insufficiently learned, what should have been obvious from their minimal
training in historical linguistics. He is stigmatized as a "liberal" (a smear-
word nowadays in this particular context), as "permissive," as one who
"has no standards," all because he conceives it to be his primary function
to record, study, and, if he is lucky, to make some significant comment
on the facts of linguistic change.

Later studies which have little or no direct concern with historico-
comparative linguistics have contributed vastly to our understanding of
language *qua* communication and will in time, it is hoped, become inte-
grated into the teaching of the schools. Ideally, however, those scholars
who are concerned primarily with the ways in which language signals,
transforms, or generates need have no direct concern with the Tweedledee-
Tweedledum decisions regarding usage over which only very recently so
many reviewers of and commentators upon *Webster's Third* have exercised
themselves, usually in ignorance of the principles and the materials for
judgment which have been laid out for us by older scholars in the historical
tradition. But it is obvious from the spate of misleading and badly informed

19

English Usage: The Views of the Literati

THERE are few touchier subjects in the world than English usage. Those who think about it at all, if they are not professional linguists, are likely to feel almost as strongly about it as they do about God and the American Way of Life; and even a few professionals are from time to time subject to states of incalescence induced by what one would expect to be, after all, only their bread and butter. The lay observer, who may be, and nowadays frequently is, otherwise well educated, almost invariably fancies himself competent to make *ex cathedra* pronouncements concerning the speech which he speaks, writes, reads, and listens to almost constantly. Most professional students of language, by the time they have acquired a modicum of maturity, have learned not to question such pronouncements when they occur, as they often do, in ordinary social contexts. There is no more effective way of losing friends and alienating people than by knowing more about language than they do, particularly the language which they themselves speak and write. It is the better part of wisdom under such circumstances to avoid the subject as one would avoid religion, politics, and the cozier aspects of sex.

But occasionally one slips up, as even the late, great Leonard Bloomfield did upon being informed by a "physician of good general background and education" that the Chippewa language had only a few hundred words. The doctor had acquired this information from a Chippewa Indian hunting guide, who really ought to have known, since his ancestors had almost certainly spoken the language fluently. Bloomfield, who, as everyone knows, was a distinguished student of American Indian languages, tried—to use his own ironic choice of words—"to state the diagnostic setting," whereupon the physician "briefly and with signs of displeasure repeated his statement and then turned his back to me. A third person, observing this discourtesy, explained that I had some experience of the language in question. This information had no effect."[1] One wonders how the doctor of the story would have responded to a layman's diagnosis of some illness or other which might have been afflicting him—for it is a fact within my own sad experience that the medical diagnoses of laymen are just about as likely to be wrong as the linguistic lore of doctors. Without specialized training it is quite easy to diagnose influenza as poliomyelitis and vice versa; the fact is that I have been guilty of doing both.

Seldom does the lay linguist, who may incidentally be quite a distinguished writer, have any sort of rationale. "Good English" may be, from his point of view, quite easy of attainment, since it involves only the consistent avoidance of certain *pro*scribed constructions—split infinitives, dangling modifiers, terminal prepositions, and the like—and the consistent employment of certain *pre*scribed ones: the supposedly proper *shall-will* distinction, "the reason is that" rather than the somewhat commoner and more idiomatic "the reason is because," and the like. This is very democratic, in that it puts good speech within the reach of every man intelligent enough to master a few simple rules. It becomes even easier in view of the patent fact that many who sit in judgment on the speech of their neighbors are addicted to only a few such prescriptions; they have usually forgotten the others learned in high school and in English 1. What they have remembered, however, furnishes a bludgeon with which to belabor those who in their opinion use "bad English." In other words, not every *only*-snooper—to use Sir Ernest Gowers's apt phrase for those who set out to pillory every instance of what they suppose to be a misplaced *only*—is also a split-infinitive sleuth; and many a *due to* bloodhound is quite impervious to the supposed bad grammar of split infinitives—he may in fact split them wide open himself without being aware of any relapse from the strictest principles of linguistic hygiene. As I have pointed out elsewhere,[2] C. S. Forester characterizes as a vulgar fellow a certain copy writer to whom "split infinitives and 'different to's' mean nothing," but himself uses in the same novel[3] "cannot help but" (p. 124), "Everyone . . . fidgeted in their chairs" (p. 127), and "why his voice changed was because he was not at all sure

1. "Secondary and Tertiary Responses to Language," *Language*, 20 (1944), 49.
2. *The Origins and Development of the English Language* (New York, 1964), p. 244 [2d edition (1971), p. 257].
3. *Plain Murder* (London, 1951), p. 102. (First published in 1930.)

that [his decision] was a wise one" (p.151)—all constructions which are stigmatized by school grammars and handbooks of good English.

Indeed the lay linguist—and those who are themselves writers are naturally likely to be more vociferous than the less articulate—is quite likely to deliver jeremiads over his particular linguistic *bête noire*, like the well-known diatribe of Professor Sheridan Baker in *College English*[4] against a harmless and historically quite respectable contraction of *am not* which is to him an especially dirty four-letter word. Attitudes toward language being thus permeated—and they usually are—with the same sort of emotionalism as pertains naturally to God, the home, the American mother, and the flag, it has become practically impossible for the professional observer of language to make a factual statement about a given locution without its being misunderstood as either a recommendation or, less frequently, a condemnation of the locution in question. In the opinion of so brilliant a scholar and writer as Professor John Nash Douglas Bush, those of us who do so belong to "a tribe of linguistic scholars who proclaim that there is no such thing as good or bad English: whatever is used is right," going on to say that "this ultra-democratic gospel was supported a few years ago by a new edition of Webster; there were some persons who vehemently denounced the abandonment of any standard, but their voices did not carry very far"—which seems to me to be the prize understatement of the year.[5] If the linguist so much as points out that "he, she, it don't" occurs quite frequently in the speech of cultivated speakers in the works of George Bernard Shaw, W. S. Gilbert, and other writers of an earlier period, this is taken as indicating a conviction on his part that present-day schoolchildren should be indoctrinated and drilled in the use of third-person singular *don't*. Actually, the student of usage is quite cognizant of the widespread unreasoning prejudice against this alternate contraction of *does not*, and merely intends to make the point that, though now old-fashioned, the form cannot be considered "bad English."

It is obvious from a good many pronouncements on language scattered throughout his *The Last Puritan* (New York, 1936) that even so sophisticated and learned a writer as George Santayana gave himself a good deal of concern over purity and impurity as linguistic characteristics. There is,

4. "The Error of *Ain't*," 26 (1964), 91–104.
5. From a commencement address entitled "This Is Worth Fighting For" delivered at Marlboro College in Vermont and reprinted in the *Chicago Daily News*, "Panorama," 6 August 1966. The friend who furnished me with the clipping unfortunately did not note the page number.

for instance, Dr. Peter Alden's wish that his son's English should be "fundamentally pure"; he goes on to say: "Did it ever strike you how little we are affected by the servants' way of talking, though we hear it every day of our lives? It's because we recognize it for a dialect apart, which is not our own. That's the way anyone to whom good English is natural must regard the common speech of the day" (p. 80).

In other words, Dr. Alden, whose linguistic judgments can fairly be taken to reflect those of his distinguished creator, believed that educated speech was pure, common speech impure. If *pure* means 'conservative, uncontaminated,' as I take it to mean here rather than being merely an endorsement of the type of speech Dr. Alden (and Santayana) happened to prefer, then it is noteworthy that from the point of view of the historical linguist precisely the opposite is true. For the folk, if they but knew the facts and were in the least interested in defending themselves from the charge of having messed up the language by adding supposed impurities of one sort or another—a charge which most of them would doubtless humbly accept as true—might with a good deal of reason point out that they have retained many characteristics of the earlier and presumably "pure" English of Alfred, Chaucer, Shakespeare, and Milton which we who speak the current Standard have lost. Every student of dialect is well aware of the fact that the folk have made very few innovations, and that it is the taboo against nonstandard constructions which is usually the innovation rather than the constructions themselves.

Subservience to, or at least faith in, the traditional school discipline in English is a very notable and potent characteristic of American English. Teacher knows best in such matters as correct grammar, though she may be regarded as a complete booby and a crashing bore in all other departments. Witness this statement of J. Donald Adams concerning the present deplorable state of the language and his remedy for it:

> Some of the editors in our leading publishing houses are apparently as ignorant of the fundamentals of good English as the writers over whose copy they labor. If you think this an unfounded assertion, open at random, as I often do, a batch of newly hatched books, particularly those known as "creative writing," and read a few pages carefully. Often they would not have passed muster by the nineteenth-century schoolmarm of the little red schoolhouse enshrined in American memory. . . . For one Maxwell Perkins, to name the already classic example of a literate book editor, there are at least two or three men or women holding editorial posts who should be sent to night school. Those who exhibit some knowledge of and regard for

good English are not unlikely the beneficiaries of the training provided by some exacting newspaper editor who himself had the benefit of an instructor free of hifalutin theories.[6]

Mr. Adams has long been a crusader for what he considers the good English of the little red schoolhouse. Elsewhere he has indicated the desirability of an "armed uprising among the Parent-Teacher Associations all over the United States" which would "demand and get the scalps of those so-called educators whose indefensible doctrines are rapidly producing a generation of American illiterates." These murderers of grammar, the so-called educators referred to by Mr. Adams, are doubtless to be identified with the "structural linguists" so vigorously lambasted by Dwight Macdonald in his notorious review of *Webster's Third* in the *New Yorker* of 10 March 1962. Those who in former days would have brandished their hickory sticks and their blue-backed spellers in "the little red schoolhouse enshrined in American memory" have been demoralized most, Mr. Adams feels, by the National Council of Teachers of English, which he believes to be the official organ of the grammar-murderers. The attitudes and activities of this subversive organization, he declares, "constitute one of the chief threats to the cultivation of good English in our schools."[7]

By virtue of the fact that they supply the data on which the scholar's conclusions about usage are based, one would expect successful literary men and women to take a somewhat cavalier attitude toward the matter of correctness. (I leave out of the question the semiliterate writers mentioned by Mr. Adams; I seldom, if ever, come upon their books.) On the contrary, many seem to regard it as the be-all and end-all of good writing. They are, in fact, even more puristic than most teachers nowadays, for even the backwoods ma'am, if there still be any such, must have felt some impact of the scholarly study of usage; or, as Mr. Adams would interpret the matter, even she has to some extent been corrupted by the National Council of Teachers of English.

Let us examine a few other linguistic pronouncements from well-known professional writers, though actually some of these dicta would be more accurately termed stylistic than linguistic. All, however, are concerned with what the writers would think of as "good English."

6. "Does Anyone Know What Creative Writing Is?" *Saturday Review*, 18 September 1965, p. 23.
7. These astute opinions were expressed in his column in the *New York Times* book review section of 20 December 1959, and are approvingly quoted by Professor Mario Pei in the *Saturday Review* of 21 July 1962, p. 44.

Thus Edmund Wilson, who self-righteously declares "I never use Webster,"[8] apparently referring to *Webster's Third*, takes a writer severely to task because "he habitually uses 'transpire' as if it meant 'occur,'" though the word has meant just that, among other things, for the better part of two hundred years. The fact that the newer meaning arose from misunderstanding is quite irrelevant as far as its present status is concerned, for many unquestionably standard constructions began as blunders. Whether or not one chooses to use *transpire* in this sense is one's own affair, and hardly a gauge of one's ability as a writer. I may say parenthetically that I have never so used it and never intend to; but my eschewal is purely a personal and stylistic matter, having no validity in lexicography or in linguistics. Word choice is, after all, a matter of style.

It is not surprising that Wilson should share the horror of many other lay linguists over *disinterestedness* in the sense 'lack of interest.' This is a usage which I personally have no more love for than do Dean Jacques Barzun and Professor Mario Pei, but it does seem to have been used by a good many distinguished people, including the hapless author who is Wilson's reviewee—a former ambassador to the Soviet Union, visiting professor at Oxford, member of the Institute for Advanced Studies at Princeton, and president of the National Institute of Arts and Letters— whose knuckles Wilson duly raps.[9]

Professor Mark Schorer, who is of considerable eminence as both teacher and writer, has declared, in reference to *Webster's Third*: "I frankly prefer the old dictionary, speaking not only as a teacher, but as a writer. Granted, language changes. But I don't see any great advantage in trying to hurry it along that way. They accept anything, because it is used."[10] As for Mr. Schorer's magnanimous acceptance of the fact of linguistic change, one is reminded of what Carlyle, or Emerson, or Thoreau, or some other good gray person is reported to have said to Margaret Fuller when she vouchsafed the information that she accepted the universe: "By gad, Margaret, you'd better." As for the preference for the "old dictionary," that is, the *New International* of 1934, Professor Bergen Evans has well said, "Anyone who solemnly announces . . . that he will be guided in matters of English usage by a dictionary published in 1934 is talking ignorant and pretentious nonsense."[11]

8. In a letter to the editor of the *New York Review of Books*, 26 August 1965, p. 26. He is apparently referring to *Webster's Third*.

9. All these linguistic animadversions occur in a review of George F. Kennan's *The West under Lenin and Stalin* in the *New Yorker*, 9 September 1961, p. 141.

10. Quoted from the *San Francisco Chronicle* in the *New Yorker*, 12 April 1962, p. 90.

11. "But What's a Dictionary For?" *The Atlantic Monthly*, May 1962, p. 62.

Let us examine a few more specimens from my florilegium of linguistic pronouncements by professional writers. The critic Brendan Gill, reviewing in the *New Yorker* a motion picture dealing with the life of Christ, has this to say: "My respect for Christianity and good grammar obliges me to call attention to the fact that among the phrases . . . put into the mouth of Christ is the barbarism 'different than.' "[12] Leaving the mouth of Christ out of the question, this particular barbarism has, according to the *OED*, also issued from the pens of Fuller, Addison, Steele, Defoe, Richardson, Goldsmith, Fanny Burney, Coleridge, Southey, DeQuincey, Carlyle, Thackeray, Newman, Dean Trench, and others of comparable distinction in English literature who, unlike Brendan Gill, are unaware that it was a barbarism.

Equally magisterial is Dorothy Parker, who has declared that "any one who, as does [Henry] Miller, follows 'none' with a plural verb . . . should assuredly not be called writer."[13] The usage in question is first recorded in the ninth century in the writings of Alfred the Great. More recent occurrences cited by the *OED*, which points out that the plural usage is "now the commoner . . . the sing[ular] being expressed by *no one*," are from the writings of such nonwriters as Dryden, Goldsmith, Burke, and Southey; and Otto Jespersen adds occurrences from St. Thomas More, Shakespeare, Dr. Johnson ("None are wretched but by their own fault"), Scott, Charlotte Brontë, Ruskin, Morris, Shaw, Stevenson, and Kipling.[14]

It is noteworthy that both Mr. Gill and Miss Parker have managed to out-Fowler Fowler, whose *Dictionary of Modern English Usage* echoes the comment of the *OED* regarding plural *none* and adds that "it is a mistake to suppose that the pronoun is singular only and must at all costs be followed by singular verbs etc."[15] As for what ought to follow *different*, Fowler says unequivocally—though in so doing he misplaces *only* by all decent little red schoolhouse standards—"That *d[ifferent]* can only be followed by *from* & not by *to* is a SUPERSTITION" (1st ed., p. 113), *to* being in this construction perhaps somewhat more usual than *than* in current British English. Fowler's reviser, however, adds that "*different than* is sometimes preferred by good writers to the cumbersome *different from that which* etc . . ." (2d ed., p. 621). It is to be hoped that my disclosure

12. 21 October 1961, p. 196. I have used this citation and the following ones from Dorothy Parker and Clifton Fadiman in "The New Fowler," *Sewanee Review*, 74 (Spring, 1966), 540–44.

13. *Esquire*, September 1961, p. 34.

14. *A Modern English Grammar* (Copenhagen, 1922), 2:171.

15. First ed. (Oxford, 1940; first published in 1926), p. 381. The statement is allowed to stand in the 1965 revision by Sir Ernest Gowers, p. 394.

of these grammatical defections of H. W. Fowler and Sir Ernest Gowers will not lay them open to the charge of being "permissive."

That good writers like Professor Schorer, Professor Bush, Mr. Wilson, Mr. Gill, and Miss Parker should believe so sincerely in the linguistic folklore which they promulgate is not really surprising to the linguist, who is quite aware of lay attitudes toward his craft and its ineffable mysteries — even if the lay commentators are talented creative writers and hence, in my candid opinion, far more important than mere linguists. Certainly, Miss Parker, to cite an example, must often have encountered plural *none* in the writings of those whose claims to be called writers she would, it is hoped, readily admit to be at least equal to her own; and Mr. Brendan Gill must likewise often have come upon *different than* and *different to* in what he would consider nonbarbaric writing. The fact seems to be — for I can think of no other reasonable explanation — that, unlike the scholarly drudge, who has been trained to observe such phenomena, they simply fail to notice carefully much of the time. But, even if they were indeed careful observers of the facts of English usage, it is likely that the traditional arbitrary appeal to some sort of supposed grammatical logic (*than* goes with comparatives, and *different* is no comparative) or to history and etymology (*none* was in the beginning singular and ought still to be) would impress them more strongly than the evidence of their own eyes and ears; so that it is probably just as well that they are unaware of the currency in high places of most of the constructions which they set out to discredit.

It is, I suspect, highly doubtful that anyone writes anything worth reading just by following rules, or that the difference between good writing and bad writing is anything so simple as this. Nevertheless, some of our literati would seem to think so. Clifton Fadiman, for instance, in a piece of direct-mail advertising sent out by the Book-of-the-Month Club offering Fowler's aforementioned *Modern English Usage* as a "book-dividend," has testified that the book in question, characterized as "the final arbiter of our language," "shows me how bad a writer I am, and encourages me to do better."

Now no one could deny that Clifton Fadiman has been a prolific and highly successful writer, and most people, including myself, would think of him as a rather good one as well. Perhaps he is here overawed by the Fowlerian charisma; perhaps he is unconsciously reflecting the humility of the *New York Times* as quoted in the same advertisement: "The most practiced writer will only too often find himself convicted of sin when he dips into Fowler."

The need for what is thought of as authority — a need which, as we have just seen, is filled in part by works like Fowler's and in part by J. Donald Adams's Miss Fidditch fiddling away in her little red school-house—is the motivation for many of the ill-informed attacks upon *Webster's Third*. This monument of American scholarship has been so much in the news since its publication in 1961 that I shall here limit myself to a single, but highly typical, reaction other than that of Professor Schorer, which has previously been alluded to. The reactor in this instance is Dr. Max Rafferty; the *Dr.* always precedes his name in the byline of his newspaper columns dealing with educational topics of one sort or another. Dr. Rafferty has been Superintendent of Public Instruction for the State of California since 1963. [Dr. Rafferty failed of reelection to this august post in 1971, since which date he has been Dean of the School of Education at Troy (Alabama) State University. T.P.] His concept of lexicography is one which not even Samuel Johnson, who never called himself doctor, would have approved, but it is still very widespread: "If a dictionary doesn't exist to set standards and maintain them, what possible use can it have? I don't know about you, but when I go to a dictionary I want to know what's right. I already know what folks ARE saying; what I want to know is what they SHOULD be saying." What Dr. Rafferty regards as the current "trend toward lexicographical futility" is, in his opinion, "just one phase in the decline of our language."[16]

Such notions as those of Dr. Rafferty may be linguistically untenable, but none of us can deny that they are tenacious. It is obvious that the good doctor believes in some absolute, God-given set of standards which have nothing in particular to do with actual usage, that is, with "what folks ARE saying." (Incidentally, I would not have said *folks* if I had meant just people—not because I regard the word as "incorrect," but because I regard the concept of folksiness as both corny and phony. But this is purely a personal matter appertaining to style, and I voice no criticism of Dr. Rafferty's use of the term. If that's what he wanted to say, that's what he should have said.) Apparently Dr. Rafferty also believes that certain folks—namely, dictionary folks—know what other folks ought to say, and that the dictionary folks are shirking their duty—nay, their responsibility—when they don't let him in on their private information, presumably derived from a linguistic Yahweh with whom they have been fortunate enough or gifted enough to establish contact.

Because the world is so full of a number of people who have presumably acquired their knowledge of linguistics either by afflatus or by osmosis,

16. *Jacksonville Florida Times-Union*, 7 June 1965, p. 6.

the lot of the professional student, traditionally a neck-shaven drudge who finds it necessary to do a great deal of homework, is oftentimes hard. Though he does not presume to instruct engineers, naturopaths, or for that matter creative writers, for whom he may have tremendous respect, in the arcana of their respective crafts, he can hardly be blamed for his discouragement over the fact that they seem to know, or at least are given credit for knowing, so much more about language than he knows, and can speak so much more authoritatively concerning it than he can.

In condemning what Sterling Andrus Leonard called "the old purist junk," we are not beating a dead dog. Antiquated attitudes based on arbitrary appeals to logic, reason, and often traditional prejudice are still very much with us; indeed, they seem to me to be very viable. "Yet the old schooling sticks," as Browning's Fra Lippo Lippi complained. Furthermore, as we have seen, such attitudes are by no means confined to the badly educated and the *petit bourgeois*; as often as not, they are held as tenets of linguistic faith by the highly literate and in some instances by the brilliantly creative and talented.

Because he is usually, at least externally, a calm fellow with little capacity for passion over matters of usage, the linguist is likely to be accused of assuming an Olympian attitude, of being "permissive" (one of the most damning of adjectives in this glorious era of our Great Republic), or of maintaining that, as far as the English language goes, anything goes. The fact is, I believe, that those of us not gifted either by afflatus or osmosis are not likely to learn much that is really worth knowing about man's greatest accomplishment—that is, language—if we succumb to the allurement of making vague, glamorized, pseudophilosophical generalizations about English usage. To do so in sufficiently authoritative tones is the surest route to linguistic mahatmadom, as Dean Barzun, Professor Pei, Dwight Macdonald, the late Wilson Follett, and other popular pundits have discovered. Nevertheless, the supposed obtuseness of the professional grammarian is such that he will doubtless go on adding one to one in his unglamorous way; and, though he may never contribute anything of much importance to the Great Society in which we are privileged to live, let alone settling *hoti*'s business or unraveling the mysteries of the enclitic *de*, he will doubtless stubbornly insist upon going on in his own way, with all his human limitations, examining the evidence on what folks— to use Dr. Rafferty's darling homespunism—say and write. What they ought to say and write must be decided by those who are presumably more gifted than he. As we all know, their name is Legion.

20

Dictionaries and Usage

IN a society which, theoretically at least, is classless, it is obviously important that everyone should have the opportunity to learn to speak and write well, whatever "well" may happen to mean. America has no courtly social caste upon which to model its manners in speech, only a school tradition— which is nonetheless potent. This tradition dates back to the days when, in colonial New England, a schoolhouse stood beside every church, or almost every church. By the latter half of the seventeenth century, these church schools passed into the jurisdiction of the state and became district schools. In the South and in the Middle states, attitudes toward learning were somewhat less zealous than among the Puritans.

The New England tradition, which was ultimately to become the American tradition, gave rise to Noah Webster, the most important single figure in American lexicography. Webster was, unlike his English predecessor Samuel Johnson, primarily a pedant. Johnson tried schoolmastering, true, but he was above all a gifted man of letters who wrote a great dictionary; Webster tried many things other than schoolmastering, but all his long life—he belonged to a Revolutionary War regiment which never heard the crack of rifle fire, and lived into the reign of Queen Victoria—he was by temperament and inclination a schoolmaster. And, with all his quirks and crotchets, coupled with an arrogance which makes it difficult for us to regard him with any degree of warmth, he may be said to have started a distinguished tradition in American lexicography.

Webster was quite fanciful in many of his etymologies, for he did not have a really expert knowledge of all the languages with which he claimed familiarity; the fact is that his knowledge of language in general was weak even for his day. He was sufficiently dogmatic to declare that it was better to be unfashionably right—remember, he was essentially a Puritan—than fashionably wrong, whatever in the world that could possibly mean. But he was a man of really tremendous energy and industry, and, in the opinion of Sir James Murray, the great first editor of the *Oxford English Dictionary*, "a born definer of words."

Beginning with the revision, after his death in 1843, of his *American Dictionary of the English Language* (1828), there have been many excellent American dictionaries for general use. There are more than a half dozen in circulation today, three of which bear Webster's name, and others are in preparation—not to mention such specialized works as the *Dictionary of American English* (the principal editor of which was a Scotsman, Sir William Craigie), the *Dictionary of Americanisms*, the *Dictionary of American Regional English*, now in preparation, and the various dictionaries of slang, argot, and vernacular.

Though "Old Noah"—one always thinks of him thus, for he seems never to have had any youth—has, of course, had nothing to do with these current dictionaries, not even those which bear his name, naive people may still say "according to Webster" when they want to settle an argument about what a word is supposed to mean. They may even proceed to cite some work which they refer to as "the dictionary," whether or not it happens to bear his name—to such an extent is Noah Webster associated with lexicography in the popular mind. Of course any definition cited today is unlikely to stem from any dictionary actually prepared by him; but his name confers a sort of authority to the notions regarding the inflexibility of language dear to the heart of the average man. Webster must in large part be credited with the veneration in which dictionaries are held.

But another force, growing out of the same tradition that gave us Webster, helps to account for American linguistic attitudes (though it must be stated emphatically that most of the attitudes to be discussed in this chapter are by no means exclusively American). This force is a widespread, though only partial, literacy which is equatable with *education* in the older sense of that word only by a tremendous stretch of the imagination; it is a result of the public school system—public school, of course, in the American sense. The American desire for schooling, if not indeed for learning, which is rather more difficult to come by, is evidenced in the early township schools and in the "little red schoolhouses," the rural schools of the nineteenth and early twentieth centuries. I cannot testify that all these were painted red, but it would seem from the American proverbial expression that most of them were.

These are supposed to have imparted a particularly sound, "no-non-sense" education in such fundamentals as "readin', writin', and 'rith-metic"—sometimes affectionately referred to as "the three *r*'s." Even highly cultivated Americans see these rural schools—which in fact must have been rather dismal institutions, as often as not presided over, in H. L. Mencken's phrase, by milkmaids armed with hickory sticks and yokels in frock coats—through the nostalgic shimmer of romance and patriotism. To question the sources of their authority is still to bring down coals of fire upon the linguist's head. It can be said for them, however, that they did try, by means of constant drill and that good old American institution, the spelling bee—a contest in which sides were chosen and each side attempted to "spell down" the other—to combat the troublesome and inconsistent matter of English spelling. Time-wasting perhaps it was; effective it may have been, though every generation tends to think that the succeeding generation is made up of miserable spellers. The bad spelling of the young is almost invariably attributed—and with some justice—to deficiencies in the educational system: "Schools aren't what they were in my day." Inasmuch as the layman usually confuses writing with language, this is taken as evidence of the deterioration of English. The spelling text used throughout the nineteenth century (still in use in a few private schools, I am told) was Noah Webster's *Spelling Book*, the "blue-back speller," first published in 1783. It must be one of the best-selling books of all times.

In view of the fact that litterateurs supply most of the data on which the scholar bases his conclusions concerning the nature of Standard English, one would expect literary men to be more or less self-assured about their usage—to assume, as English writers did for the better part of a thousand years, that what they write is indeed "good English." On the contrary, many seem to regard hoary old precepts as the *summum bonum* of what they have been trained to think of as grammar. Thus, a well-known and highly successful American writer has stated that consulting H.W. Fowler's *Modern English Usage*—which is actually somewhat more "liberal" than many an American school text—made him realize how bad a writer he was and encouraged him to do better, just as if one ever "did better" merely by following handbook precepts. A few are, in fact, considerably more puristic in their attitudes, if not actually in their practice, than most teachers nowadays; for even the most benighted teacher must by now have felt some slight impact of the scholarly study of language as it is used—or, as some would put it, have to some extent been corrupted by the National Council of Teachers of English. Note, however, this statement by an

American writer and critic, himself a teacher of English for a single year (1913–1914 —long before the rise of enlightened attitudes toward usage in this country, and only a few years after the first meeting of the National Council of Teachers of English, which has long fostered such enlightened attitudes): "Some of the editors in our leading publishing houses are apparently as ignorant of the fundamentals of good English as the writers over whose copy they labor," going on to say that many of the books being printed nowadays "would not have passed muster by the nineteenth-century schoolmarm of the little red schoolhouse enshrined in American memory." I really do not know what the gentleman has in mind. The books that I read which are published even by disreputable American publishers contain few if any of the purist's supposed errors in grammar, though their style may frequently be halting and dull and their choice of words not precisely what mine might have been. But that is another matter entirely.

There can be little doubt that the inadequately educated, unsophisticated teacher of the near past—the schoolmarm dedicated to her little red schoolhouse, and her metropolitan counterpart—has to a large extent fostered the layman's confused notions about English usage, his belief that there are many rules governing English which must not be broken by those who aspire to write and speak well, despite the fact that great writers and speakers have in fact broken them without compunction, often without even any awareness that such rules existed. Because of the general belief that these rules are the stock-in-trade of the teacher of English, teachers are often expected to make decisions about relatively unimportant matters of English usage.

It is a popular assumption that, as in morals, so in language there is invariably a sharp line of demarcation between "right" and "wrong." (Whether this is altogether true in the moral sphere need not concern us.) It follows from this assumption that there must be no schisms in language. It is generally supposed to be the scholar's business to determine, by some appeal to logic, analogy, Latin grammar, or historical development, or simply by afflatus, what choice between alternative constructions one *ought* to make. Consequently he is often consulted respectfully by business and professional men whose attitude toward him in other circumstances might well be somewhat condescending. He is, moreover, thought incompetent, or at the least disobliging, if he refuses to falsify the facts of usage as he knows them from firsthand observation. As for the variant constructions *it's me* and *it's I*, for instance, he will be aware that educated speakers might use either form: the valet Jeeves would be more apt to choose the less natural *I* than his master

Bertie Wooster. The plain fact is, however, that the occasion for either rarely arises. In answer to some such questions as "Who's there?" one would, for instance, ordinarily merely announce one's name.

A caste dialect in the European sense is largely a matter of pronunciation and intonation, though word choice is often quite important. Because of the size, the settlement history, and the cultural history of the United States, no single type of pronunciation has ever been able to establish itself as a standard comparable to what is known as Received Pronunciation, recorded principally by H. C. Wyld and Daniel Jones and referred to as *U* (for upper-class) by A. S. C. Ross, and subsequently by the Hon. Nancy Mitford in her widely publicized article "The English Aristocracy," in *Encounter.*

The American uses the pronunciation of the region in which he has in his early childhood acquired his speech habits; thus, the Chicagoan speaks in one way, the Bostonian of the same status in another, the Virginian in another, and the Texan in yet another; yet the differences are not very great, for American English has always been noted for its uniformity. With the exception of Gullah, spoken by blacks living along the coastal region of South Carolina and Georgia, both on the Sea Islands and on the mainland, there are no types of American English which are not readily understandable in all parts of the country, though a certain tolerance is sometimes necessary. To the layman's ear many of the differences, at least away from the Atlantic coast, are so subtle as to be practically indiscernible, though everyone can tell a speaker from the Deep South from one from the Middle West. There are, of course, types of American pronunciation which are regarded as substandard; but these are more noticeable in the metropolitan than in the rural areas and are due to a number of factors which it would be irrelevant to discuss here.

There is thus a good deal of truth in the statement of an English journalist that "in America, where it is grammar, not accent, that places you, anyone can learn the grammar." Consequently, much of the teaching in the lower schools has been largely concerned with the inculcation of grammatical precepts calculated to imbue the pupil with what is nowadays referred to as status, to put him into possession of what is assumed to be the prestige dialect. *Status* is perhaps only another word for *class*, but in this case it is class based upon the mastery of a fairly simple set of precepts—nothing so difficult as the acquisition of a caste "accent"—rather than upon birth and breeding.

The linguist's main contention about prescriptive teaching, which in itself he has not the slightest objection to, is that its precepts should be properly based—that is, based on the *actual* usage of reputable speakers and writers rather than notions of what *should* be or arbitrary appeals to such extralinguistic factors as logic, analogy, the historical development of the language, and the like. From appeals of this sort have come taboos, some of them more or less confined to the classroom, against such usages as these:

he don't (now old-fashioned in cultivated speech, but frequent a generation ago until a schoolteachers' crusade blacklisted it)

ain't I (a variant of British *aren't I*)

reference by the plural pronoun to the indefinite pronouns *everyone*, *someone*, and the like (as in *Everyone cheered the returning hero, and he waved his hand to them*—just try substituting the prescribed *him* for *them* in that sentence)

due to as a compound preposition (as in *Due to his lack of foresight, the battle was lost*)

the so-called split infinitive (that is, the insertion of a word, usually an adverb, or a phrase between *to* and the verb form)

the disregarding of the *shall-will* distinction (artificial for Americans)

the terminal preposition (as in *What is the world coming to?*)

these (or *those*) *kind* (or *sort*)

the reason is because

like introducing a clause

different than (or *to*)

supposedly misplaced *only* (as in *He only arrived a few minutes ago*, purists preferring us to say *He arrived only a few minutes ago*)

supposed misuse of *who* for *whom* in such a sentence as *Who are you waiting for?* (which also offends by its terminal preposition)

All these locutions actually occur, some perhaps infrequently, in the discourse of educated speakers, British as well as American, when they are not thinking of the schoolmaster's ruler hovering over their knuckles. Some occur as well in the works of highly respectable authors. My files, necessarily somewhat more limited than those of the editors of the *Oxford English Dictionary* and *Webster's Third*, abound in illustrative citations. But there are many circles—not very interesting or lively circles, it is true—in which the breaking of such taboos might cause eyebrows to lift. The ambitious young person not yet established in his career had best watch his words; they need not be interesting words, stylishly put together, but they must be "correct" ones, as correctness is conceived in such circles.

The old teaching—the "old purist junk," as the late Sterling Andrus Leonard once called it—lingers on, despite enlightened dictionaries and the efforts of such objective students of usage as Leonard himself, the late

George Philip Krapp, the late Porter Perrin, Albert H. Marckwardt, Robert Pooley, Kemp Malone, the late Charles Carpenter Fries, Margaret Bryant, and a good many others whose findings have fallen upon deaf ears in many pedagogical circles. The usual reaction to any studies which demonstrate the great discrepancy between textbook rules and the actual usage of recognized speakers and writers is abusive attack upon those who have made such studies—an attack often fortified by newspaper editorials pointing out that the English language is rapidly deteriorating. A frequent assertion is that such scholars, who have merely examined the same evidence that is there for all to examine, are "permissive"—a voguish adjective nowadays, with pejorative connotations; with them, it is said, "anything goes." Nothing could be further from the truth.

The critical reception of *Webster's Third* when it first appeared in 1961— a work based on sound editorial principles which do not actually depart much from those of the great *Oxford English Dictionary*—indicates that many of our most eminent critics believe that a dictionary ought to be a law book, and moreover one which incorporates all their own crotchets, prejudices, and misconceptions rather than a record of the usage of writers and speakers of the language who are persons of some prominence in modern life, though not necessarily concerned with the arts and sciences. Despite the considerably greater enlightenment shown by the English critics, the fact remains that many persons on both sides of the Atlantic still conceive of some *ideal* English language, its rules embalmed forever in moldy textbooks, whose standards everyone should continually aspire to speak up to and to write up to. The distinguished efforts of a generation of scholars who have devoted themselves to the study of English usage have as yet made little impact on the public mind—and I refer here to the educated public, of course, for no one else cares much one way or the other. Perhaps it will require yet another generation to take heed of what has already been done. By then, other changes will have occurred in the language, though fortunately they will be comparatively slight.

When, a number of years ago, certain American cigarette manufacturers declared in their advertising slogan that their cigarettes *taste good like a cigarette should*, there were storms of protest from the purists, who had been taught to believe that, according to some God-given law, *like* could not be thus used as a conjunction—though it had been so used many times before by not contemptible writers, among them Robert Southey, Charles Darwin, Cardinal Newman, William Morris, and George Bernard Shaw. Fowler, usually regarded as a custodian of the purity of the English language, says of the construction in his *Modern English Usage:* "It is the established

way of putting the thing among all who have not been taught to avoid it.
. . . But in good writing this particular *like* is very rare, and even those
writers with whom sound English is a matter of care and study rather than
of right instinct, and to whom *like* was once the natural word, usually
weed it out." One wonders just what is gained by so doing.

And so it goes. Students have made great progress in establishing what
is good English, assuming that we accept as a definition of good English
the usage of those whom we should expect to speak and write good English—
and I know of no better definition. In any case, this usage is amply recorded
in the myriad pages of the *Oxford English Dictionary*, in Otto Jespersen's
Modern English Grammar, in the works of other great continental Angli-
cists, in the works of many English and American scholars, in the valuable
materials of the Linguistic Atlas of the United States and Canada, in scores
of learned articles and notes in such American journals as *American
Speech*, the *English Journal*, and *College English*, and in our on-the-whole
excellent dictionaries.

It is ironic that, in a period which has produced the liveliest linguistic
research since the nineteenth-century work of Rasmus Rask, Jacob Grimm,
and Franz Bopp, popular attitudes should lag so far behind. Arbitrary notions
about English usage which date from the eighteenth century should, one
would suppose, have been dissipated by now. But, on the contrary, they
have retained so much of their original potency that any questioning of
their validity for all sorts and conditions of men is regarded as a linguistic
heresy. But what the social scientists have called "cultural lag" is in no
sense peculiar to America, nor to linguistic attitudes.

21

Sweet Are the Usages of Diversity

IN its title J. J. Lamberts's new book[1] ironically recalls Bishop Lowth's famous *A Short Introduction to English Grammar* (1762)—a title which James Sledd, also ironically, used verbatim for his own 1959 grammar. The two books are quite differently oriented, though Lamberts is no more in the Lowthian tradition than Sledd; rather, he is in the enlightened tradition of Jespersen, Pooley, Fries, Perrin, Bryant, and the Evanses, Bergen and Cornelia—unhappily in eclipse at the moment in the more rarefied atmosphere of linguistic theory. This tradition holds that good usage is the more or less unstudied, natural usage of cultivated speakers and writers. In a society dedicated to what is throbbingly referred to as the democratic way of life, "cultivated" is equated with "educated," which is in turn equated with "schooled," though it is doubtful that the equations are really exact. But this is a matter beyond the scope of the present review.

Scholars working in this tradition—a tradition by now regarded as ancient and honorable everywhere save in the popular mind, where prescriptivism continues to be held in reverence—do not believe that "whatever is, is right." They are quite aware, for instance, that cultivated speakers of English do not any longer say "you was," even though their equally well-bred (and in some instances equally well-educated) ancestors did so; and they record the fact without emotion.

They have no concern with setting up an arbitrary and inflexible standard; their concern is with the facts of usage and the relative social status of those facts, the frequent "illogicality" of which disturbs or has disturbed the presumably more orderly and logical minds of, say, Lowth, Lindley

1. J. J. Lamberts, *A Short Introduction to English Usage* (New York: McGraw-Hill, 1972).

Murray, Noah Webster (who, incidentally, defended singular "you was" on logical grounds), Wilson Follett, Jacques Barzun, and Theodore M. Bernstein. They accept the diversity of usage at any given time in history, so that it does not particularly pain them that some speakers pronounce *ration* to rime with *fashion*, whereas others of comparable status rime it with *nation*—though the scholarly traditionalists are most of them aware that the first is the "historically correct" pronunciation of this French loanword and hence, pedants as they are likely to be at heart, are likely to prefer it for themselves. This is no more than reserving their own right to talk as they please, and not as someone else, no less tempted by the world, the flesh, and the devil,–and probably no wiser than they are, thinks they should talk. But they respect equally the right of others to talk as they please, even though certain locutions, certain types of speech—it would be easy to cite here some of my own prejudices, but these are of no importance—may make them wince a little, particularly when these emanate from high places. They do not regard themselves as law-givers, and they do not believe that the English language, or any other language for that matter, is going to perdition. They do not equate linguistic change with deterioration, or diversity with disorder and chaos.

If they are both older-generation and crustily conservative, like the present writer, third-person singular *don't* may come to them as naturally as it did to writers and speakers of the near past,[2] but they are likely to avoid it (except among intimates, who will think them merely eccentric rather than ignorant), if only because they are humane and kindly men and hence chary of causing pain to refined sensibilities. (But does it really matter all that much? Is the delectable Yum-Yum any the less delectable because she comments, upon hearing that Japanese widows of executed men are buried alive, "It—it makes a difference, don't it?" Although there is every reason to believe that any equally well-bred young English lady of Gilbert's day would have used the same contraction of *does not*—Yum-Yum's Japanese ladies' seminary must have been as strict in matters of linguistic deportment

---

2. And presumably of the not-so-near past as well, though examples of either third singular *don't* or *doesn't* are difficult to find in earlier writing. Those that do occur are, as their colloquial nature would lead us to suspect, in dialogue. The late Karl Dykema, in "An Example of Prescriptive Linguistic Change: 'Don't' to 'Doesn't,' " *English Journal*, 36 (1947), 372, cites an occurrence of third singular *don't* as early as 1697, but none for *doesn't* before 1818, both antedating the earliest citations in the *OED*. It is likely that the august Bishop Lowth, who died in 1787, would have used third singular *don't* if he was ever so informal as to use contractions. Both forms are obviously earlier than any citations. It is, nevertheless, highly probable that third singular *don't* is considerably older than *doesn't*, which, if it occurred at all, must have been considered a somewhat questionable neologism, perhaps even an erroneous form, in Lowth's day.

as any English one—recent editors of *The Mikado* purify Yum-Yum's grammar by changing her *don't* to *doesn't*. As Jane Austen, an impeccably brought-up young lady, said in another connection a generation or so earlier, "It don't signify.")

Such elderly and conservative speakers for similar reasons are likely to prefer the English pronunciations of many Latin words and phrases, pronunciations hallowed by centuries of cultured tradition and preserved in *et cetera* and a few legal phrases like *habeas corpus*.[3] But they are willing to eschew such traditional pronunciations as ['pɜ 'si] for *per se*, ['saɪnɪ kwe 'nɑn] for *sine qua non*, [ɪn 'mɪdɪ,æs 'riz] for *in medias res*, ['e praɪ'ɔraɪ] for *a priori*, and ['diəs ,ɛks 'mækɪnə] for *deus ex machina*, simply to save the feelings of those who use the schoolbook pronunciations; they may even screw themselves up to calling boy graduates [ə'lʌmni] and girl graduates [ə'lʌmnaɪ], though to do so amounts not only to a rejection of a tradition which they may respect, but also to a complete reversal of their former practice.[4]

As scholars they are perfectly well aware that such pronunciations of learned words and phrases as they may happen to prefer for one reason or another (mainly because they learned them that way) are now hopelessly old-fashioned. As individuals, and presumably free souls, they may not really like change, just as they may not really like the law of gravity; but as students of language they find the observation and recording of linguistic change the breath of life. And, as such an observer and recorder of trivia, I am here bound to point out that in this matter of Latin pronunciation my own observations, some of them recorded years ago, do not accord with Lamberts's statement that "except for working out classroom exercises . . . or declaiming select passages from Caesar or Cicero or Virgil, a person normally avoids school-book Latin pronunciation" (p. 120). The traditional, that is, English, pronunciations of such Latin words and phrases as I have recorded in the preceding paragraph would be certain to cause incredulous amusement and not a few lifted eyebrows in most academic circles with which I am acquainted. When I once read a paper before a group of teachers of English the title of which included the word *literati*, I was careful to pronounce the word as the chairman of the meeting

---

3. It has been lost in *fieri facias*, thus destroying Nashe's pun: "Purseuants with red noses . . . a purseuant . . . with the verie reflexe of his firie facias." For other examples of the punning possibilities (none of them very good) of the traditional English pronunciation of *fieri facias*, see the *OED* entry.

4. It is notable that the newer pronunciations of *alumni* and *alumnae* give the schoolbook (or "reformed") pronunciation only to the inflectional endings; there is nothing "Latin" about the central vowel occurring in the syllables bearing principal stress.

pronounced it—that is, [ˌlɪtərˈɑtɪ]—though I would normally have said [ˌlɪtəˈretaɪ]; adopting the new pronunciation caused me no pain, even though so to pronounce the word was no part of my so-called cultural tradition— a tradition which, *pace* Lamberts, is moribund if not indeed quite dead. Even the hybrid pronunciations which Lamberts cites, like those for *alma mater*, *curriculum vitae*, and *magna cum laude*, indicate clearly the way the wind is blowing. I have attended a good many graduation exercises in my time, ever a slave to duty as I conceived it; and I have seldom if ever heard any university president say anything but [ˈmɑgnə] for *magna* or [ˈlaudɪ] for *laude*, though the intervening *cum* wavers between traditional [kʌm] and "Latin" [kum]. To those who must use the phrase *alma mater*— usually the heads of alumni associations—the second element is invariably [ˈmɑtər]; traditional [ˈmetər] would nowadays sound like a mistake. The vowel of the first syllable of *alma* is, however, as often as not [æ] (influence of the girl's name?).

The musty prescriptions for linguistic elegance inherited from the eighteenth century and set forth in such works as Wilson Follett's *Modern American Usage* (1966) remain today in most circles as awe-inspiring as they were over two centuries ago, when Robert Lowth[5] compounded them more effectively than any of his predecessors had done. The modern commentator who attempts to demonstrate by means of concrete evidence that many of them fail to describe the English usage of any period, including Lowth's own, is condemned for being "permissive" (a voguish word which I am too cynical to take seriously), if not downright subversive, by people who are otherwise fairly well informed but who prefer to believe, with Lowth, that our most eminent writers and speakers are liable to make the most egregious blunders through lack of attention to the rules that he prescribed, no matter by whom promulgated. (Most of them have of course never heard of Lowth, or even of Lindley Murray, Goold Brown, Richard Grant White, and others who carried the torch for "correct English" as they conceived it to be.) To the jaded observer, it is amusing that an abhorrence and fear of permissiveness in matters of linguistic usage should continue to thrive in an otherwise permissive and Spock-marked generation.

5. The distinguished emeritus professor of Romance languages who wrote the introductory essay "Good Usage, Bad Usage, and Usage" in the *American Heritage Dictionary* (1969) and was a member of its famous "Usage Panel" calls him John Lowth, at least in the first printing of that work. I find no previous record that Lowth was ever named John. But, with the authority of the *American Heritage Dictionary* to support it, the rechristening has, not surprisingly, gained ground, occurring also in Anthony Wolk's "Linguistic and Social Bias in *The American Heritage Dictionary*," *College English*, 33 (1972), 934. Sic transit gloria episcopi.

Wilson Follett believed that "the great classics are no better off [than modern literature] when they rely on habit or technique without self-inspection" (p. 19), that is, with no regard for the rules, and he is not alone. His attitude toward English usage, like that of those who carried his work to completion after he went to his Great Reward in 1963, is exemplified in such a declaration as the following: "Let three thousand say *one of those who believes* while only three say *those who believe*; and as long as the three thousand do not also say *we believes, you believes, they believes*, the three thousand will be wrong from the only point of view that is relevant here, the point of view of form" (p. 25). *Modern American Usage* was highly praised on its publication by such eminent authorities as Sir Denis Brogan, Kingsley Amis, Cyril Connolly, V. S. Pritchett, Malcolm Cowley, Clifton Fadiman, and Mark Van Doren, among a good many others quoted in the publisher's announcement; the (London) *Times Educational Supplement* called it "a powerful counterblast to the 'descriptive' school of linguists and the support which they claim to have secured in the third edition of Webster's Dictionary." (Support for what?)

But even the aspirant to linguistic sanctification may slip up occasionally, the pitfalls attendant upon speaking and writing one's native language being what they are, or are supposed to be. Wilson Follett, always on the side of the angels, of whose number he is now one—doubtless saddened by the careless colloquialisms which besmirch the lips of his fellow cherubim and seraphim, whose original classical Hebrew must by now have undergone some degree of change—declares in the introduction of his aforementioned vademecum for the timorous that "*amorous* can only be used of persons" (p. 7). This rule, unknown to a number of quite distinguished writers (see the *OED*, s.v. *amorous*, def. 4), is laid down after a severe reprobation of the phrase "amorous Hindu sculpture," where Follett—and I too, for that matter—would have chosen *erotic*. But that is beside the point, which is that many fellow precisians, including 70 percent of the Usage Panel of the *American Heritage Dictionary*, would gleefully single out for reprobation Follett's use of *can* in the statement of his rule; after all, his previously cited occurrence of *amorous* in reference to sculpture proves that it *can* indeed be used of sculpture. Schoolteachers of Follett's generation, if they were like those of my own generation, must surely have drilled their classes in the supposedly proper use of *can* and *may*. The hapless moppet of my day who was so lacking in grammatical self-inspection as to ask, "Miss Fidditch, can I be excused?" was, unless his condition seemed very desperate indeed, required to mend his grammar before the requested permission for relief was granted. It therefore seems happily still sublunary. Theodore M. Bernstein's "Bernstein on Words" (originating with the *New York Times*) is doubtless only the most widely read of a number of syndicated newspaper columns on English usage, all prescriptive and authoritarian. The spirits of Robert—or John—Lowth, Lindley Murray, Noah Webster, and Wilson Follett are by no means completely at rest; their toil was not in vain. The hand of the schoolmarm is perhaps somewhat less heavy than it used to be, not necessarily because the current and doubtless prettier Miss Fidditch is so much more sophisticated than the prototypical marm, but mainly because of the radical sociological changes that have occurred in recent years—but there can be no doubt that the prototypical attitudes linger on. He who presumes to cast doubt upon the divine inspiration of the purifiers and their rules is by no means beating a dead dog; old Fido Fidditch has plenty of vitality and viability left in him.

The Writings of Thomas Pyles

1937

1. "Rejected Quarto Two Readings in the New Shakespeare *Hamlet*." *ELH* 4: 114–46.

1939

2. "Tempest in Teapot: The Reform in Latin Pronunciation." *ELH* 6: 138–64. (Also published separately as a portion of "A History of the Pronunciation of Learned Latin Loan-Words and Foreign Words in English," Johns Hopkins doctoral dissertation, 1938, preceded by a table of contents and summary of the entire work and followed by a vita.)
3. Review of *Hamlet: A Critical Edition of the Second Quarto*, by T. M. Parrott and Hardin Craig. *MLN* 54: 205–7.

1941

4. (With S. V. Larkey, M.D., editors.) *An Herbal (1525)*. New York: Scholars' Facsimiles and Reprints. xxiv [+72] + 86 pp. (Also published in a special limited edition by the New York Botanical Garden.)

1942

5. " 'Dan Chaucer.' " *MLN* 57: 437–39.

1943

6. "The Pronunciation of Latin Learned Loan Words and Foreign Words in Old English." *PMLA* 58: 891–910.

1944

7. "The Romantic Side of Dr. Johnson." *ELH* 11: 192–212.

1945

8. "A New Meteorological Theory of Stress." *MLN* 60: 497–98.
9. Review of *The Miracle of Beatrice*, translated by Adriaan J. Barnouw. *Books Abroad* 19: 307.
10. Review of *One Language*, by R. S. Jaque. *Books Abroad* 19: 310–11.

1946

11. Review of *From These Roots*, by Mary Colum. *Books Abroad* 20: 92.
12. Review of *À Paris tous les deux*, by M. Dekobra. *Books Abroad* 20: 69.
13. Review of *The Jew and His Language Problem*, by D. Goldblatt. *Books Abroad* 20: 94–95.
14. Review of *A Handbook of Basic English*, by T. B. Haber. *Books Abroad* 20: 95.
15. Review of *Publications of the Society for the History of Germans in Maryland*. *Books Abroad* 20: 204.
16. Review of *Dictionary of Word Origins*, by J. T. Shipley. *Books Abroad* 20: 212.

1947

17. "The Pronunciation of Latin in English: A Lexicographical Dilemma." *American Speech* 22: 3–17.
18. "Onomastic Individualism in Oklahoma." *American Speech* 22: 257–64.
19. Review of *A la découverte de Shakespeare*, by Abel Lefranc. *Books Abroad* 21: 59–60.
20. Review of *Life in the USA*, by H. Moriarta. *Books Abroad* 21: 90.
21. Review of *Twentieth Century English*, by W. S. Knickerbocker. *Books Abroad* 21: 450–51.
22. Review of *Les Grands Lyriques anglais*, by F. Rose. *Books Abroad* 21: 433.
23. Review of *Anglo-Saxon Saints and Scholars*, by E. S. Duckett. *Oklahoma City Daily Oklahoman*, *Sunday Literary Supplement*, 16 March, p. D-3.
24. Review of *How People Talk*, by Miriam Chapin. *Oklahoma City Daily Oklahoman*, *Sunday Literary Supplement*, 26 October, p. D-3.
25. Review of *A Treasury of New England Folklore*, by B. A. Botkin.

Oklahoma City Daily Oklahoman, *Sunday Literary Supplement*, 14 December, p. D-3.

26. Review of *The Layamon Texts*, by N. Bøgholm. *Studies in Linguistics* 5:79.

1948

27. Review of *German Universities—Through English Eyes*, by S. D. Stirk. *Books Abroad* 22: 93.

1949

28. "Innocuous Linguistic Indecorum: A Semantic Byway." *MLN* 64: 1–8.
29. "Linguistics and Pedagogy: The Need for Conciliation." *College English* 10: 389–95.
30. "Ophelia's 'Nothing.'" *MLN* 64: 322–23.
31. "Margarita, Marianna, and the Countess of Blessington." *Notes and Queries* 194: 209–10.
32. "That Fine Italian *A* in American English." In *Philologica: The Malone Anniversary Studies*, edited by Thomas A. Kirby and Henry B. Woolf (Baltimore: Johns Hopkins University Press), pp. 290–95.
33. "Bollicky Naked." *American Speech* 24: 255.
34. "Alas for the South!" *South Atlantic Bulletin* 15: 13–14.

1950

35. "Southern Scholars and the Foundations." *South Atlantic Bulletin* 16: 10.

1951

36. Review of *Beowulf in Modern English*, by Mary E. Waterhouse. *Books Abroad* 25: 172.
37. Review of *Leave Your Language Alone!* by Robert A. Hall, Jr. *ETC: A Review of General Semantics* 8: 155–56.

1952

38. *Words and Ways of American English*. New York: Random House. vii + 310 pp. (From the 4th printing on, issued as a paperback.)
39. "'Choctaw' *Okeh* Again." *American Speech* 27: 157–58.
40. "*Latch On*." *American Speech* 27: 291.
41. Review of *Studies on the Accentuation of Polysyllabic Latin, Greek, and Romance Loan-Words in English*, by Bror Danielsson. *MLN* 67: 266–67.

42. Review of *The Secular Lyric in Middle English*, by Arthur K. Moore. *Books Abroad* 26: 399.
43. "Linguistic Law-Givers." *Saturday Review*, 21 June, p. 13. (From chapter 4 of item 38 above.)

1953

44. "British Titles of Nobility and Honor in American English." *American Speech* 28: 69–79.
45. Review of *British and American English Since 1900*, by Eric Partridge and John W. Clark. *MLN* 68: 580.
46. Review of *Shakespeare's Pronunciation*, by Helge Kökeritz. *U.S. Quarterly Book Review* 9: 426–27.

1954

47. *Words and Ways of American English*. London: Andrew Melrose Ltd. 240 pp. (Item 38 above, with numerous revisions.)
48. "The Dance of Words." Review of *Plain Words: Their ABC*, by Sir Ernest Gowers. *Saturday Review*, 23 October, p. 30.

1955

49. "The English of VIPs." *College English* 16: 356–61.
50. "More on *Hubba-Hubba*." *American Speech* 30: 157–58.
51. "Still More on *Hubba-Hubba*." *American Speech* 30: 305–6.
52. Review of *Purity of Diction in English Verse*, by Donald Davie. *MLN* 70: 541–42.
53. Review of *Usage and Abusage*, by Eric Partridge. *MLN* 70: 608–9.

1956

54. "Tall Talk, Turgidity, and Taboo." In *A College Treasury*, edited by P. A. Jorgensen and F. B. Shroyer (New York: Scribner's), pp. 134–46. (From chapter 6 of item 38 above.)
55. Review of *Selections from Beowulf*, by J. C. Pope; *Selections from Chaucer*, by H. Kökeritz; *A Guide to Chaucer's Pronunciation*, by H. Kökeritz. *MLN* 71: 297–99.

1957

56. "Noah Webster, Man and Symbol." In *Weigh the Word*, edited by C. B. Jennings, Nancy King, and Marjorie Stevenson (New York: Harper), pp. 167–72. (From chapter 5 of item 38 above.)
57. Review of *The Words We Use*, by J. A. Sheard. *MLN* 72: 66–71.

58. Review of *Hands Off Pidgin English!* by Robert A. Hall, Jr. *MLN* 72: 147–49.
59. Review of *Grundzüge der englischen Sprache und Wesenart*, by Walther Azzolino. *MLN* 72: 537–38.
60. Review of *A Concise Dictionary of the American Language*, by Arthur Waldhorn. *American Speech* 32: 125–28.
61. Review of *Tarheel Talk*, by Norman E. Eliason. *Language* 33: 256–61.

1958

62. "Subliminal Words Are Never Finalized." *New York Times Magazine*, 15 June, pp. 16, 55, 57, 58.
63. *"The Real McCoy."* *American Speech* 33: 297–98.
64. "A New Book on American English." Review of *American English*, by A. H. Marckwardt. *American Speech* 33: 195–98.

1959

65. "American Pronunciation." In *Modern Prose: Form and Style*, edited by William Van O'Connor (New York: Crowell), pp. 315–32. (From chapter 10 of item 38 above.)
66. "Bible Belt Onomastics; Or, Some Curiosities of Anti-Pedobaptist Nomenclature." *Names* 7: 84–100.
67. "Bible Belt Onomastics." Bobbs-Merrill Reprint Series in Language and Linguistics, Language–77. (Reprint of item 66 above.)
68. Review of *Airship, Aeroplane, Aircraft*, by Svante Stubelius. *Language* 35: 558–61.

1960

69. "Words and Meanings." *The Eleusis of Chi Omega*, February, pp. 26–31.
70. "Task Force Makes Breakthrough." *American Speech* 35: 155–56.

1961

71. "Bible Belt Onomastics." In *English as Language*, edited by Charlton Laird and Robert M. Gorrell (New York: Harcourt, Brace and World), pp. 44–50. (Reprint of most of item 66 above.)
72. "Purity by Prescription." In *The Craft of Writing*, edited by Derek Colville and J. D. Koerner (New York: Harper), pp. 35–42. (Chapter 11 of item 38 above.)
73. Review of *Balloon, Flying-Machine, Helicopter*, by Svante Stubelius. *Language* 37: 292–94.

1962

74. "Slang." *Collier's Encyclopedia* (New York: Crowell-Collier) 21: 69–70.
75. "Early American Speech: Adoptions from Foreign Tongues." In *Introductory Readings in Language*, edited by Wallace L. Anderson and Norman C. Stageberg (New York: Holt, Rinehart and Winston), pp. 93–111. (Chapter 3 of item 38 above.) Revised edition, 1966, pp. 65–82.

1963

76. "Some Characteristics of American English and Their Backgrounds." In *Perspectives in Language: An Anthology*, edited by John A. Rycenga and Joseph Schwartz (New York: Ronald), pp. 52–63. (Chapter 3 of item 38 above.)
77. "The Influence of the Frontier on the American Language." In *Exposition and the English Language*, edited by James L. Sanderson and Walter K. Gordon (New York: Appleton-Century-Crofts), pp. 276–80. (From chapter 6 of item 38 above.)
78. "American and British Differences in Pronunciation." In *Exposition and the English Language*, edited by James L. Sanderson and Walter K. Gordon (New York: Appleton-Century-Crofts), pp. 302–6. (From chapter 10 of item 38 above.)
79. Review of *American Political Terms: An Historical Dictionary*, by Hans Sperber and Travis Trittschuh. *American Speech* 38: 223–26.
80. Review of *Explorations in Shakespeare's Language: Some Problems of Lexical Meaning in the Dramatic Text*, by Hilda M. Hulme. *Shakespeare Quarterly* 14: 469–70.

1964

81. *The Origins and Development of the English Language*. New York: Harcourt, Brace and World. viii + 388 pp.
82. "The English Language: A Brief History." In *An American Rhetoric*, by W. W. Watt (New York: Holt, Rinehart and Winston), chapter 10, pp. 411–49.
83. Review of *English Place-Names in* -stead, by Karl Inge Sandred. *Names* 12: 232–34.

1965

84. "The Role of Historical Linguistics." *College English* 26: 292–98.
85. "*Highball* for *Tall Glass*." *American Speech* 40: 76–77.

86. "Inkhornisms, Fustian, and Current Vogue Words." In *All These to Teach: Essays in Honor of C. A. Robertson*, edited by R. A. Bryan, A. C. Morris, A. A. Murphree, and A. L. Williams (Gainesville: University of Florida Press), pp. 1–14.

1966

87. (With John Algeo.) *Problems in the Origins and Development of the English Language*. New York: Harcourt, Brace and World. 274 pp.
88. "Mencken's *American Language*, First Edition: The Preface." In *An American Primer*, edited by Daniel J. Boorstin (Chicago: University of Chicago Press), 2: 794–801.
89. "How Dilapidated Is Delapidated?" *CEA Critic* 28: 12.
90. Review of *The Mother Tongue*, by Lancelot Hogben. *College English* 27: 518.
91. Review of *South Carolina Names*, edited by C. H. Neuffer. *Georgia Review* 20: 370–71.
92. "The New Fowler." Review of *A Dictionary of Modern English Usage*, by H. W. Fowler, 2d edition revised by Sir Ernest Gowers. *Sewanee Review* 74: 540–44.
93. "American and British Word Usages." In *From Paragraph to Essay*, alternate edition, edited by Woodrow Ohlsen and Frank L. Hammond (New York: Scribner's), pp. 20–21. (From chapter 9 of item 38 above.)

1967

94. "English Usage: The Views of the Literati." *College English* 28: 443–44, 449–54.
95. Review of *Modern American Usage*, by Wilson Follett et al. *College English* 29: 168–70.
96. "Later American English: Coinages and Adaptations." In *The World of Words*, edited by Barnet Kottler and Martin Light (New York: Houghton Mifflin), pp. 75–92. (Chapter 7 of item 38 above.)
97. "Some Characteristics of American English and Their Backgrounds." In *The World of Language*, edited by Robert N. Hudspeth and Donald F. Sturtevant (New York: American Book Co.), pp. 167–80. (From chapter 3 of item 38 above.)

1968

98. *The English Language: A Brief History*. New York: Holt, Rinehart and Winston. 60 pp.

99. "Mencken's *American Language*, First Edition: The Preface." In *An American Primer*, a one-volume paperback reprint of item 88 above (New York: New American Library), pp. 819–26.

100. "Comment and Rebuttal: A Reply." *College English* 29: 483–84.

101. "The Background of English." In *From Source to Statement*, edited by James M. McCrimmon (New York: Houghton Mifflin), pp. 364–69. (From chapter 4 of item 81 above.)

102. "Early American Speech: Coinages and Adaptations." In *The Writer's Reader*, edited by Wilma R. Ebbitt and Wm. T. Lenehan (Chicago: Scott, Foresman), p. 93. (From chapter 1 of item 38 above.)

103. "Taboo and Euphemism." In *Language and Literature Reader*, edited by William Heffernan and James Degnan (Beverly Hills, California: Glencoe Press), pp. 194–98. (From chapter 11 of item 81 above.)

1969

104. "English Usage: The Views of the Literati." In *First Perspectives on Language*, 2d edition, edited by William C. Doster (New York: American Book Co.), pp. 96–107. (Reprint of item 94 above.)

105. "Dictionaries and Usage." In *Linguistics Today*, edited by Archibald A. Hill (New York and London: Basic Books), pp. 127–36. (From a lecture broadcast on the Voice of America Forum Series.)

106. Review of *The American Heritage Dictionary of the English Language*. *Chicago Sunday Sun-Times Book Week*, 21 September, p. 6.

107. "Dictionaries and Usage." In *Linguistics*, edited by Archibald A. Hill (Voice of America Forum Series; Washington: USIS), pp. 145–54. (Same as item 105 above.)

108. "A Dictionary Designed for Middlebrow Users." *Northwestern Report*, Fall, pp. 52–53. (Reprint of item 106 above.)

109. "Letters and Sounds: A Brief History of Writing." In *Language and Its Written Uses: A Curriculum for English, Grade 9*, by the Nebraska Curriculum Development Center (Lincoln: University of Nebraska Press), Student Manual pp. 176–94, Teacher Manual pp. 87–117. (Chapter 2 of item 81 above, and from chapter 2 of item 87 above.)

1970

110. "How Meaning Changes." In *About Language*, edited by Marden J. Clark, Soren F. Cox, and Marshall R. Craig (New York: Scribner's), pp. 232–34. (From chapter 11 of item 81 above.)

111. (With John Algeo.) *English: An Introduction to Language*. New York: Harcourt, Brace and World. x + 367 pp.

112. "The Indo-European Homeland." In *Modern English Reader*, edited by Robert Gorrell, Charlton Laird, and Ronald E. Freeman (Englewood Cliffs, New Jersey: Prentice-Hall), p. 30. (From chapter 4 of item 81 above.)

113. "Tall Talk and Turgidity." In *Modern English Reader*, edited by Robert Gorrell, Charlton Laird, and Ronald E. Freeman (Englewood Cliffs, New Jersey: Prentice-Hall), pp. 270–80. (From chapter 6 of item 38 above.)

114. "American and British Word Usages." In *English Then and Now*, edited by Alan M. Markman and Erwin R. Steinberg. (New York: Random House), pp. 331–41. (Chapter 9 of item 38 above.)

115. "William Dwight Whitney." Review of *Whitney on Language: Selected Writings of William Dwight Whitney*, edited by Michael Silverstein. *American Speech* 45: 108–15.

116. "Sweet Are the Usages of Diversity." Review of *A Short Introduction to English Usage*, by J. J. Lamberts. *American Speech* 45: 252–60.

1971

117. *The Origins and Development of the English Language*. 2d edition, revised. New York: Harcourt Brace Jovanovich. x + 413 pp.

118. "Words and Meanings." In *Aspects of American English*, edited by Elizabeth M. Kerr and Ralph M. Aderman, 2d edition (New York: Harcourt Brace Jovanovich), pp. 147–60. (From chapter 11 of item 81 above.)

119. "Getting Named in the Bible Belt." In *Readings about Language*, edited by Charlton Laird and Robert M. Gorrell (New York: Harcourt Brace Jovanovich), pp. 98–102. (From item 66 above.)

120. "The Backgrounds of English." In *Readings about Language*, edited by Charlton Laird and Robert M. Gorrell (New York: Harcourt Brace Jovanovich), pp. 363–72. (From chapter 4 of item 117 above.)

121. "Words and Meanings." In *Words on Words: A Language Reader*, edited by W. Bruce Finnie and Thomas L. Erskine (New York: Random House), pp. 42–59. (From chapter 11 of item 81 above.)

122. "Early American Speech: Adoptions from Foreign Tongues." In *A Various Language: Perspectives on American Dialects*, edited by Juanita V. Williamson and Virginia M. Burke (New York: Holt, Rinehart and Winston), pp. 69–86. (Chapter 2 of item 38 above.)

123. "The Porn Is Green." Review of *A Supplement to the Oxford English Dictionary*. *American Speech* 46: 237–46.

1972

124. "English Usage: The Views of the Literati." In *Contemporary English: Temporal, Regional, and Social Variations*, edited by David L. Shores (Philadelphia: J. B. Lippincott), pp. 160–69. (From item 94 above.)

125. "The Auditory Mass Media and U." In *Studies in Linguistics in Honor of Raven I. McDavid, Jr.*, edited by Lawrence M. Davis (University, Alabama: University of Alabama Press), pp. 425–34.

126. "Kemp Malone." *Language* 48: 499–505.

127. "The Conservatism of American English." In *The Techniques of Reading*, 3d edition, by Horace Judson (New York: Harcourt Brace Jovanovich), pp. 346–49. (From chapter 9 of item 81.)

1973

128. Review of *The Names of Towns and Cities in Britain*, compiled by Margaret Gelling, W. F. H. Nicolaisen, and Melville Richards, edited and introduced by W. F. H. Nicolaisen. *Linguistics*, no. 102: 122–24.

129. *The English Language: A Brief History*. With questions and assignments prepared by Jayne C. Harder and annotated by Nobuyuki Higashi (Tokyo: The Eihōsha Ltd.). (Same as item 98 above, with preface and annotations in Japanese.)

130. "Kemp Malone, Onomatologist." *Names* 21: 131–32.

131. (Special editor.) *Names* 21, number 3 (September), Kemp Malone Souvenir Issue.

132. "British and American English." Review of *British Self-Taught*, by Norman W. Schur; *Dictionary of Modern British and American English*, by Givi Zviadadze; and *Concise Pronouncing Dictionary of British and American English*, by J. Windsor Lewis. *American Speech* 48: 108–17.

1974

133. *The Origins and Development of the English Language*. International edition. New York: Harcourt Brace Jovanovich. x + 413 pp. (Reprint of item 117 above.)

134. "Some Characteristics of American English and Their Backgrounds." In *Language and Culture: A Book of Readings*, edited by Robert B. Glenn, Stewart A. Kingsbury, and Zacharias P. Thundyil (Marquette: Northern Michigan University Press), pp. 158–66. (Chapter 3 of item 38.)

135. "Early American Speech." In *American English*, by Virginia Mc-

David (New York: Random House), pp. 68–75. (Abridged extracts from item 38.)

1977

136. ''Early American Speech: Adoptions from Foreign Tongues.'' In *Language: Introductory Readings*, 2d edition, edited by Virginia P. Clark, Paul A. Eschholz, and Alfred F. Rosa (New York: St. Martin's), pp. 163–80. (Chapter 2 of item 38.)